analogies
_p' — se_

D0876937

CHALLENGE OF PSYCHICAL RESEARCH

A Primer of Parapsychology

the text of this book is printed
on 100% recycled paper

CHALLENGE OF PSYCHICAL RESEARCH

A Primer of Parapsychology

BY GARDNER MURPHY

with the collaboration of Laura A. Dale

ILLUSTRATED

HARPER COLOPHON BOOKS

Harper & Row, Publishers

New York, Evanston, and London

In Gratitude to

FREDERIC W. H. MYERS

ELEANOR MILDRED SIDGWICK

WALTER FRANKLIN PRINCE

This Colophon paperback edition reprints Volume XXVI of the WORLD PERSPECTIVES series, which is planned and edited by RUTH NANDA ANSHEN. Dr. Anshen's Epilogue to this reprint appears on page 293.

First HARPER COLOPHON edition published 1970
by Harper & Row, Publishers, Inc.

Contents

Preface

IN THE library of my mother's father, George A. King, I read at the age of sixteen Sir William Barrett's little book, *Psychical Research*. "Granpa King," as well as my father and my mother, all felt strongly that there was "something in" psychical research; indeed, had a fair reading knowledge of the new field of inquiry. I started with a bias for, rather than against. The opportunity to work with L. T. Troland at Harvard a few years later, and the help given me by leaders of the Society for Psychical Research in London, especially Miss Isabel Newton, in 1919, and by Professor J. H. Hyslop at the American Society for Psychical Research, got me started; and I read intensively and extensively in the field all during my first years as a psychologist. The Richard Hodgson Fellowship at Harvard gave me a stipend with which I tried to study telepathy, and with which I had some sittings with Mrs. L. E. Piper.

After a long illness in which I could not be active in the field, I began again in 1934, the year in which J. B. Rhine's *Extrasensory Perception* appeared. I got a great deal of help and inspiration from visiting Dr. Rhine at the Parapsychology Laboratory at Duke University and meeting many of his associates. In 1941 a "palace revolution" at the American Society for Psychical Research gave me the opportunity to share with research-minded people, especially with Mrs. Laura A. Dale. The degree of my indebtedness to her is far greater than can ever be expressed, despite many specific references to her work, her ideas, and to her collaboration.

In a period of contact with the Richard Hodgson Fellowship Committee at Harvard, I had met several who felt it would be a good idea for me to teach a summer session course in psychical research there in 1942. Among the group who took the course, Dr. Gertrude R. Schmeidler became excited about experimental research, and embarked upon a research career in the field to which

one will find references in the present volume. Two other collaborators who guided me in the evolution of research concepts
must be mentioned: Dr. Ernest Taves and Dr. Joseph L. Woodruff.
With the latter I am still in constant and grateful contact. These
are among my chief living sources of inspiration. Among those
passed on I must emphasize the extraordinary pioneer leaders of the
Society for Psychical Research in London, the reading of whose
works is absolutely fundamental for serious knowledge of psychical
research, especially Frederic W. H. Myers and Eleanor Mildred
Sidgwick. All this gives some idea of the furniture of my mind as
I face the task of trying to write something about psychical research.

Nearly ten years ago Arthur Rosenthal of Basic Books asked me
if I would like to write a systematic manual, treatise, or guide to
parapsychology. I replied that I was not ready, and that it would
take some years to become ready. Then came, three years ago, an
invitation from Ruth Nanda Anshen to write a book for her *World
Perspectives* series, in which a wide variety of modern approaches
to newly discovered or marginal areas of fact or theory are being
presented for the thoughtful general reader. Arthur Rosenthal gen-
erously agreed that my acceptance of this latter responsibility for a
book of this sort would *not* interfere with the more ambitious book
just mentioned above; in fact, that the one might be considered a
precursor to the other. I agreed to this. I suggested to Dr. Anshen
that instead of a treatise I should prepare a collection of basic
source materials in psychical research, introducing these with brief
explanations as to their sources and meanings, and concluding with
comments and interpretations, the theme always to be: "What may
a serious, modern thinker believe about the evidences that are offered in this field? What is credible; what is knowable; what, if
anything, can be concluded?" The aim is not to survey the whole
field, and it is certainly not to instill opinions in the reader. The
aim is to give a primer of working materials with which the reader
may struggle. If he wishes to go further, the specialized literature,
to which reference is made at many points in the present book, can

be used. Sometime, if all goes well, I shall have the larger book in hand, for which this is, in a remote sense, an introduction. In the meantime this is my effort to show the reader what I believe to be classes of serious evidence available for the various kinds of alleged psychical happenings, with enough commentary to make intelligible to the reader why these were chosen, and why I believe that there are genuine challenges to be met by serious reflection and responsible individual decisions rather than editorial summaries and generalizations alone.

In addition to what has been said about the help given me through all these years by Mrs. Dale, I wish expressly to thank her for the constant assistance given as to the best materials to use, the pitfalls to be warned against, the clarifications necessary. She has again made herself indispensable to my efforts. I wish also to thank Dr. Anshen for her generous and liberal policy in letting me write a book so different in spirit and form from most of the books usually devoted to this subject; to Lorraine Ayers for her care and competence in preparation of the manuscript; and to the following publishers, editors, and authors for permission to reprint the various materials indicated below:

George Allen and Unwin, Ltd., London, and Grune and Stratton, New York, for permission to reprint from Jan Ehrenwald, *New Dimensions of Deep Analysis*, 1954, 39–44.

Yale University Press, for permission to reprint from S. G. Soal and F. Bateman, *Modern Experiments in Telepathy*, 1954, 132–167; and to reprint from Gertrude Raffel Schmeidler and R. A. McConnell, *ESP and Personality Patterns*, 1958, 21–27, 32–34, 42–45, 46–48.

American Society for Psychical Research, for permission to reprint from Walter Franklin Prince, Four Peculiarly Characterized Dreams, *Journal of the American Society for Psychical Research*, 1923, Vol. 17, 82–101, and Laura A. Dale, The Psychokinetic Effect: The First A.S.P.R. Experiment, *Journal of the American Society for Psychical Research*, 1946, Vol. 40, 1–29.

Journal of Parapsychology, Duke University Press, and J. B.

Rhine, for permission to reprint from J. B. Rhine and J. G. Pratt, A Review of the Pearce-Pratt Distance Series, *Journal of Parapsychology*, 1954, Vol. 18, 165–177; Margaret Anderson and Rhea White, A Further Investigation of Teacher-Pupil Attitudes and Clairvoyance Test Results, *Journal of Parapsychology*, 1957, Vol. 21, 81–97; J. G. Pratt and H. Forwald, Confirmation of the PK Placement Effect, *Journal of Parapsychology*, 1958, Vol. 22, 1–19.

Society for Psychical Research (London) for permission to reprint from Mrs. Henry Sidgwick, Notes on the Evidence Collected by the Society for Phantasms of the Dead, *Proceedings of the Society for Psychical Research*, 1885, Vol. 3, 95–99; J. G. Piddington, A Series of Concordant Automatisms, *Proceedings of the Society for Psychical Research*, 1908, Vol. 22, 59–77; J. G. Piddington, Three Incidents from the Sittings: Lethe, the Sibyl, the Horace Ode Question, *Proceedings of the Society for Psychical Research*, 1910, Vol. 24, 87–104; Sir Oliver Lodge, Evidence of Classical Scholarship and of Cross-Correspondence in Some New Automatic Writings, *Proceedings of the Society for Psychical Research*, 1911, Vol. 25, 113–195; G. W. Balfour, The Ear of Dionysius: Further Scripts Affording Evidence of Personal Survival, *Proceedings of the Society for Psychical Research*, 1918, Vol. 29, 197–243; Eleanor Mildred Sidgwick, An Examination of Book-Tests Obtained in Sittings with Mrs. Leonard, *Proceedings of the Society for Psychical Research*, 1921, Vol. 31, 253–260. Mrs. Henry Sidgwick, Phantasms of the Living: An Examination and Analysis of Cases of Telepathy between Living Persons (etc.), *Proceedings of the Society for Psychical Research*, 1924, Vol. 33, 423–429 (see especially pp. 413–419).

G. M.

Birchlea,
Ashland, N.H.
August, 1959

CHALLENGE OF PSYCHICAL RESEARCH

A Primer of Parapsychology

I.

Introduction

HALF of the problem of achieving a "world perspective" is the problem of integration. How may the eager, restless gropings into many odd corners be induced to yield a coherent and unitary view of our world? How may synthesis, co-ordination, insight, meaning be achieved? Most of the volumes in this *World Perspectives* series are concerned with perspectives in this sense.

There is, however, another task of equal importance. This is the response to new voices, undeciphered symbols, odd discoveries for which no place can at present be found; the investigation of that which defies today's order and rationality; the resolute and unfrightened recognition of what appears out of place, irrational, meaningless, an affront to reason. In the history of discovery, there have always been the blur and the horror of that which refuses to be assimilated; observations which, however carefully repeated and checked, fall into no predetermined place in the jigsaw puzzle which we conceive to be nature.

Psychical research, or parapsychology, consists of observations recorded in a form which aims at order and intelligibility, but which cannot by any stretch of the imagination be subsumed under the science of today. Shall we accept that which cannot be assimilated? The issue is an old one. When Aristotle discussed dreams which seemed at times to foretell the future, he felt that it was his business to consider the evidence, but neither to include the evidence as a part of the texture of his treatise on *Psychology*, nor on the other hand to reject the narratives as inherently unworthy of attention.

It was not, however, until the nineteenth century that serious and systematic investigation of psychical or paranormal events—telepathy, prevision, apparitions of the dying and deceased, the movement of objects in a manner unknown to the physical sciences—began to take shape.

The primary factor launching modern psychical research was the existence at Cambridge University, England, of a group of scholars who felt that it was "nothing less than a scandal in this enlightened age" (Henry Sidgwick's words) that the serious reports of serious people regarding such experiences should have received no scientific investigation. The physicist, William Barrett, the clergyman, W. Stainton Moses, the classical scholar, F. W. H. Myers, succeeded in launching in London, largely with the help of this group of Cambridge scholars, a strong and effective research group which within a few years numbered in its ranks many of the outstanding British intellectuals, with a definite program of investigation into problems varying as widely as experimental telepathy, a census of hallucinations, and the observation of spiritist mediums in or out of trance. William James played a major role in launching a similar organization in the United States. Such societies have until recently been the major instruments in the investigation of paranormal phenomena.

Despite the reluctance of the academic world to admit that such incredible reports might be worthy of serious investigation, a few efforts were made at Harvard, at Stanford University, and elsewhere, until in 1930, with the support of William McDougall and the vigorous leadership of J. B. Rhine, a parapsychology laboratory was established at Duke University, from which a continuous and very considerable volume of research publication has followed. The three main sources from which the present volume has drawn its examples are the Society for Psychical Research in London, the American Society for Psychical Research in New York, and the Parapsychology Laboratory at Duke University. A fourth important example, the laboratory of the Parapsychology Foundation in New York, will soon be heard from.

KINDS OF EVIDENCE

The purpose of this volume is to attempt for the busy non-specialist reader one step toward a perspective on the nature of the assertions made about paranormal phenomena, the kinds of evidence with which a serious modern person must concern himself, the positive fulfillments and frustrations involved in such investigations. The aim of the book is not to convince, and it is not to survey. Conviction, for a disciplined mind, could arise only on the basis of extensive evidence and authentication, much more detailed than can be offered in a book of this character. A real survey would necessitate serious consideration of the *Proceedings* of the S.P.R. since 1882 and the same number of volumes of the S.P.R. *Journal*, and likewise an impressive amount of material from the A.S.P.R., and from the *Journal of Parapsychology*, appearing since 1937; a considerable literature in French, German, Italian, and Dutch; and a few volumes of classic importance (the lighter material in this field will receive no attention in our present volume).

This serious literature, the literature of the journals, is hardly known at all. The difference between psychical research as a serious discipline and as a form of "common knowledge" is enormous. If a reasonably well-informed and thoughtful person were to wander up and down the highways and byways of the civilized world, listening to street-corner conversations, stopping in coffee houses and the lobbies of hotels, reading a fragment here and there in each of many popular magazines, and scanning judiciously what the papers, and the radio and television programs had to offer, he would get the following preliminary impressions, which he would try to sort out and understand:

A large number of people, especially in the lower educational levels, but with a good sprinkling of average or higher levels, believe themselves to have received impressions regarding distant realities which did not reach them through their sense organs, or through their normal processes of drawing inferences. They report that they have caught impressions of distant catastrophes to loved ones, or have had curiously exact and detailed premonitions of future events. It is not hard to find people who do automatic writing or operate a Ouija board which, communicating in the first person singular, purports to offer messages from the deceased. A smaller number, but still a considerable number of persons, report that they have seen apparitions of the deceased while in good health and under conditions of good illumination; or that they have seen objects move without any easy physical explanation; or have received through spiritist mediums information purporting to come from deceased persons which they regarded as correct and characteristic, and not easily explained away.

If now our thoughtful investigator followed through on these street-corner impressions by undertaking to talk about such experiences, he would often encounter among his interlocutors considerable excitement and vigorous asseveration on the one hand, and on the part of many of their friends much coolness, hostility, and scoffing. He may conclude that these are phenomena precious to many, but full of absurdity or of dangerous implications to many others. Looking still more closely, he would find that many of the persons who vouch for these matters are poorly informed as to the nature of science; that they are confident about amazing phenomena of which there are no records; that cross-examination may yield damaging results. He would find that the automatic writing, if taken in considerable quantity just as it comes, is mostly childish, and that those small fragments of it which are interesting, coherent, and make a reasonable claim to be communication from the deceased, usually reproduce items which are known to the writers themselves and therefore have no great psychological interest. The witnesses to these occurrences are indeed frequently unaware that automatic acts like writing, gesticulating, doodling, even talking and singing, may occur without full conscious control. The material communicated is often just what is wanted by the writer. In such a situation it may at first be hard for our thoughtful observer to see why one should take psychical research seriously.

Yet if he persists our observer will here and there encounter an individual who knows of the existence of the research in this field which began with the founding of the (London) Society for Psychical Research, as described, in 1882. Indeed, from the 1880's until the time of the First World War the English-speaking public got some glimmerings through newspapers and books regarding efforts associated with a few celebrities like William James, Oliver Lodge, Gilbert Murray, the Earl of Balfour, who were known to be party to such studies. The vigorous books of James H. Hyslop in the United States exemplified a literature that did something to give a popular awareness of psychical research. J. B. Rhine's extensive laboratory attack upon the problems of psychical research at Duke University was marked by the appearance of his volume, *Extrasensory Perception,* in 1934, followed by a series of popular books based largely on the technical research literature appearing in his new *Journal of Parapsychology,* and at times by severely technical books such as J. B. Rhine and J. G. Pratt: *Parapsychology: Frontier Science of the Mind,* Springfield, Illinois, 1957, Charles C Thomas. Rhine's influence has not only transformed the experimental approach used in most psychological laboratories which have investigated such problems; it has made a considerable dent upon thoughtful scientists. While Alexis Carrel was a voice crying in the wilderness when he wrote *Man, the Unknown* in 1935, today extrasensory perception is accepted without apology by scientists of the stature of C. J. Herrick, Evelyn Hutchinson, Julian Huxley, Henry Margenau, E. W. Sinnott, and there is a widening interest in new work in the field. Moreover, among thoughtful people everywhere, insofar as one can judge from the response to lectures, mass media, and books, knowledge of serious work has increased a little and standards have gone up a little.

The present volume is aimed at two kinds of people: the professional scientist and the thoughtful lay reader. Within a small volume I cannot waste space on diffuseness and generalizations. I have decided to try to show what psychical research is by giving *documented examples of the kinds of data available* in relation to a few main kinds of problems, selecting from the classics and the near-classics of the field, and asking always this one recurrent question: what can a thoughtful reader think about these things? My aim is to offer exhibits of data; to suggest ways in which the data may be interpreted; and to leave the reader to decide—or to decide not to decide—what to make of it all. He may decide: "It's all rubbish." He may decide: "It *could* be; but who knows?" He may decide: "Here is an area that calls for more and better research." Or he may take one of the many directions which it is not my task—or my privilege —to foresee.

II.

Spontaneous Cases

ONE OF the first tasks of the newly organized Society for Psychical Research in London was to investigate at first hand the reports of telepathy and related happenings. By telepathy, Frederic W. H. Myers meant: "The communication of impressions of any kind from one mind to another, independently of the recognized channels of sense."[1] A committee from the Society for Psychical Research gathered cases and presented them in the first huge collection published by Edmund Gurney, Frederic W. H. Myers and Frank Podmore under the title *Phantasms of the Living.*[2] The following is the first case reported in that study:[3]

. . . I [Edmund Gurney] will open this preliminary batch of narratives with just such a case . . . as pure an instance of transference of sensation, unattended by any idea or image, as can well be conceived. The parties concerned are Mr. Arthur Severn, the distinguished landscape painter, and his wife; and the narrative was obtained through the kindness of Mr. Ruskin. Mrs. Severn says:—

[1] *Human Personality and its Survival of Bodily Death,* two volumes, London: Longmans, Green, and Co., 1903. Vol. 1, xxii. Telepathy is thus one example of *paranormal* interaction with the environment, today often called *psi.*

[2] Two volumes, London, Trubner and Co., 1886.

[3] Vol. 1, 187–189.

"Brantwood, Coniston.
"October 27th, 1883.

"I woke up with a start, feeling I had had a hard blow on my mouth, and with a distinct sense that I had been cut, and was bleeding under my lip, and seized my pocket-handkerchief, and held it (in a little pushed lump) to the part, as I sat up in bed, and after a few seconds, when I removed it, I was astonished not to see any blood, and only then realized it was impossible anything could have struck me there, as I lay fast asleep in bed, and so I thought it was only a dream!—but I looked at my watch, and saw it was seven, and finding Arthur (my husband) was not in the room, I concluded (rightly) that he must have gone out on the lake for an early sail, as it was so fine.

"I then fell asleep. At breakfast (half-past nine), Arthur came in rather late, and I noticed he rather purposely sat farther away from me than usual, and every now and then put his pocket-handkerchief furtively up to his lip, in the very way I had done. I said, 'Arthur, why are you doing that?' and added a little anxiously, 'I know you've hurt yourself! But I'll tell you why afterwards.' He said, 'Well, when I was sailing, a sudden squall came, throwing the tiller suddenly round, and it struck me a bad blow in the mouth, under the upper lip, and it has been bleeding a good deal and won't stop.' I then said, 'Have you any idea what o'clock it was when it happened?' and he answered, 'It must have been about seven.'

"I then told what had happened to *me,* much to *his* surprise, and all who were· with us at breakfast.

"It happened here about three years ago at Brantwood, to me.
"JOAN R. SEVERN."

In reply to inquiries Mrs. Severn writes:—

"There was no doubt about my starting up in bed wide awake, as I stuffed my pocket-handkerchief into my mouth, and held it pressed under my upper lip for some time before removing it to 'see the blood,'—and was much surprised that there was none. Some little time afterwards, I fell asleep again. I believe that when I got up, an hour afterwards, the impression was still vividly in my mind, and that as I was dressing I did look under my lip to see if there was any mark."

Mr. Severn's account, dated November 15, 1883, is as follows:—

"Early one summer morning, I got up intending to go and sail on the lake; whether my wife heard me going out of the room I don't know; she probably did, and in a half-dreamy state knew where I was going.

"When I got down to the water I found it calm, like a mirror, and remember thinking it quite a shame to disturb the wonderful reflections of the opposite shore. However, I soon got afloat, and as there was no wind, contented myself with pulling up my sails to dry, and putting my boat in order. Soon some slight air came, and I was able to sail about a mile below Brantwood, then the wind dropped, and I was left becalmed for half-an-hour or so, when, on looking up to the head of the lake, I saw a dark blue line on the water. At first I couldn't make it out, but soon saw that it must be small waves caused by a strong wind coming. I got my boat as ready as I could, in the short time, to receive this gust, but somehow or other she was taken aback, and seemed to spin round when the wind struck her, and in getting out of the way of the boom I got my head in the way of the tiller, which also swung round and gave me a nasty blow in the mouth, cutting my lip rather badly, and having become loose in the rudder it came out and went overboard. With my mouth bleeding, the mainsheet more or less around my neck, and the tiller gone, and the boat in confusion, I could not help smiling to think how suddenly I had been humbled almost to a wreck, just when I thought I was going to be so clever! However, I soon managed to get my tiller, and, with plenty of wind, tacked back to Brantwood, and, making my boat snug in the harbour, walked up to the house, anxious of course to hide as much as possible what had happened to my mouth, and getting another handkerchief walked into the breakfast-room, and managed to say something about having been out early. In an instant my wife said, 'You don't mean to say you have hurt your mouth?' or words to that effect. I then explained what had happened, and was surprised to see some extra interest on her face, and still more surprised when she told me she had started out of her sleep thinking she had received a blow in the mouth! and that it was a few minutes past seven o'clock, and wondered if my accident had happened at the same time; but as I had no watch with me I couldn't tell, though, on comparing notes, it certainly looked as if it had been about the same time.[4]

"ARTHUR SEVERN."

So now I ask what the attitudes of thoughtful modern persons might appropriately be to reports of this sort. First of all, are they coincidences?

Well, it is difficult indeed to say exactly what a coincidence is. Unrelated happenings? But are any two events in the universe utterly unrelated? On the other hand, how can two events be proved to be related? To use an old, but not too shopworn illustration, the *random* pounding of typewriter keys might generate the proposition that "on January 19, 1988, 119 pink elephants will march, playing trombones, down Pennsylvania Avenue," and it still might be "coincidence" if the event came off as predicted. It is not possible to *exclude* the application of the concept of coincidence.

The early investigators tried to cope with the coincidence problem in the following way. Is an event the *cause* of a personal experience; e.g., was the blow of the tiller the cause of Mrs. Severn's experience? If *not*, we can say "coincidence." In the case of appari-

[4] This does not square exactly with Mrs. Severn's memory of what Mr. Severn said. [G. M.]

tions perceived at the moment of the death of those whose forms are seen, we can refer to "coincidence," if we know roughly *how many* people now living can be expected to die on a given day, and if we find that the number who do actually die on the day when their apparition is seen is comparable to what would be expected on the basis of chance alone. The number of instances of apparitions of the dying available for analysis by the early S.P.R. group was many times the number which should be expected to occur in the British Isles in the period in question, if coincidence, that is, the absence of a causal relation, was to be held to be a reasonable interpretation. Cases in which it was known that the dying person was ill or in danger could be excluded without affecting the weight of the material. Does this kind of thinking really help in the deciding whether Mrs. Severn's "blow in the mouth" was a "coincidence"? Many will feel that there are too many of these cases. But any pretense of an exact statement is illusory.

It is clearly of the utmost importance to have contemporary records or records written shortly after the events described, and to have independent confirmation of the fact that the experience had been reported before the facts bringing the confirmation could be known. It will be noted that in the case just cited, this specification is not met, although written authentication is obtainable from both of the principals in the case.

Perhaps until we come to cases in which genuine statistical analysis is feasible, it may be better to place our emphasis on three issues: the adequacy of the corroboration of the experiences, to see what probably actually happened; second, the psychology of the process—clear or confused, cold or emotional, confident or hesitating, etc.; third, a tentative interpretation of the meaning, or function, or purpose, the *work done* by the experience, in the hope that after interpreting these spontaneous cases and experimental cases we may begin to have a glimmering of understanding of them.

CONTEMPORARY CASES

Some hundreds of these cases have been examined and published in *Phantasms of the Living* and in "The Census of Hallucinations,"[5] and since that time something like a dozen good cases per year, on the average, have been presented by the S.P.R., and a comparable number by the A.S.P.R. A resurgence of interest in the problem of these "spontaneous cases" has occurred in recent years, both on the American scene and internationally. A case[6] gathered and analyzed by Mrs. Dale, formerly Research Associate at the A.S.P.R., is an example of an impression so commanding that it led to immediate action, despite the nuisance caused and the ridicule and hostility to which it gave rise. The case was reported to the Society in a letter from the daughter of the percipient.

> Bessemer, Louisiana
> [Undated; received in
> March, 1957]

. . . Two years ago my parents went away on a short vacation. Shortly after they left on their trip my small son became very ill and had extremely high temperature. Early the next morning I was surprised to see my mother and father driving into the driveway. Mother rushed in and said, "I had a terrible dream. I dreamed I kissed Billy and he was burning with fever and when I turned around John (my brother) was standing there with a big hole in his head, pouring blood." I told her that Billy was terribly sick but that my brother John had gone to work as usual that morning and was just fine. In less than an hour my brother, a lineman for Southern Bell Telephone Company, had been brought home by his foreman with a big hole cut above his left eye, and bleeding profusely. . . .

> Yours truly,
> (Signed) JANET STONE
> (MRS. H. M.)[7]

[5] *Proceedings of the Society for Psychical Research,* 1894, Vol. 10, 25–422.
[6] This and several of the cases to follow are in a group which came in to the A.S.P.R. as a result of a request for such cases appearing in the press early in 1957.
[7] Permission was granted by the members of the family to use their actual

❦

In answer to Mrs. Dale's request, Mrs. Stone asked her mother, Mrs. Helen C. Turner, also of Bessemer, Louisiana, to dictate a first-hand account of her recollection of the dream and the attendant circumstances. This account follows:

❦

During the night I dreamed that I walked into Billy's room and picked him up from his bed and sat down in a rocking chair. I kissed his forehead and he was burning with fever. He seemed to be very limp and he did not know me. While I was sitting there rocking Billy I was crying because he seemed almost dead. My son John came to the door of Billy's room, and leaned up against the frame of the door with his hand to his head. I asked him what was wrong and he said he fell from a telephone pole. Actually, I had had a secret fear of his falling since he took the job as lineman with Southern Bell Telephone Company. In the dream he said, "I fell and I feel a little sick at my stomach." Then he moved his hand and blood began pouring from a hole above his eye. In the dream I screamed, and he said, "Now I think I'm going to be all right." It was a terrible dream, one of those dreams when the feeling of terror lasts even after awakening. I didn't sleep any more and I got up very early the next morning and went home. The dream I had was re-enacted completely. I went directly to my daughter's house hoping the whole thing had been only a dream but I did go into Billy's room and picked him up. I kissed his forehead and he was burning with fever and did not know me. While my daughter dressed so we could take Billy to the doctor I asked about John and she told me that he was all right. In the meantime John had fallen from a pole while he was at work and had been brought home from work. His wife was terrified when she saw him, and she knew

---

names if the case was published in the *Journal* of the A.S.P.R. For the purposes of this book, however, I have used pseudonyms and changed geographic localities. [G. M.]

we had returned home. She ran across the backyard screaming for me and my son followed her. When they came into the house I saw that the second part of my dream had come true. Almost every dream I have comes true either directly or indirectly. Almost always they are of an ordinary nature, not signs of disaster like this one. I have dreamed of relatives whom I haven't seen for years only to hear from them the next day. Maybe I get a wedding invitation from one, or maybe I have unexpected company. Every night I go to bed I hope that I will not have a dream!

Mrs. Stone also answered the following questions sent to her by Mrs. Dale:

1. If possible, we would like to have the exact date of the occurrence.

    I cannot give the exact date but it was in the month of November, 1952. I am able to set the date because our son Billy was four. My brother's little girl was born in October after which they stayed at my Mother's for a month. Also my brother went with Southern Bell in October of that year.

2. At the time of the dream, did you and your parents live together? If not where did they live?

    My husband and I lived in an apartment on the rear of the lot where my parents' home was located. My brother and his wife were living with my parents at the time.

3. How long were your parents planning to remain away from home on this vacation?

    My father had taken only half of his vacation during the summer and they had planned to be away from home about five days. They were planning to visit my father's parents first, then to visit several aunts and uncles spending only a day with each one.

4. How long had they been gone and where were they at the time of the dream?

They left on Friday morning about seven-thirty and were spending the first night with my grandparents, whose home is about seventy-six miles from our home. . . . It was not possible to reach them because my grandparents had no phone.

5. Had they ever before cut short a vacation due to a dream or "hunch" of your mother's?

No!

6. When your mother last saw Billy, prior to leaving for the trip, was he apparently in perfectly good health?

Yes.

7. How long was it after your mother left that Billy fell ill? What was the nature of the illness?

My parents left at seven-thirty Friday morning and Billy did not get sick until late afternoon when he began vomiting and running a temperature which got steadily higher and finally reached 105. He had a severe case of tonsillitis.

8. When Billy fell ill, did you think of your mother and wish that she were there to help you?

Not at first but later in the night as his temperature ran higher and higher and I could not break it with aspirin, enemas, or any of the methods I had ever heard of, I began to panic. Because then I did not know that it was tonsillitis, and as a young mother with an only child, I feared the worst thing I could imagine. I was quite desperate and neither my husband nor I went to bed at all that night. I prayed a lot and it is quite possible that I thought of my mother but I cannot be sure. I do know that whenever Billy had been sick before I had relied heavily on my mother's experience with children and on her assurances that nothing seriously was wrong with him.

9. Was your brother living with you at the time?

As I said, he and his wife and baby were living with my

parents, because the baby was small and Elizabeth, his wife, is an orphan and had no mother to help her until she regained her strength.

10. Did your father object to cutting short the vacation and was it difficult for your mother to convince him to turn back home?

Yes, he objected very much and so did my grandfather. Finally, Mother told my father that she was going to take the car and go home and that he could come later on the bus. My father's relatives with whom they were staying thought the whole thing was pretty ridiculous. My grandmother thought someone had offended my mother, but since she has been in the family for twenty-some odd years and had never behaved in such a way they soon realized that she really felt that something was wrong, and my father brought her home, but she said the silence in the car all the way home was pretty uncomfortable. If the feeling had not been so strong I am sure she would not have caused and persisted in creating such an awkward situation.

❦

The following is also from the current A.S.P.R. collection analyzed by Mrs. Dale, as reported in a letter from the percipient:

❦

27 Selwin Grove[8]
Dover, Delaware
June 1, 1957

I read, with great interest, your story of mental telepathy. You requested stories of such events dating back [no more than] five years. This, then, will be of no help to you as it happened a good many years ago, but it is an experience I will never forget.

This happened while I was a freshman attending ——— College

[8] In this case we were requested to use pseudonyms. Therefore, names and addresses have been changed. [G. M.]

in Wilmington, Delaware. While attending church services with Mr. and Mrs. W. L. Scott and their son Paul, I was listening to the minister who was about mid-point in his sermon. Suddenly, for no reason I can explain, I glanced up to the front left corner of the church and clearly saw a big plane screaming, flames streaking out from behind, to the earth. I gasped. I didn't hear another word of the sermon. I couldn't take my eyes from that spot on the wall. When the congregation stood to sing a hymn I remained seated with a horrible feeling of helplessness. (The Scotts told me I sat staring at the wall and didn't answer when they asked me if I was ill.)

After church I ran to the dorm and told my roommate, Louise Tracy, that something had happened to Tom Richter. He was a gunner on a B-17 and had been a childhood friend and neighbor. Louise laughed when I told her what I had seen and felt in church. She told me to forget it. I couldn't, and I couldn't get over my depressed (for want of a better word) feeling. Several months later my mother paid me a visit. When I told her I knew something had happened to Tom she told me she had come to tell me he was missing in action. She wanted to tell me before I learned via returned letters to him.

I wrote to Tom's base in England (7th Air Force) and a friend replied that the last he had seen our friend, was when his plane was falling through the air in flames as they were returning from a raid on Frankfurt, Germany. The day his plane was shot down and the day I saw it fall was the same. That gunner is now back home after having been a prisoner of war until the war ended.

This has remained vivid in my memory. I cannot understand why or how it happened. I am most anxious to know more about this. . . .

Very truly yours,
(Signed) SARAH CRAMPTON
(MRS. T. S.)

ｾ

In answer to Mrs. Dale's questions, Mrs. Crampton replied as follows:

1. What was the exact date—or the approximate date if exact date is not recalled—of the experience?

    A Sunday in February, 1944.

2. About how long did the vision of the falling plane, which you saw in the corner of the church, seem to last?

    It lasted only a short time, but I couldn't seem to move my eyes from that spot for quite a while.

3. Did this vision seem to be fully externalized—out in space— or more something that you saw with your "mind's eye" and inwardly?

    Very definitely externalized. It was horrible.

4. As soon as you saw this vision, did you immediately interpret it as meaning that something had happened to Tom Richter?

    Very definitely so. I had no reason to be thinking of him, but it just seemed to be his plane (which, of course, I'd never seen). He was one of two fliers I knew.

5. Did you tell the Scotts about your vision when they noticed your unusual behavior and asked you if you were ill?

    No, I couldn't say anything. I remember tears in my eyes and a strange feeling of no one being around. (All voices were far off.)

6. If "yes" to the above, would it be possible for you to get a word of corroboration from them concerning this matter?

    ———

7. When you told your roommate, Louise Tracy, that you knew something had happened to Tom Richter, did you also tell her about the vision?

    Yes, I told her I had seen the flaming plane. She laughed it off and left the dorm. I spent the rest of the afternoon trying to shake the pressing feeling of complete helplessness.

8. If you are still in touch with Miss Tracy, would it be possible for you to get a word of corroboration from her?

    She lives in Wisconsin now, but we still correspond and I

am sure, if she remembers the incident, she will gladly corroborate it.[9]

9. Do you by any chance still have the letter Tom's friend wrote you from England describing the details of the fatal crash and giving the date, which coincided with the date of your vision? If not, would it be possible for us to get a statement from this friend concerning the details?

No. I had no reason to save the letter or the newspaper clippings. He was in the 7th AAF in England and so was Tom Richter. Tom's plane was the lead plane and was also the first to be shot down.

10. You say that "several months" after your vision your mother came to tell you that Tom was missing in action—she did not want you to learn of this by way of returned letters. Was this the first you heard of the tragedy? Why were you not told sooner?

Yes, this was the first news I had. The following weeks brought letters returned marked "missing in action." I was not told sooner because "missing" persons were searched for before the notices were sent out. I guess no one thought I would be too upset about the news and saw no reason why it should interest me that much, but Mom knew that as a child I had been very fond of Tom and was afraid I'd be shocked to have letters returned with such a notation.

11. Did you write Tom any letters *after* you had the experience?

That same night, and every night after that, even though they were never mailed. When he was found in a prisoner-of-war camp I was allowed to write one short note a month. I received one card on which three lines were written.

[9] On June 6, 1957, Mrs. Crampton sent Mrs. Dale a letter received from her former roommate, Miss Tracy, to whom she had written to inquire whether she recalled the incident. Miss Tracy wrote: ". . . yes, I do remember the incident you speak of, but only the vague details . . . you were terribly upset at the time, but I can't remember how long afterwards your mother came to college telling you that Tom had been shot down. . . . " [G. M.]

12. Were Tom's parents eventually informed that he was killed (as I presume he was) and if so, when did they receive this information?

I am afraid I misled you. Tom was a prisoner until the end of the war when he was released and returned home (in quite a state). His parents were informed first that he was Missing in Action and later that he was a P.O.W.

13. Anything else that might occur to you to tell us about this striking experience, and also anything you might want to say concerning your relationship with Tom, would be greatly appreciated.

I can think of nothing further. As to my relationship with Tom, he moved to our neighborhood when we were both 9 years old. He was ahead of me in school and he attended Military Academy not far away through high school. I saw him on holidays and a few weeks in the summer. I was in five bands in Washington, D.C., and so was he in the summer. He left for the Air Corps while I was completing high school. His mother has always said it was because of me that he enlisted (we had never had any dates but I dated others) and held me responsible for his being shot down and taken prisoner. When Tom returned home we did date some because he liked to "talk out" his experience. When I told him about seeing his plane in flames, he too laughed. I returned to college and he married and is now living somewhere in Delaware. He was like a part of the family and spent much time at our house listening to records and talking to us.

Another recent case with corroboration is the following:

11 Freedomtown Place[10]
Westphalia, New York
February 18, 1957

. . . I write in response to the invitation that appeared in *This Week* Magazine, N.Y. *Herald Tribune,* Feb. 17, 1957, along with an article "Telepathy is a Fact," by Dr. Gardner Murphy.

I refer to an experience which occurred during July, 1954, when my daughter Jessie was spending the summer in El Cajon, California.

On Wednesday afternoon, July 28, 1954, I heard Jessie call me as if she were terribly frightened. My first impulse was to run to the door, but I resisted the urge for a second or two, thinking "How ridiculous!" However, the feeling was so compelling that I went to the back door and looked down the walk leading to it. Of course she wasn't there.

I was quite distressed for I suddenly knew for certain that Jessie was in extreme danger. I think I prayed.

The uneasiness became less pressing and some time later, I knew that Jessie had been near water when "it" happened.

It is strange, but I never felt the need to call my parents with whom Jessie was staying—I knew that I was being kept informed.

My daughter remained in my thoughts throughout the next two days. Friday night I learned in the same inexplicable manner that she was all right.

I told my husband of the sequence of events on Saturday morning.

What happened: While on a fishing trip with her grandparents on Wednesday Jessie had returned to the car for something. Apparently she couldn't resist the temptation to drive it. She managed to release the emergency brake, causing the car, which was parked on a hill, to start down. The folks were about a block away and did not reach her until the car with $300–$400 damage came to a halt on rocky terrain, flinging Jessie out as it did so. She was stunned, bruised, and scratched and there was the possibility of internal injuries.

[10] In this case also we were asked to use pseudonyms. [G. M.]

X-rays were taken and the folks were notified on Saturday that Jessie was all right.

My parents did not tell me of the incident until mid-August lest I be upset about it. They were not going to say anything about it at first, but feared that Jessie might mention it and either be punished for it or cause needless alarm.

My daughter was 9 years old at the time.

She says that she called "Granny" but I suspect that in her moment of fear she probably said "Mommy" for that is what I heard.

Yours truly

(Signed) (Mrs.) HARRIET RAYNOR

❧

Mrs. Dale answered this letter in the usual fashion and asked some questions. The questions and Mrs. Raynor's answers follow:

❧

1. At about what time on the afternoon of July 28, 1954, did the experience occur?

   After 1 and before 3 P.M. I cannot now be more specific.

2. Where were you and what were you doing when you heard your daughter's voice?

   I was in my kitchen doing housework, dishes, etc.

3. Was anyone else with you when you heard your daughter call? If so, did they also hear the voice?

   No, I was alone in the house at the time.

4. Was the sound completely externalized, as if it were a "real" voice calling, or was it more a matter of hearing it with your "inner" ear? If completely externalized, where did it seem to be coming from?

   I felt at the time that it was real, coming from outdoors, perhaps from the front or the side of the house, where my little girl would probably have been if she were at home. I am now inclined to believe that the sound was mentally received.

5. At about what time did the accident occur?

In the afternoon. My mother commented that they arrived home about 4:30 P.M. as a rule, but they were delayed on this particular occasion by the accident, finally arriving back home at about 7:30 P.M.

6. You say that on Friday night (following the accident) you learned "in the same inexplicable manner" that your daughter was all right. Do you mean that you again heard a voice? Or was it an impression—or a dream?

I felt that someone had spoken to me to that effect. It was not a dream. I "recognized" the voice and was at ease at last. To explain—I knew that it was not wishful thinking on my part but that Jessie was truly all right for I had been informed with authority. It was not my daughter's voice nor that of any living person that I know.

7. You say you learned of the accident in mid-August. Did your parents write to you about it?

I telephoned my daughter on her birthday (Aug. 11th) and learned about it from them at that time.

8. Was this a unique experience in your life, or have you had other psychic experiences?

[Mrs. Raynor describes a few rather vague impressions, etc., etc.]

❦

In answer to Mrs. Dale's request for corroboration from her husband, Mr. Raynor wrote as follows:

❦

"My wife told me of her 'dream.' At that time I did not give it much thought. It did upset her at the time and I tried to discount it, but when the letter came from Mom about the accident it did make me wonder."

❦

Mrs. Raynor comments on her husband's corroboration as follows:

❦

"With reference to my husband's comment—I believe I did tell him that I dreamt of the accident, his attitude being such that he would have scoffed at the true account of what happened."

❦

Inconsistencies: Percipient says she learned of the accident when she *phoned* her daughter on her birthday. The husband says the accident was described in a *letter* from his mother. But probably this discrepancy is more apparent than real—there was probably both a phone call and a letter.

Remarks: Activity on the part of the mother rather than the child is indicated—note that the mother structured the impression in terms of the child calling *her* whereas in reality the child called her *grandmother*. This appears to be a case of a clairvoyant impression externalized in the form of an auditory hallucination. . . .

Shall we allow ourselves here a few words of theoretical interpretation?

We have no *good* theory of telepathy. I should like, however, to quote from Mrs. Sidgwick[11] a passage which seems to throw some light on the process, suggesting that in all telepathy there is a *two-way* communication: both individuals are really agents, and both percipients.

❦

. . . There are two stages in the process of manifestation of telepathic communication at which failure, that is, incompleteness, may occur. There may be incomplete contact between the two minds concerned; and when that contact is subliminal, as I imagine is gen-

[11] Mrs. Henry Sidgwick, Phantasms of the Living: An examination and analysis of cases of telepathy between living persons (etc.), *Proceedings of the Society for Psychical Research*, 1923, Vol. 33, 23–429.

erally the case, there may be incomplete emergence in either mind from the subliminal to the supraliminal consciousness. The contact could not be really complete—it could not extend to the whole content of either mind—without loss of individual personality, but short of this it may presumably vary in completeness through all possible degrees. Emergence into the conscious again varies probably in degree. It certainly varies in method, as it may occur through remembered dreams, through waking hallucinations, through motor automatism such as automatic writing, or through conscious but non-externalized waking impressions of various degrees of definiteness, such as those described. . . . It probably often happens that there is telepathic communication which does not emerge into the normal consciousness at all. We cannot therefore tell where failure occurs, nor why or how any particular case differs from the normal type. But this is, of course, equally true whether we think of the process as transmission of thought or as merging together of minds —what we might perhaps call transfusion of thought.

I have quoted Mrs. Sidgwick, partly because even in our groping blindness we need a theory that can be tested. Earlier I suggested that in studying spontaneous cases we need to emphasize:

1. Corroboration, authentication of what actually happened; this purpose has been sought by showing how the analyst, e.g., Mrs. Dale, does her work.
2. The psychology of the process; this has been sought through letting the agents and percipients talk in their own way, and to offer hints as to their feelings, attitudes, and ideas.
3. Meaning, purpose or *function* of these experiences. Mrs. Sidgwick's conception of a "transference" of thought, just quoted, is an effort at definition of function in this sense. Such a concept is useful in systematizing the study of spontaneous cases, in keeping our eyes open to processes that might be overlooked, and in setting up experiments in telepathy in which

"reciprocal action" and "transference" can appear if they are real events in nature.

A good many of the interesting cases are *dream* cases. Dr. Walter Franklin Prince, historian and Episcopal clergyman, who became a professional psychical researcher, has given us an exceptionally vivid account of some of his own dreams, bearing on two ancient questions: (1) "Is there a distinctive quality of paranormal dreams marking them off from ordinary dreams?" (2) "Can dreams predict the future?"

౽

Four Peculiarly Characterized Dreams[12]

These dreams are related because they are marked by characteristics which distinguish them amid the dreams of a lifetime as a separate class, characteristics which in part fall within the purview of psychic research.

1. The qualities of emotionality and vividness of imagery to a superlative degree. (1) *Emotionality*. The first roused feelings of aesthetic beauty and sublimity in the highest degree, certainly equalling if not exceeding, those produced by the grandest spectacle I have ever actually witnessed, and revivable years afterward apparently to the degree that memory of such an actual scene is capable of reviving the original emotions which it created. The other three dreams[13] produced superlatively intense feelings of tragic horror, and in one case of terror. In all of these instances, I woke to experience still the emotions appropriate to one who has just witnessed a scene of disaster and death, while for years following each successive dream its sense of horror dimmed only in about the same degree, I am confident, that would have been the case had the scene been an actual one. (2) *Vividness of Imagery*. All four dreams were startlingly vivid in their imagery. In all cases, as will be stated

---

[12] W. F. Prince, *Journal of the American Society for Psychical Research*, 1923, Vol. 17, 82–101.

[13] Only two of the dreams are presented here. [G. M.]

more in detail, the imagery lived on in my memory, for weeks and months almost unimpaired, but as the months lengthened to years with dimming details, as would be the case after similar actual experiences, while the salient outlines will doubtless continue etched in my memory through life.

In both respects, it seems to me that all the rest of my dreams, compared with these four, must be as the glow-worm to the lightning flash. The great mass of my dreams are but vaguely remembered in waking if at all, and leave no trace beyond a few hours. Of course I have had bad dreams as well as pleasant ones, but certainly none to compare, either in vividness of imagery or in emotionality, with those I am to narrate. It is a fact that I cannot at the present moment remember the particulars of any other dream of my lifetime, unless it is one which I recorded because of some odd psychological details which it contained, such as mathematical calculation or puns, and then the memory is not of the dream itself but of the written account of it. But the very fact that the first three of the special class were, unfortunately, not recorded at the time, but continued to live on with salient outlines indelibly fixed, like actual experiences, is a witness to the difference in their quality.

2. Two of the four dreams proved to be complexly coincidental with events which happened very soon afterwards, and a third coincided with an external fact not then known, strikingly but not complexly, and in a manner much less evidential of any supernormal quality that anyone may choose to ascribe.

3. No other dream of my lifetime, so far as memory serves—and it is probable that memory would not fail had there been one—ever caused me to inquire whether there might be any telepathic or supernormal connection between it and external events. Such slight coincidences as there may have been did not appear for a moment otherwise than as the result of normal knowledge, inference or chance. The fact to which I wish to call attention here is that the two dreams which contained complex and extraordinary coincidences, as well as the third which contained a coincidence of slighter character, all belonged to the group which is marked off by the

qualities of intense emotionality and vivid imagery. There must have been countless thousands of dreams, remembered briefly on waking, and that the three singularly coincidental ones should all belong to the little group of four so characterized is a noteworthy coincidence in itself. It might be that the emotionality and vividness of this group, existing in so disproportionate a degree, were indicative of some factor contained in that group and not in the mass of dreams experienced by the same individual.

I may add that I have always been fond of analyzing my dreams, and have generally been able to discover, in the thoughts and experiences of the previous day, and in their apparent utilization of emotional complexes in the storehouse of memory, some ground for them and some reasons for their details. It is a fact that I made such efforts, contemporaneously, in connection with every one of the four dreams, but with no satisfactory results. . . .

III. *Dream of a Collision of Railway Trains: Complexly Coinciding with an Event a few Hours Later.*

During the night following the day Jan. 7th, 1902, probably towards morning, I dreamed that I was looking at a train, the rear end of which was protruding from a railway tunnel. Then, suddenly, to my horror, another train dashed into it. I saw cars crumple and pile up, and out of the mass of wreckage arose the cries, sharp and agonized, of wounded persons. I could distinctly see some pinned under the wreckage. Then other persons hurried up, and seemed to be occupied in trying to get the imprisoned persons clear. And then what appeared to be clouds of steam or smoke burst forth, and still more agonizing cries followed. At about this point I was awakened by my wife, since I was making noises indicative of distress . . . my brain seemed to echo with the after-effects of the crash, the hissing steam and the frenzied screams. It was many minutes before they quite subsided. The dream was related to my wife before I went to sleep again.

At 8:18 that morning, not more than six, and probably not more than four hours after the dream, the Danbury express train, standing with its rear end at the entrance of the Park Avenue tunnel in New York City (the dream occurred in New Haven, about seventy-five miles distant), was struck by the locomotive at the head of the White Plains local train, which crashed through the rear cars of the standing train, crushing them like paper, and killing or wounding a large number of people. The crash, according to the newspapers, was heard half a mile away. And then, one account states, "to add to the horror of it all, the steam hissed out from the shattered engine upon the pinned down unfortunates," and "the steam rose in clouds from the tunnel opening." According to another account, it was after men had begun to cut away the wreckage that the steam pipes burst and fire, also, broke out, all these particulars following in the exact order of the dream.

At that date I had not begun psychical research in a scientific way, and the dream was not recorded at the time. But

1. The dream was related at once to Mrs. Prince.

2. When, during my absence the next afternoon, a neighbor described to her the disaster which he had just read of, she at once recognized the parallels, and said, "Dr. Prince dreamed that this morning just as you have described it," and she is a woman far from disposed to accept signs and wonders.

3. When I saw the newspapers the next day, I was struck by the likeness between the details which I had dreamed and those which actually took place.

4. I retained no copy of the printed account, and never saw one after a day or two following the tragedy. Yet seven years later, in response to a request made by Dr. Hyslop of his readers, for "psychical" experiences, I wrote out the dream as above, and asked him to look up the newspapers which described the event, confident that my dream, whose outlines were still etched in my memory after the manner of a real occurrence, would be found to tally. Probably he filed the letter, but forgot to do as suggested, and it was not until I came into the office of the Society, in 1917, that the comparison was made. It vindicated my memory.

5. In 1917, at my request, Mrs. Prince wrote her recollection of

the dream and the accompanying circumstances, unprompted and without recourse to any printed or written memoranda. It proved that her memory had retained the chief features to an unusual degree, together with the important fact that she recognized the similarity to the actual disaster when the newspapers came out the next day, and so told a named neighbor. The reason why her memory was so tenacious is doubtless the fact that, leaving the house about the hour of the accident, I did not return all that day and the following night; she had no explanation of my absence, since a message which I sent stating why my return was delayed was not delivered; so she sat up all night in great anxiety, thinking much of the dream and fearing that some accident had happened to me.

All the documents connected with this case are to be found in the *Journal* for February, 1919, together with a full discussion, and it will suffice here to set down the coinciding particulars.

(1) A collision of railway trains; (2) In a tunnel; (3) At the tunnel entrance; (4) A rear end collision; (5) The killing and injuring of people by the first impact; (6) The added horror of "steam or fire"—what I saw in the dream being dense clouds of what might have been steam or smoke, and what occurred being that the steam-pipes burst and also the wreckage took fire; (7) The further infliction of death and injury by the steam; (8) The fact that men rushed in and began cutting away the debris and saving the unfortunate *before* the steam and flames broke forth; (9) Temporal proximity—the disaster proving to have been not more than six and probably not more than four hours after the dream; (10) Comparative proximity of place—the collision occurring not in some other country or some distant part of our vast land, but within seventy-five miles, in a locality familiar to me.

This dream was, and is reported simply and solely as a coincidental one, which, up to the point when I was awakened by my wife, presented no divergences from the salient features of the accounts of the survivors which I could detect. Of course they told many incidents which I would not have been in a position to observe, even had I been an actual witness from the point of view in the dream.

I was again unable to discover, in any of my late thoughts or experiences, any favoring causes for the dream, much less for its astonishing vividness and emotionality.

IV. *Dream of the Decapitated Woman: Complexly Coinciding with an Event about Twenty-four Hours Later.*

Date of Dream, Nov. 27, 1917. Told to two persons before the coinciding event. Recorded soon after. Corroborated.

This dream has not hitherto been reported, and will be given in full, with the supporting documents.

Document 1.

New York, Nov. 30, 1917.

On the night following Nov. 27, I dreamed that I had in my hands a small paper with an order printed in red ink, for the execution of the bearer, a woman. I did not seem to have any distinct notion of the reason for her condemnation, but it seemed that I inferred that it was for a political offense, and some thought of the French Revolution seems faintly connected with it; though it may be that I was only reminded of the execution of such as ᴹadame Roland. The woman appeared to have voluntarily brought the order, and she expressed herself as willing to die, if I would only hold her *hand.*

I remember her looks quite well; she was slender of the willowy type, had blonde hair, small girlish features, and was rather pretty. She sat down to die without any appearance of reluctance, seeming fully calm and resigned. It was not clear where we were, but she seemed to me to be in a chair. I should have thought her about 35.

Then the light went out and it was dark. I could not tell how she was put to death, but soon I felt her hand grip mine (my *hand*), and knew that the deed was being done. Then I felt one *hand* (of mine) on the hair of the head, which was loose and severed from the body, and felt the moisture of blood. Then the fingers of my other *hand* were caught in her teeth, and the mouth opened and shut several times as the teeth refastened on my *hand,* and I was filled with the horror of the thought of a severed but living head. Here the dream faded out.

I used years ago to have dreams occasionally of adventures in which I was the afflicted one, with wild beast, as prisoner, as person awaiting execution, etc. (Scarcely a detail of any of these remains in memory. The nearest I come to recollecting any is that in one I was to be drowned by other persons.) I attributed these to my then habits of worrying. I do not now recollect any such dream relating to another than myself, and no dream of the kind in which I figured for at least two years, prior to the dream of Nov. 27–28. (None since to Jan. 20, 1923.)

Yesterday, at about 1 P.M., on my way home from Manhattan, I bought a "Telegram," and found the article appended to this (See Document 4), relating to Mrs. Sarah Hand.

WALTER F. PRINCE.

Signature appended at 12:10 P.M., immediately after writing. Read by me Nov. 30, at 12:15 P.M., 1917.

GERTRUDE O. TUBBY.

(Written later on the same day, by W. F. P.) In the morning I was reminded of the story of Marie Antoinette to the effect that when the executioner held up her head the eyes opened and shut several times, as if to indicate that the head was conscious. It is possible that my vague memory of some woman connected with the French Revolution, in the dream itself, was really this emerging.

It is almost unknown to me to have unpleasant dreams which cast a shadow over the following day, but in this case, not for the following day only, I would find myself dwelling upon the dream details, and particularly the gruesome one of the head being alive after severance. It was on this account that I told the dream to Miss Tubby in the morning, after I had reached the office. On the morning of the 30th, the earliest possible opportunity after I learned of the tragical event which really took place, I asked her to set down what she remembered of what I had told her.

Document 2.

44 East 23rd St.,
10:45 A.M., Nov. 30, 1917.

On the morning of Tuesday or Wednesday, Nov. 27th or 28th, Dr. W. F. Prince told me at the office of the A.S.P.R. that he had dreamed, the previous night, a most gruesome dream, such a gruesome dream as he had not dreamed for a long period— whether months or years I do not precisely recall. He recounted it to me and I recollect it about as follows, after his asking if I remembered it, and on my recollection proving vague asking me if "execution" would help me any; and then, as I proceeded, whether "hand" would help me any.

Some woman was to be executed by beheading. She asked Dr. Prince to hold her hand while she was being beheaded, stating that she felt it would be "all right" if he would only do so; she would not be afraid. He felt the horror of it that would be natural, but consented to assist her as she had asked. He witnessed —or was present, at any rate, at the execution, felt her grip his hand in a spasm of reaction as the head was severed from the body, and turned and picked up her head as it rolled off.

The jaws opened and closed several times and in doing so the teeth once—or more?—bit down on his finger.

On awaking, he could find no physical explanation for the dream experience, his hand being free. He recalled a point in the history of an execution, to which he referred in our conversation —I cannot recall whose—where the eyes had opened and closed several times after the head was severed and Dr. Prince could not quite see how that one bit of information could so stir up his consciousness as to account for his dream. He expressed himself as being at a loss to account for the fact that he does sometimes have such horrible dreams as this.

GERTRUDE O. TUBBY.

Miss Tubby states that I told her on the morning of the 27th or 28th; as the dream was not until the night of Nov. 27th, it was therefore on the 28th that I narrated it, as I have stated. The dream of another person seldom makes much impression on the hearer's memory, hence, to evoke anything that might really be in her memory, I uttered the two words, "execution" and "hand"; but I ask any reader what chance there was of her being able to write down so near a parallel from these two verbal cues, unless she really remembered. Of course, too, she did not remember every detail exactly. I did not dream of picking up the head, but simply felt that it was loose—severed from the body. But substantially her memory proved correct.

I not only told the dream to Miss Tubby on the 28th, but I told it to Mrs. Prince on the morning of the 29th, before we set out to attend a church service in Manhattan, and before I could have seen any printed account of the corresponding event, which was first printed in the afternoon papers. I asked Mrs. Prince to write out her memory of the dream, and on the third following day, unprompted in the meantime, she did so.

Document 3.

[Flushing, Long Island.]
December 2nd, 1917.

Thanksgiving morning my husband, Walter F. Prince, complained about not sleeping well for two nights and said perhaps it is because of a horrible dream I had night before last. I dreamed I was with a party of people and one young lady for some reason had to be executed by having her head cut off. She said to my husband, I think I would not mind it much if you were to hold my hand. He did so and after the head was severed from the body the mouth kept opening and shutting as if it were alive. He said it was so horrible he could not get it out of his mind.

When we were on the way home from The Cathedral of St. John the Divine, Thanksgiving Day, he exclaimed, "A woman by the name of Hand committed suicide and left a note saying her head would live after her body was dead," or something like this. He read this from the paper which he held in his hand.

LELIA C. PRINCE.

Mrs. Prince remembered less than Miss Tubby, but fortunately retained some of the most important particulars. Like Miss Tubby, she imported one detail into the dream which was not originally there; the woman appeared alone, and not with a "party." But the two corroborations, taken together with my own narrative, and the documents to follow, furnish all the proof that could reasonably be expected as to the essential features of my dream, that it was experienced before the event which took place at midnight of the 28th, as will be seen, and narrated to one person before the event and to another before the publication of the event.

As my wife and I were returning to our home in Flushing, L.I., on the early afternoon of Nov. 29th, I read in *The Evening Telegram* of the same day the following:

Document 4.

HEAD SEVERED BY TRAIN AS WOMAN ENDS HER LIFE

Deliberately placing her head in front of the wheels of a train that had stopped at the Long Island Rail Road Station at Hollis, L.I., so that the wheels would pass over her when it started, a woman identified by letters in her handbag as Mrs. Sarah A. Hand, thirty years old, of No. ——— West ——— St., ended her life early to-day. In the handbag, beside the letters, was found a letter rambling in its contents, that predicted the existence of life in her body after death and that her head would still continue to live after it had been severed from her body.

The husband of the woman, ——— Hand, was notified at the ——— Street address, and he went to Hollis in a taxicab. He said his wife had been missing from home since November 27. Since the death of her little girl several months ago, he asserted, Mrs. Hand had acted strangely.

Further details appear in an article which was printed in the *Long Island Farmer:*

Document 5.

DEMONSTRATED A THEORY

WOMAN WHO BELIEVED HER HEAD AND HER BODY COULD RETAIN
LIFE IF SEPARATED CAUSED BEHEADMENT BY CAR WHEEL
WAS INSANE SEVERAL YEARS

Mrs. Sarah A. Hand, 30, of Manhattan, had a theory that her body and her head could live independently of each other. Her friends said she was crazy; but she had the courage of her convictions. So, late Wednesday night, she went to Hollis and, to prove her contention, lay down on the Long Island Rail Road tracks and permitted a train to run over her neck, cutting off her head as cleanly as though the job had been done with an axe. The finding of her head and body, and of a letter beside it, revealed the theory and its execution. The letter read as follows:

"Please stop all trains immediately. My head is on the track and will be run over by those steam engines and will prevent me from proving my condition. You see, my body is alive without my head, and my head is alive without my body. It is suffering where it is, and if smashed in small bits will suffer just the same. So please, I beg, stop all trains so my head will be saved from this terrible torture. My head is alive and can see and talk, and I must get it to prove my case to the law. No one believed me when I said I would never die and when my head was chopped off I would still be alive. Everyone laughed and said I was crazy, so now I have proved this terrible life to all. Please call my husband up at Audubon ———, or Academy ———, N.Y.

"Please have all trains stopped to save my head from being cut in fragments. I need it to talk to prove my condition and have the doctor arrested for this terrible life he put me in."

This missive was not signed. It was in a plain envelope, addressed "To whom it may concern."

Mrs. Hand's body and head were seen by the crew of an eastbound train that left Hollis at 11:15 o'clock Wednesday night. She had placed her neck across the outside westbound rail, close to the station. The station has an elevated concrete platform. It is believed Mrs. Hand crouched for some time under this platform, out of sight of anyone, waiting for a train to stop at Hollis.

When one did, it was evident by the position of her body that she crawled out from her shelter and put her head under the wheels. She lay on her stomach, gripping the ties with her hands, to prevent the wheel pushing her along the rail. As a result, the wheel cut her head off without inflicting any other mark or injury except a deep scratch on her face.

Her husband was notified and hurried to Jamaica. He told the authorities that his wife had been deranged for several years. On an occasion she became much interested in a murder trial in progress in Georgia, where the family then lived. The trial preyed on her mind, and, when her son was born, she conceived the idea that he would be a murderer. The mother's mental condition grew steadily worse. Hoping a change of scene would be beneficial, her husband came to New York.

Recently, he said, his wife had been in a sanatorium. She begged to be taken home for Thanksgiving, so he took her out of the sanatorium last Saturday, sending for his mother to watch over her. On Tuesday she seemed perfectly normal, and went to visit a sister in Manhattan. She never reached her sister's. Following her disappearance her husband spent all his time searching morgues and hospitals. He also sent out a general police alarm. He said he did not know why she had traveled to Hollis, as she knew no one there.

Near the body was a butcher's knife and cleaver, bright and new. It is thought Mrs. Hand intended at first to demonstrate her theory with them, but finally decided that a railroad train would sever her head more effectually. She had written two other letters besides the one found, but afterwards tore them into pieces so small they could not be put together. These pieces lay beside the butcher's tools under the railroad platform. There was also a pocketbook containing $1.50 and some small personal belongings.

While very likely some details in this account, especially in regard to the woman's history, may be erroneous, it can hardly be doubted that the main facts pertinent to our present purpose are correct. The letter found in the handbag is a document in itself, an unimpeachable exhibit.

A letter addressed to the husband was not answered, and a friend of mine, Mrs. Libby, volunteered to try to get information regarding the age and appearance of the dead lady. She had her maid call up the house, with the following result, written on December 30th.

Document 6.

I will now give the maid's exact words.

"A man answered the 'phone. I asked to speak to Mrs. Hand, if she was in. I said I was speaking for a friend who had written her at that address and had not received any answer. Friend wanted to know if she was still living there; had heard that she had moved there from her last address. She said that she had been living there since October.

"I said, 'Are you a blonde?' She said, 'No, I have dark hair.'

"I said, 'Then perhaps you are not the right party. The person my friend wrote to was slender, blonde, and about thirty-five years old.' She said, 'I am not slender, but my son's wife was slender.'

"I said, 'Will you give me the address of your son's wife?' Answer was, 'My son is living here. I live with him. His wife is dead. She has been dead about a month.'

"I said, 'Was your son's wife a blonde?' 'No, but she was slender, she was considered good-looking and had goldish-brown hair.' The lady sighed.

"I said, 'Did she die in the city or in Long Island?' The answer was, 'She died in Long Island.' Another sigh as though I had asked questions enough. I said, 'Thank you, very much. Goodbye.'"

Document 7. Statement by W. F. Prince.

I did myself finally succeed in obtaining a short interview with the husband and his mother, on Jan. 10th, 1918, and in seeing a portrait of the dead lady. It proved that she was 31 years old at the time of her death. She was said to have a sweet smile, such as characterized the lady of my dream, which is, of course, not an uncommon fact. I certainly should not have picked the portrait out as one representing the lady of the dream, though it is possible that the portrait, with its particular style of arranging the hair, did not resemble her so much as the woman herself did. This must remain forever unascertainable. It was confirmed that the tragic event took place at the going out of the 11:15 train, on the night of Nov. 28th. I also learned that the woman had some acquaintance with Flushing, making it a little more likely that she might actually have been there on the night of my dream. Neither her head nor her body was mutilated. I was also informed that her mind was affected by childbirth, and that on this account she had been in a sanatorium until shortly before her disappearance. At about 3:30 P.M., Nov. 27th, she stepped out, saying she would be right back. Her actions and whereabouts are utterly unknown from that moment until her body was found. She had spoken to her husband several times about her head being taken off, and causing her to feel better, and she had told him that he would see that she was right and he was wrong.

Coincidences Between the Dream and the Event.

The Dream.	*The Event.*
1. (a) A woman,	1. (a) A woman,
(b) apparently about 35 years old.	(b) about 31 years old,
(c) slender,	(c) slender,
(d) with very light hair;	(d) with "golden-brown" hair (Semi-coincidental particular),
(e) was rather pretty.	(e) said to be pretty. (Portrait, however, not recognized by me.)
2. (a) Carried the order of	2. (a) Her death was volun-

execution, and was "willing to die,"

(b) and she went to the place of "execution."

3. (a) The "execution" was bloody (not electrocution, strangling, *et al.*),

(b) by decapitation,

(c) and the head seemed to be entire afterwards.

4. The "execution" took place in darkness.

5. The word "hand," or the idea of a hand, kept appearing. The woman asked me to hold her hand, then her hand gripped my hand, then my hand felt her hair, then her teeth fastened on my hand.

6. (a) After decapitation, the head acted as though, and impressed me very disagreeably that it was, still alive.

tary and willed by herself,

(b) and she went to the place of suicide.

3. (a) Her death was bloody,

(b) by decapitation,

(c) and, as the woman hoped it would be, the head was not "smashed."

4. The head was cut off at about 11:15 in the night.

5. The woman's name was Sarah A. Hand.

6. (a) She left a paper declaring that her head would live apart from her body, and asserting that she had previously maintained that "when my head was chopped off I would still be alive."

(b) The acts which manifested life were in connection with the mouth (gripping my hand).

(b) The act, which the note found with the body stated that the still living head would perform, was also one connected with the mouth (talking).

7. The dream took place in a house on Franklin Place, near Bowne Avenue, Flushing, L.I.

7. The event occurred near the railroad station in Hollis, L.I., about six miles from Flushing.

8. The dream was during the night of Nov. 27–28, 1917.

8. The event took place less than twenty-four hours afterward, at about 11:15 P.M., on Nov. 28, 1917.

I have specifically stated that I did not recognize the portrait of Mrs. Hand, though unable to say that the actual woman, especially when she smiled, would not have resembled more the woman of the dream. I have also stated that the actual hair was darker than in the dream-image, though "golden-brown" suggests some resemblance. In the dream the woman seemed to sit down, but it was only an inference that she sat in a chair, as I saw none. At least the impression of sitting implied a descent from her first or standing position. The actual woman must have lain down or crouched on all fours. I certainly saw no engine in my dream, but I also saw no other means of "execution," so this feature is negative.

THEORETICAL.

Something may be added regarding the theories which can be maintained, to explain these dreams.

A. *Chance Coincidence.* Some will think that, however remarkable the combination of coincidences in the "execution" dream, including one so unusual as that of the living severed head, and the approximations in time and space, it came about simply by accident. That the same person had another dream with similar complexities of coincidence, will not alter their opinion. They will urge that two such accidental groups of coincidence might occur in the course of the thousands of [dreams occurring in] a lifetime. To this I might agree, not without misgiving, but for the fact that the two complexly coincidental dreams as well as a third which had the appearance of being coincidental though in a far less impressive manner belonged to a group of four, self-selected by qualities of vividness of imagery and intensity of emotionality unshared by the thousands; and for the fact that no coincidences worth attention were ever noted amid the thousands outside of this class of four. If it be said that other dreams as vivid and emotional may have been forgotten, I reply that the very fact that these remain in my memory as actual experiences would do is itself a witness of the differentiating qualities which I assert that these possessed. I have already asserted the perhaps peculiar fact that, aside from a few dreams recorded in note books, and remembered simply as records, I can recall to-day not a dream of my lifetime out of the class referred to,—nothing but a few subjects and a few vague details. Weeks pass without a single dream remembered on waking, and I do not believe that I have had a dream in the five years following that of the "execution" which has left a trace after three days. If it be conjectured that I remembered the dreams of the particular class because I afterwards noted the coincidences, I reply that the dream of the bombardment is remembered as vividly as any of the four, yet not a scrap of coincidence has ever been found in it. That the only coincidental dreams should be found in the vivid and emotional class of four, seems to me to multiply thousandsfold the impressiveness of the fact that two of these should be so complexly and remarkably coincidental.

B. *The Psycho-Analytical Solution.* Psychoanalysts will say that could they subject me to their processes they could probably account for the four dreams on the basis of former experiences, complexes and submerged wishes of my own. Granting that they satisfied themselves that all the factors of these dreams were thus accounted for, and even that the reasons for the differentiating qualities of vividness and emotionality of the four were laid bare; still, they would not have proceeded one step toward accounting for the coincidences with external facts and events shown in so high a degree by two of the dreams, or for the fact that the dreams containing such coincidences belonged solely to the small group so differentiated.

C. *The Telepathic Solution.* This may most readily be applied to the dream of the "execution." The suicide was evidently planned before the woman left her house, as she took a "butcher's knife and cleaver" with her, as if her first wild idea was to cut off her own head. Whether or not the note found by her body, saying that her head would be living after cut off, was already written, we know that she had already expressed such thoughts to her husband. She may have planned to kill herself at night, etc. She left her home in the afternoon before the dream, and, since it was learned that she had some acquaintance with Flushing, may actually have been near the dreamer at the time of the dream.

But it can hardly be supposed that the events of the railroad collision were consciously or latently in the mind of any living person, several hours before the occurrence. . . .

§

I have nothing to add to Doctor Prince's discussion of the theoretical possibilities. The dream which precedes the event might be called precognitive. On the other hand, assuming that the dream is paranormal, it could have expressed *telepathy* from Mrs. Hand before her death, or *clairvoyance* regarding the tragedy already unfolding.

TELEPATHIC DREAMS AND PSYCHOANALYTIC PRACTICE

Since Freud raised the question whether unconscious dynamics could manifest themselves in telepathy between psychoanalyst and patient, or between either of these and some third party, there has been a considerable volume of serious work by analysts on the problem, notably a series of papers immediately after World War II by Drs. Ehrenwald, Eisenbud, Pederson-Krag, Ullman, and others. These and related materials were assembled, criticized, and evaluated from various points of view in a book edited by George Devereux entitled *Psychoanalysis and the Occult*.[14] We shall not try to recapitulate the themes already regarded as a challenge— or an annoyance—to the analyst. Rather, we shall report here a case from Jan Ehrenwald, *New Dimensions of Deep Analysis*,[15] in which one of his patients had a curious dream; she dreamed that night what looks almost like a carbon copy of what her analyst had been doing:

. . . Her analysis soon revealed a marked fixation on her father. In her behaviour towards the therapist she sought to repeat the old pattern: she was anxious to please, and tried her best to entertain me with her chatter during the treatment sessions. Her positive transference was unmistakable and ushered in a symptomatic improvement of her condition. At that time, on March 10, 1948, she produced the following dream:

"I went to my dressmaker's with Henry's sister Anne. The dressmaker showed me her place and said the apartment was to let. We looked at it. It consisted of a beautiful long, well-shaped living room, spacious, with high ceiling. It opened out to a nice open terrace where the sun shone. It was long; it stretched along the whole building across the front . . . some 50 feet or so. It had a brick wall and the floor was made of planks with cracks in between. There was not much furniture in the room, not so much as you would have if you would furnish it yourself. There

14 New York, International Universities Press, 1953.
15 London, George Allen and Unwin, 1954; New York, Grune and Stratton, 1955.

was quite a lot of space left between the things. It was not a cluttered room. There was no carpet, only oriental rugs, a big one in the middle with figures like the one you have here in the office. There were smaller rugs at either end. But they covered only part of the floor, much of it was showing. There were also a few mahogany chairs and an open fireplace. A french door and two french windows opened to the terrace. A dingy little hall led into the bedroom and into a bathroom. I thought this would be the apartment I would like to live in, except that it did not have a maid's room and no extra bathroom. Still, I was wondering how that little dressmaker could afford such a nice apartment. . . ."

The patient's associations shed little light on the deeper meaning of the dream. She had always considered Anne, Henry's sister, her rival for his affection. Anne was therefore a representative of the patient's own sister, Mary, with whom she had in vain competed for her father's love. Her dressmaker was a somewhat masculine woman whom she nicknamed Bangs on account of her hairdo. She had a tiny apartment on the second floor of an apartment house in Upper Manhattan. She rated her dressmaker either high or rather low in her favours, according to the way she had catered to her sartorial needs. This was the connecting link between Bangs and myself, whom she expected to cater to her psychological needs. The patient had been looking for a new apartment where she could live by herself—not with her tiresome old aunt, as she did at present. Here ended her chain of associations. They revealed nothing about the reason for the appearance in the dream of the detailed picture of the apartment, its precise layout and furnishings, and still less about its relevance to the patient's problems.

But we shall presently see that more light can be thrown on the dream by considering the psychological situation on my side of the picture. A week before the dream occurred, on March 3rd, I had moved into a new apartment in a residential suburb of New York. It was in a large unfinished apartment house and I had been glad to settle down in it comfortably after nearly ten years of nomadic existence during the war. On the night of the dream my brother and his wife had arrived from the country to visit us for the first time in our new home. They shared my enthusiasm. It was a dark rainy night but we stepped out on the terrace which belonged to the apartment. A french door and two french windows opened to the terrace from the living room. It ran across the whole building from one end to the other—between two street blocks—though only a stretch of about 50 by 22 feet was our own. The living room extending into the hall was spacious and high, 34 by 12 feet. It was only scantily furnished at the time the dream occurred. It contained bookshelves on one side; a settee, three easy chairs, two end tables and a small coffee table. On the other end, in the hall, there was only a studio couch and a large unpainted wooden chest. There was no carpet in the apartment, but the floor of the living room was covered by one larger and two smaller oriental rugs, leaving much of the wooden floor uncovered. These rugs were of the same type as I had in my office. A small "dingy" hall led from the living room to the bedroom. It also opened to the bathroom and a second bedroom, occupied by my daughter. The furniture was modern, functional, bleached walnut. There were no mahogany chairs, no fireplace. The main entrance was not from the dingy hall but from the staircase into the hall-living room. The apartment and terrace were on the second floor. The terrace formed the ceiling of the garages belonging to the house. It had a brick wall. At the time the dream occurred the wooden casing of its cemented roof had not yet been removed. It was unfinished and covered with a layer of tarred paper. At one place there was a gaping hole in the floor.

I have to add here that the dreamer located the apartment she saw on the second floor. She made a drawing of its layout as reproduced here (Fig. 1).

It will be noted that her sketch suggests an apartment in a small house, some 50 feet long ("the terrace runs from one end of the house to the other, some 50 feet long"). This is at variance with the fact that both my own and the dressmaker's apartments are in large apartment houses. On the other hand, the fact is that Ruth had lived as a child with her father in a self-contained house of

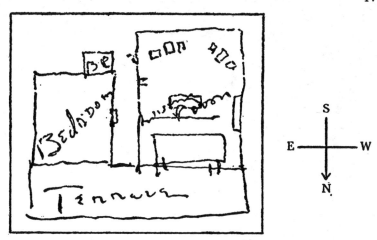

Fig. 1   Ruth's sketch of her "dream apartment."

the Colonial type. The mahogany furniture seen in her dream was the same, she said, as they had at home. The fireplace, too, reminded her of their sitting room in X. There was no terrace.

In spite of these differences, the similarity of the apartment seen by the patient in her dream and my own apartment is striking enough. The majority of the elements mentioned are independent features of whatever apartment they may belong to, although it may be stated that some are inter-related (several rugs—the floor showing in between; location of bedroom and bathroom, etc.). On the other hand, the whole layout of the place, the references to the large terrace with the parapet running across the house, with the french door and windows opening into it; the oriental rugs, etc., are so specific that the correspondences cannot reasonably be attributed to chance alone. Indeed, the chance hypothesis would explain nothing in our case. On the contrary, it would rather bar the way for a proper understanding even of the familiar psychoanalytic aspects of the dream.

The corresponding features can be listed in the table below:

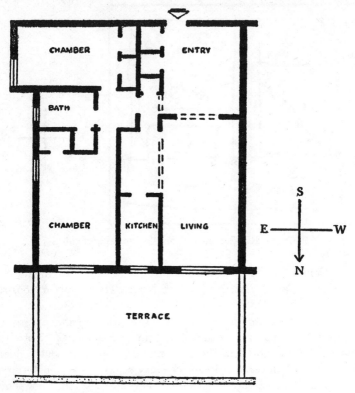

FIG. 2   Floor plan of the therapist's apartment.

Dream	*Reality*
(1) Spacious high living room.	(1) Spacious high living room.
(2) French door and windows to terrace.	(2) French door and windows to terrace.
(3) Very large terrace running across the house.	(3) Very large terrace running across the house.
(4) Brick parapet on terrace.	(4) Brick parapet on terrace.

(5) Scanty furniture in living room "not as you would furnish it yourself."

(6) Oriental rugs "like here in the office."

(7) One large rug, two smaller ones on both sides.

(8) Leaving floor uncovered in places.

(9) Bedroom located to the east of living room.

(10) Bathroom located to the east of living room.

(11) Dingy little hall connecting (9) and (10) with living room.

(12) No maid's room.

(13) No second bathroom.

(5) Scanty furniture in living room (European taste).

(6) Oriental rugs of the identical type.

(7) One large rug, two smaller ones on both sides.

(8) Leaving floor uncovered in places.

(9) Bedroom located to the east of living room.

(10) Bathroom located to the east of living room.

(11) "Dingy" little hall connecting (9) and (10) with living room.

(12) No maid's room.

(13) No second bathroom.

For the sake of the records I have to add here that the patient had been completely ignorant of my personal circumstances before and during the whole course of the treatment. She did not know my private address or telephone number, she had been unaware of my moving to a new apartment and could by no conceivable "normal" ways of communication have learned about its size, layout and furnishings.

☙

The question has already been raised whether it contributes to our understanding of such phenomena to ask whether they are "coincidences." Perhaps a more meaningful question would be whether they are more numerous than we should expect when we take into account the volume of dreams produced by patients, the volume of experiences of analysts on the days preceding the dreams, and the mental connections already likely to occur as a result of the conscious and unconscious interchanges between analyst and patient in the course of therapy. Those who have tried to gather data on the frequency of dreams of various sorts, and to estimate how much might be guessed by patients regarding the experiences of their analysts, will be the best witnesses as to the soundness or unsoundness of referring to an experience like this as a coincidence. If it be held that the normal associative connections offer relatively little explanation, and that very few dreams could be expected to correspond as closely as this one does to a waking experience of another person, then we shall incline toward the establishment of a category which we may call "more than coincidence." Yet this will not in any sense be an explanation. In fact, we must, like Dr. Ehrenwald, discuss the meaningful connections between the experiences of the two parties in any given case, with emphasis upon the symbolic, unconscious implications. Unconscious desires and defenses against them, for example, may contribute to a web of associations between patient and analyst which will only later emerge in the analytic process, or may not emerge at all. It is not Dr. Ehrenwald's belief that the value of such investigations lies in chalking up a striking number of cases going beyond "coincidence," but rather that we have here a way of understanding the dynamics of interpersonal relations: "new dimensions of deep analysis."

III.

Experimental Telepathy

THE GATHERING of spontaneous or "anecdotal" material never satisfies a scientist. Even if he should work in a field in which nature permits little or no control of her performances—a field like geology or astronomy—he reaches out to find something which he can take apart, examine closely, cause to happen over and over again. If he is a geologist he can bring back stones to be studied in a laboratory of petrology or mineralogy. He may subject some of his specimens to high pressures or he may observe them under high-power microscopes as special techniques are applied to them. Even if his subject matter is that of the heat at the interior of a star, he can, in a certain sense, bring to himself through the telescope and spectroscope some of the phenomena which can then be worked out in the terrestrial laboratory of physics. He is determined, come what may, to get experimental control over his phenomena if he can. The biologist turned at this fork of the road well over one hundred years ago, making experimental biology a sort of highway upon which more and more of the old problems of life have been forced to tread, and the experimental psychologist soon agreed to walk with him. Indeed, experimental method in psychology was central in the new psychology which took shape in the physiological laboratories of nearly a hundred years ago, and together with evolutionary and statistical modes of thinking and the study of abnormalities and defects, has served to give a broad picture of psychological processes under various conditions of stimulation and stress. It is where there is experimental intervention—where we can make phenomena happen according to our plan—that we feel we understand the psychology of perceiving or remembering or think-ing. Experimental psychology in these fields has done much to give us the scaffolding of what will in time become a science.

Parapsychology has, of course, been committed to the same out-look and for the same reasons throughout the whole modern period. We have given examples of spontaneous phenomena gathered in the closing years of the last century and samples from our continuing studies of these spontaneous cases, partly to give the raw matrix which nature throws at us; the kinds of experiences regarding which we can hope to know more by setting up special conditions, indeed by defining experiments. It no longer sounds odd to speak of ex-perimental telepathy; in fact, many of us are not very sure that there is great sense in talking about any other kind of telepathy, since the non-experimental can be disposed of with various types of shoulder-shrugging activities and by the process of crawling into that very large shell in which we wish neither to assert nor to deny that which we cannot experimentally control. Most investigators in parapsychology are committed to a maximal use of the experi-mental method. This means, then, that experimental telepathy will now come into the forefront for a number of pages, samples being chosen first from the more primitive, and then from the more so-phisticated experimentation of modern times. It is, of course, the more primitive and impressionistic studies, antedating the period of exact statistical control, that will have to give us our dramatic in-troduction to the experimental method. If the reader will bear with a few of the reports dealing apparently with the transmission of impressions from one mind to another without recourse to any sta-tistical control, he may at least begin to see more clearly the kinds of problems that demand attention, and may be more alert to what can be accomplished by the better-controlled and statistically more sophisticated studies which follow.

We begin with an early report from René Warcollier.[1]

[1] *Experimental Telepathy*, Boston, Boston Society for Psychic Research, 1938, 25–28.

From among our best percipients we chose the person who was to act as agent. She relaxed into the passive state, the usual state for *percipients*. A characteristic object was then, in darkness, placed in her hand, and her descriptions were recorded. Percipients in a distant room recorded their impressions. The results rewarded our trouble.

In one experiment, the object was presented to the agent, under the conditions described, by D. The object was the lower jawbone of a woman found in the crypts of St. Etienne du Mont. Only D, in this case an *active* agent, as distinguished from the passive agent (who received the object in her hand), knew the nature of the

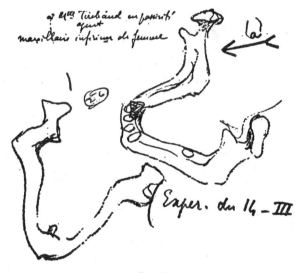

FIG. 3

object, shown in Figure 3. It is obvious that the image itself was not transmitted, but that what the agent *thought* of the object was. The thoughts of the passive agent are found in her description of her part in the experiment. She felt the object and said, "Horns of a little deer, or rather of a roe; not made of wood. I put it

against my forehead—idea of a mountain, wild animal, wild spring-
ing, very difficult to catch. In the middle of a little point, the nail
by which it is attached, a little movable knob, like a joint. It is a
stag's horn." The association of ideas is evident.

And what did the percipients receive? In a room at a distance,
R., one of the percipients, drew the Greek letter gamma. R. W.,
another passive percipient, drew a tined *pitchfork*, a *claw*, and
antlers. These are shown in Figure 4. The experiment was a

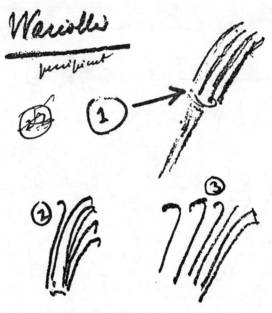

Fig. 4

complete success. The *thought* provoked by mistaken interpretation
in the passive agent's mind was transmitted, while the actual object,
and what the experimenter knew about it, were not transmitted.

In this case the explanation of clairvoyance cannot be applied.
The phenomenon is one in which the state of consciousness of the
passive agent plays an important rôle. To employ a term from

physical science, a certain "potential" of thought is involved.

To continue with the above experiment. The hour was now 6:00 P.M. At 9:30 that evening, March 14, 1925, I was to send a message to the American group in New York with whom we had been experimenting for three years. I had tried on that evening not to concentrate my thought upon any object, but to remain passive, and to note whatever images might pass through my mind, in order

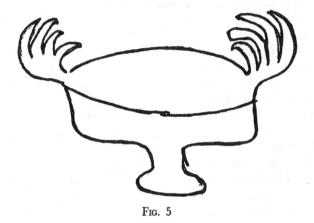

FIG. 5

to see whether they would be the ones transmitted to America. I eliminated the image of the stag's horn of our experiment at six o'clock . . . and the only image which I visualized clearly at the fixed hour of 9:30 was a glass funnel, a memory-image from the morning. At the same hour a percipient in New York drew a sort of funnel with handles, which he called a Visigoth helmet, upside down. Another percipient in New York, at the same moment, drew a large compote glass with handles, as she remarked, "like the *horns of a stag.*" Her drawing is illustrated in Figure 5. Here the factor of the intentional disregard of an image, whose importance we had, in fact, suspected, played its part. . . .

But this intriguing study does not sound much like a modern parapsychological experiment. What about rigorous experimental method and statistical analysis? The following is an early effort to meet this challenge.[2]

๕

Our subject, a young man of twenty-three, a student of mathematics and physical sciences, became aware of his telepathic talent on the occasion of the public performances of Rubini, a young Austrian, who through his demonstrations revived in Holland an interest in paranormal gifts.

I hasten to state immediately that the talent of the student, whose name was Van Dam, has seemed to us very real. While the experiments of Rubini leave some doubt as to the genuine telepathic origin of his acts and performances (which in themselves are very remarkable), in the case of Mr. Van Dam we have been able to give the experiments such form that, in my opinion, no possibility of sensory communication was allowed.

I shall not speak of the experiments with Rubini, as they are very well known. The method is to follow the telepathic subject, fixing one's thoughts upon the object which must be found, changed from one place to another, etc. The telepathic subject takes the hand of the man who guides him, or the end of a steel chain, which is also held by the other person, or indeed, he works without contact, without material link. In all these cases, even in this last, all sorts of circumstances may have an influence. Thus, all investigators are in agreement that from such procedures nothing can be ascertained to establish genuine telepathy. . . .

[2] H. I. F. W. Brugmans, Une communication sur des expériences télépathiques au laboratoire de psychologie à Groningue faites par M. Heymans, Docteur Weinberg et Docteur H. I. F. W. Brugmans, *Le Compte Rendu Officiel du Premier Congrès International des Recherches Psychiques,* Copenhague, 1922, 396–408. [A communication regarding the telepathy experiments in the Psychological Laboratory at Groningen . . . , *Proceedings* of the First International Congress of Psychical Research, Copenhagen, 1922.] The report here is a free translation from the French by G. M.

I shall not speak of experiences of the Rubini type that we made likewise with Van Dam. We began each session with experiments of this sort because our subject believed that he was better disposed after such experiments. I cannot say whether it is exclusively a subjective opinion or whether the subject's opinion was in accordance with reality. Since, in any event, auto-suggestion is a real factor as an idea force, we have felt required to act in accordance with the opinion of our subject. These experiments of the Rubini type have always been successful. The eyes of the subject were always blindfolded. These experiments were done without contact. It is needless to say that the experimenter who led the subject, who walked with him, inhibited so far as possible the expression of his thought. Sometimes we have carried out very complex experiments, as for example finding a rubber stamp in the midst of a pile of objects, finding then the box containing the ink used for stamping, opening this box and then making all the necessary manipulations to stamp a specially marked piece of paper in a certain spot.

. . . I shall not speak further about this. It is always possible that there were sensory influences. The eyes were blindfolded but auditory influences were possible. . . .

Our desire was to eliminate the walking, through which the subject could always influence and disconcert the one who led him. Our idea was to get the subject to choose from among about ten objects as the subject sat before them. Then, no more walking, and in addition the possibility of gauging the results attributable to chance. Instead of this group of about ten objects, we ended up at last with a sort of checkerboard (see Fig. 6) with forty-eight little compartments in which the horizontal direction gave the letters from A to H, and the vertical direction, the numbers 1 to 6.

The small compartment was chosen each time by lot. We had eight letters and six numbers, and each time before beginning the experiment we had drawn twice, and among the three of us only he who was to influence the hand of the subject knew the result of the drawing, such as A2 or G3.

6	6	6	6	6	6	6	6
5	5	5	5	5	5	5	5
4	4	4	4	4	4	4	4
3	3	3	3	3	3	3	3
2	2	2	2	2	2	2	2
A	B	C	D	E	F	G	H

FIG. 6   Board used in telepathic experiment at University of Groningen, Netherlands.

The eyes of the subject were always blindfolded. In addition, he was always seated in a sort of little cubicle closed on three sides (see Fig. 7). Through a slit the hand alone was visible. All the rest was hidden by a curtain. In addition, the subject was placed in a room other than that containing the experimenters. We were in a room above his room. We could follow the movements of his hand through a hole filled by two sheets of glass with an air cushion between. . . .

Thus, as you see, there were three precautions: Blindfold, cubicle, and the use of another room. During the experiments the subject's room was well lighted, while ours was pitch dark.

As to the results of the experiments, first I shall give a general view, and later the details.

FIG. 7 Apparatus used for telepathic experiment at University of Groningen, Netherlands.

28 May	30 Experiments	8 Successes
11 June	24 Experiments	11 Successes
25 June	18 Experiments	16 Successes
9 July	36 Experiments	9 Successes
9 September	33 Experiments	4 Successes
10 September	16 Experiments	7 Successes
17 September	30 Experiments	5 Successes
Total	187 Experiments	60 Successes

Just now I told you that the experiments were made in two rooms. That was half of the truth. I did not give you the whole of it, to avoid distracting your attention. Now the correction. After each series of six experiments, using the two rooms, we made six experiments in the same room in which our subject sat. We wished to know about the influence of distance. In the two rooms the distance was about three meters; in the same room about a half a meter. Among the experiments in two rooms, 32 out of 80, or 40%, were successful. Of the experiments in one room, 23 out of 77, or 30%, were successful. Perhaps this is a chance difference. In any event, a greater distance did not reduce the phenomenon. Indeed, the two rooms present advantages. If as "conductor" (if the word be permitted) one finds oneself in another room from the subject, it is unnecessary to inhibit expressive movements. In the same room (though the subject had his eyes blindfolded and was placed behind a cardboard cubicle) one controls one's expressive movements. All the same, I believe that the better results with the two-room procedure is a consequence of the absence of this inhibition.

All three of us acted to guide the hand of the subject. All three served as "conductors" and with success. There is no notable difference from one experimenter to another. However, one of us who is short-sighted had scant results in the two-room experiments, but in the same room had fine results.[3]

[3] When I asked Dr. Brugmans whether this could have been clairvoyance —direct perception of the items chosen rather than telepathy from the experimenter's mind—he said, "No, we could *push* the hand this way and

The experiments were made after giving our subject 30 grams of alcohol; at other times two grams of bromide; at other times nothing at all. The bromide was given three quarters of an hour before beginning the experiments; the alcohol ten minutes before. As we have given the bromide only once, I shall not speak of this. As to the alcohol, we may say that it improves the results considerably. Without it we obtained 22 successes in 104 cases, or 21%; with alcohol we obtained 22 out of 29, or 75%. Looking back, the result is not surprising. We know that alcohol overcomes the normal inhibition of the individual. The reduction of self-control and the presence of more superficial thoughts are symptoms of the lack of inhibition. If we wish to describe the same thing in Otto Gross' terminology we may say: Secondary process is reduced and at the same time primary process is increased.[4] This means that the individual has no longer an internal life in the same sense; the internal psychic life which at times takes up so much energy that there is hardly anything left for the sensory life. Under the influence of alcohol the internal life is not so exigent and in consequence, the individual is more open to sensory impressions.

Now our experiments have taught us that the telepathic impressions partake of the character of ordinary sensory impressions. If psychic energy is taken up by our internal life, our preoccupations and problems, inhibition is apparent, and the sensory life is impoverished. It is likewise very probable that in this state the telepathic messages find, so to speak, a closed door. On the other hand, if by

---

that. C'est telepathie." A modern student might wonder if there could be a direct "mental push," the "psychokinesis" discussed on pp. 156–182 below. In Brugmans' era telepathy was the challenging question; these modern questions about clairvoyance and psychokinesis were relatively rarely raised.

If the question be raised whether there is any cogent evidence for telepathy which *excludes* interpretation in terms of clairvoyance as an alternative, I should personally emphasize the evidence (see pp. 152–153, below) that some agents ("senders") regularly succeed in transmitting impressions to certain percipients ("perceivers") while others fail, although the physical stimuli available for clairvoyance remain the same. [G. M.]

[4] This is not far from Sigmund Freud's use of the terms *primary* and *secondary process* in his *The Interpretation of Dreams*, 1900. [G. M.]

virtue of a natural or artificial cause the inhibition is slight, the impressions from outside find an opportunity to dominate and the telepathic influence is among the factors found in this category.

Thus, if we use our entire psychic energy for our practical life, our problems and preoccupations, there is nothing left to receive the messages which seek a place in our awareness. Our awareness is like a fortress well defended. It is less completely closed in sleep, and the proof of this is the fact that spontaneous telepathic cases are found more often in dreams. I have, moreover, the impression that the mental state of hystericals and neurasthenics offers a relatively favorable situation. We need a state of awareness which suffers from a handicap. Alcohol is a crude method of realizing, to some degree, artificially, this state of mind.

I do not wish to weary you with numbers. We have seen that the correct squares were chosen more often than would be expected, on the basis of chance probability. . . . Sixty hits in a total of 187. Probability would have given us only four. As you see, each of our seven sessions gave results above chance expectation. If we have not committed some error (and it is to ask your opinion regarding matters which we may have overlooked to which I would especially draw your attention) the existence of telepathy is established. . . .

In this classical experiment from the Netherlands, there are several questions which might be of interest to the careful analyst of the data.

(1) What did the experimenters do when the subject tapped, not directly on a square, but on a line between two squares or on a corner marking the intersection of four squares? (2) What was the distance from the upper room to the hand? From the photograph it may perhaps be estimated at about five feet, and the checkerboard apparently had squares about an inch big. (3) While one would think that there might be occasional cases of uncertainty, it is clear that the theory of probability would incline us not to expect as many hits as were obtained, even if all the uncertain cases were counted

as hits—indeed not by a wide margin, since only four hits would be expected in 187 trials. Still, we wish that the matter had been fully analyzed. (4) We wish we knew whether a record of the slips drawn by lot was made prior to the record of the subject's actual response. Probably so, but it is unfortunate to be left guessing in this matter. (5) The old question: could one or indeed two of the experimenters have been in collusion with the subject, or would it have been physically possible for one or two of the experimenters to "fake" the results? These questions do not appear to be answerable. The more elaborate modern plans for preventing fraud on the part of investigators had apparently not been thought of. Some readers will be worried by these considerations; others will not.

When it comes to understanding what actually happened, we have the clues regarding the deep relaxation (almost a trance state) of the subject, so often reported in telepathy experiments. Indeed, from the *Second* International Congress of Psychical Research (not used here) we have a report by Brugmans on the deep relaxation of the same subject, as shown by galvanic skin reflex, which indicates that the subject could tell pretty well when he was relaxed, in this sense of the term. Yet, this does not help us a great deal because we have here no real physiological explanation, just as we are left without a psychological explanation.

WHATELY CARINGTON'S WORK[5]

Much of the modern experimental work with telepathy and related processes limits the experimental subject to a specific range of objects among which he must choose. There may, for example, be numbers from one to one hundred; or there may be the letters of the alphabet; the fifty-two playing cards; the states of the Union; or a fixed list of flowers, birds, etc. All experiments conducted with materials of this sort permit some sort of statistical control. There are, however, two rather serious psychological objections. First, they call for a more or less cut-and-dried choice among existing pos-

[5] *Thought Transference: An Outline of Facts, Theory and Implications of Telepathy,* New York, Creative Age Press, Inc., 1946, 54–71.

sibilities. The subject is not free to let his mind roam and think of anything he likes, because there is no way of scoring his success. (Though he may think of something very unusual we do not know how many of these very unusual things would come up by chance alone in the course of experiments of various kinds.) The other psychological difficulty with the fixed or limited range of materials is that the subject may become so bored with the limited possibilities that his attitude toward the experiment is no longer positive. Granting the enormous difficulties in setting up a "free" procedure, it is to the very great credit of Whately Carington, a Cambridge University scholar, to have developed a suitable technique for the use of free material in telepathy experiments.

Carington's usual procedure was to open a large dictionary at random, preferably by inserting a pen knife; select the first "drawable" word, that is, a word which could be embodied in a drawing; make the drawing; place the drawing on his desk; and go out, locking the door. By prearrangements with his subjects scattered through a considerable region, even all of Great Britain, he could require that impressions received by the subjects be drawn, and sent in to him within a certain period.

Now as to the statistical treatment of the data. He decided first that it was necessary to have a large pool of empirical material as to what people in such experiments actually think of, and this could easily be derived. Suppose a subject correctly guesses anteater and claims a huge success on the ground that anteaters are thought of relatively rarely; and claims some credit also for a cat and an albatross. If a thousand people take part, it is not difficult to show that the cat should get very limited "credit," because so many dozens of people reported cats. The albatross should get a great deal more and the anteater more still, because these are rarely submitted. And consequently if the subject's guess actually coincides with a drawing of an anteater placed upon the desk in that particular experiment, we know what the "chances" of a successful hit on such an object are. We proceed now to give credits to all the objects reported by all the persons taking part in all of the series of the experimental trials. If there are many anteaters in the course of an experiment in which anteater was actually drawn by the dictionary method, and very few anteaters in *other* experiments preceding and following this particular experiment, we may pile up a considerable amount of "credit." Whereas, if the subjects waste their guesses either on very common objects or on rare objects which were not actually shown at the time of the particular experiment, they will have to be penalized. The total credit is going to depend on the number of hits weighted by the rareness value of the item.[6] We have then a crude but forthright way of demonstrating whether items drawn by percipients at the time of certain experiments coincide with the materials actually used in those experiments better than with material used in previous or subsequent experiments.

Carington successfully repeated his experiments on numerous occasions, notably in an "inter-university" experiment involving Scottish and English universities. Each university group scored higher on the materials set up for it to guess than on the material set up for the *other* groups. It has been clear, however, from subsequent work that it takes a very large amount of material (many subjects and many guesses) to yield a statistically significant result, and a satisfactory repetition of the Carington experiments with large quantities of material has not yet been reported.

and past a certain point anything is significant!

---

[6] This is actually a mathematical oversimplification. The mathematical formula and its rationale are described in detail in W. Carington, Experiments on the Paranormal Cognition of Drawings: III. Steps in the Development of a Repeatable Technique, *Proceedings of the American Society for Psychical Research*, 1944, Vol. 24, 3–107.

IV.

Experimental Clairvoyance

IN THE closing years of the nineteenth century and the first three decades of the twentieth, the term *telepathy* was used essentially as defined by Myers, as quoted on page 7 above; it was conceived that the essential core of many paranormal ways of making contact with the environment lay in the transmission of a sense-impression, idea, or feeling from one person to another, and sometimes (as in the quotation on pp. 24–25 above from Mrs. Sidgwick) by virtue of a sort of reciprocity or attunement of two minds. There remained, however, both in spontaneous cases and in experimental cases, the possibility (which was for the most part ignored) that contact was really made not between one mind and another, but between a mind and an object which it perceived (cf. p. 59, fn.)

If, for example, there is a genuine paranormal capacity to perceive underground water or precious metals—I say *if* because it is not my interest to discuss this type of evidence here—the positive results might have to be explained in terms of clairvoyance rather than telepathy. Psychical research was slow to grasp this point. When, in the early days of psychical research, a report strongly suggested that a sensitive person was making contact, not with another *mind,* but with an *event,* or *physical object* (as in the alleged instances of successful specification of the deep water sources to which geology could give no clue), it was said that if any positive result emerged, it would necessarily be due to action from the *mind* of someone familiar with the event, such as the presence of the water. The process of detection of *things* or *events,* rather than the contents of the minds of other persons, was, in general, designated by the term clairvoyance. But clairvoyance was in bad odor. The situation changed abruptly when, using simple and ingenious tests, J. B. Rhine at Duke University reported that the perception of concealed or distant cards whose order was unknown to any living person could be investigated by a technique which fairly well ruled out telepathy. The resulting data from recent years are therefore not, even in a forced use of the term, comparable to the main paranormal data from the first fifty years of psychical research. The claims regarding clairvoyance must be evaluated on their merits, not smuggled in as secondary types of telepathy.

Rhine began vigorously some thirty years ago to study both telepathy and clairvoyance. The circumstances under which the long series of telepathy and clairvoyance experiments were initiated at Duke University are as follows: Rhine, a forester with a Ph.D. in botany, and his wife, interested in the same fields, had encountered some impressive reports of paranormal events and decided that these should be followed up. They made their way to Harvard, where, in 1926, Professor William McDougall had been serving since 1920. Both in his British and in his American periods of service he was known to champion the reality of various ideas quite repugnant to mechanistic psychology, and to be favorable to the telepathy hypothesis. He and Rhine believed in one another from the beginning, and when McDougall was called to a chair of psychology at Duke University, Durham, North Carolina, the Rhines followed him there. Here, McDougall offered warm encouragement and made a professional opportunity in parapsychology available. From 1930 to 1934 the Rhines carried forward pioneer experimental investigations in telepathy and clairvoyance and related problems. Many students served as laboratory subjects, and during the latter part of this period graduate students in the psychology department acted as assistants. Believing from the start in a standard statistical method permitting the comparison of all results against an objectively known "mean chance expectation" (the average score which one ought to be able to make in a telepathy or clairvoyance test if one were simply guessing and exercising no telepathy and

biography of Rhine?

clairvoyance), Rhine determined to use five symbols in a "balanced

FIG. 8

deck" of twenty-five cards, each deck containing five of each of these symbols. For many purposes thereafter he and other parapsychologists have used somewhat different kinds of decks; instead of five of each kind, each card is drawn from a very large or from virtually an infinite number of cards, or each card determined by random numbers[1] so that there might be not five of each kind, but very few of one and very many of another kind. In most experiments there is a p value of one-fifth, i.e., *one chance in five,* of getting a given call right, if nothing but guessing is involved.[2] We have already seen in the Brugmans experiment the essential conception of a chance control upon the number of hits that can be made. But with the Rhine procedure we have, year in and year out, a standard p value of one-fifth, so that as we vary the motivation, the practice effects, the influence of drugs, fatigue, etc., we have a relatively simple way of comparing statistically the success under each condition.

Finding that group experiments were in general rather unsuccessful, Rhine emphasized individual experiments, acting as investigator himself and later using a considerable number of graduate students as investigators, sometimes directly under his supervision, sometimes, as will be seen later, acting on their own.

[1] Mathematicians have prepared lists of random numbers, in which each digit is in the long run followed with equal frequency by every other digit.
[2] It does not seem feasible to treat all the statistical issues in this volume. The interested readers will find many excellent elementary manuals of statistics.

Whereas most investigators in the field had for several decades found it difficult to get results much better than what would be expected by sheer chance, Rhine from the beginning got very much higher scores. After a very casual preliminary experiment (in which there might be ways of telling from the backs of the cards what figures were printed on them or in which there might be reflections, faulty shuffling and other sources of error), it was in general his practice to follow with strict experiments under controlled conditions. The main types of controls used to exclude "sensory cues," that is, ways by which some sense impression of the material aimed at might be available to the subject, included first, screens separating the subject from the cards; second, opaque envelopes; and third, long-distance conditions.

Several undergraduate and graduate students at Duke University became interested and had soon established spectacular positions for themselves as successful subjects. One of these, Hubert Pearce, was a subject in several extraordinary successful experiments, of which one will now be described. This "Pearce-Pratt" investigation carried out near the beginning of Rhine's work at Duke was reported briefly in his volume, *Extrasensory Perception*,[3] and in much greater detail in an article in the *Journal of Parapsychology* in 1954. This article is worth quoting substantially as printed, giving not only the original raw data but many circumstantial details.

A REVIEW OF THE PEARCE-PRATT DISTANCE SERIES OF ESP TESTS[4]

A number of considerations have contributed to our decision to present the original and subsequent work identified with what has come to be known as the Pearce-Pratt Distance Series of ESP tests, carried out in 1933–34 at the Parapsychology Laboratory at Duke University. One reason for the review is the need expressed by some

[3] Boston, Boston Society for Psychic Research, 1934.
[4] J. B. Rhine and J. G. Pratt, *Journal of Parapsychology*, 1954, Vol. 18, 165–177.

students of the subject for a more complete and detailed account of the original experiment than is to be found in any one publication. The first part of the series, what is known as Subseries A, was published in the monograph *Extrasensory Perception* written in 1934 by J. B. R. (6).[5] This section was all that was completed at the time the monograph was written. In 1936 a brief account of the series and its total results was given in an article by J. B. R. in the *Journal of Abnormal and Social Psychology* (8), and in 1937 a condensed version of this article was included in the first number of the *Journal of Parapsychology* (7).

Another reason for the present undertaking is the fact that almost immediately upon publication the Pearce-Pratt Series received special attention. It represented a methodological advance over earlier experimental work in parapsychology; and both for the laboratory group associated with the experiment and for those who were attempting to appraise and criticize the evidence for extrasensory perception, the series had to be considered. Moreover, as new questions were raised about the series, further analyses of the data resulted. Most of these analyses were reported as they were completed, but to the student of today it would be a difficult undertaking to run them all down.

There is the further point that it is now possible to appraise the experiment and its results in the light of the developments of the intervening twenty years, the most productive period of parapsychology. It was considered an advantage to older students as well as new, therefore, for the authors to assemble for re-examination the factual matter that has accumulated around this single experimental series.

Something should be said regarding the general background of the research. First, there is the all-important aspect of personnel. It should not be forgotten that without Prof. William McDougall's appreciation of the problem and his tolerant and courageous interest in seeing it investigated under good conditions in a psychology

[5] The numbers in parentheses refer to the references appearing at the end of this section. [G. M.]

laboratory, the experiment would not have been possible. J. B. R. was at the time an assistant professor in the department of which Professor McDougall was head; it was generally understood in those days that research in parapsychology was approved by the Department. J. G. P. was a graduate student in psychology, specially employed as research assistant to J. B. R. From the viewpoint of objectivity, it should be noted that J. G. P. had not at that time shown special interest in the problems of parapsychology, and in fact worked on other problems for his graduate researches. It was not until some years later that he decided to devote his energy to parapsychology.

The subject, Hubert E. Pearce, Jr., was at the time a student in the Divinity School at Duke. He had introduced himself to J. B. R. approximately eighteen months earlier and had stated that he believed he had inherited his mother's clairvoyant powers. In ESP card tests given by J. G. P. and J. B. R. during the intervening period he had exceeded the average score to be expected from chance in practically every experimental session under a wide variety of conditions. During that period he had participated in tests involving nearly 700 runs through the standard deck of ESP cards, averaging approximately 32% successes as compared with the mean chance expectation of 20%. Nothing like this prolonged series of tests had ever been made up to that time, and H. E. P.'s performance was recognized even then as highly exceptional.

The Distance Series was the first step involving different buildings in the separation of H. E. P. from the target card he was attempting to identify. The move was not so much a strictly necessary requirement for the exclusion of visual cues as it was a matter of providing a conspicuously wide margin of safety against the possibility of such cues. The use of different buildings, incidentally, was convenient for the independent recording of the subject's responses and the card sequences. It became easily possible at the same time to provide for duplicate recording and independent checking.

To those of us who had participated in the long series of earlier tests with H. E. P. under gradually improving conditions of test and observation, this further advance in experimental conditions was hardly required. The essential safeguards had already been approximated. There is, however, a tendency of the mind, when confronted with so incredible a hypothesis as that of ESP, to exaggerate the possibility of alternative factors such as visual cues, recording errors, the loss of records, and the like. The revolutionary character of the ESP hypothesis, then, made necessary a range of precautions that were not normally considered a part of the routine of experimental psychology. This atmosphere of critical apprehension concerning the adequacy of the design needs to be taken into account, for it was a part of the actual situation in which the experiment was conducted.

Some idea of the state of mind prevailing at the time can be gained from the circumstances leading to the planning of Subseries D. Subseries A, B, and C had been designed on the assumption that no error was possible that could favor the ESP hypothesis—not unless the two men, J. G. P. and H. E. P., were deliberately to conspire to produce a fraudulent set of results. Wisely (and accurately) anticipating that there would be those who would find it easier to suspect collusion than to accept ESP as established, Professor McDougall recommended that J. B. R. identify himself with the actual performance of at least a short subseries of the distance tests in order that a theory of collusion would have to involve all three of the participants in the experiment. On the basis of this plan Subseries D was conducted with J. B. R. actively officiating with J. G. P.

Actually the primary research objective in the experiment was to compare the effect of short and long distance on the results. In the planning of the test series, this concern with the role of distance was the essentially novel feature of the experimental design. In most of the tests in which H. E. P. took part during the preceding period, the target cards had been within a yard of him. It was considered a sufficient first step to introduce a distance of at least a hundred times that unit as one that should reveal any effect of distance on any possible radiant energy that conceivably intermediated in the operation of ESP. Later in the series this distance was increased still farther. While, then, for the general public and the critic especially, the Pearce-Pratt Series came into focus as a conclusive demonstration of the *occurrence* of ESP, to the workers in the Parapsychology Laboratory it became the first definite step in the testing of the hypothesis of the *non-physical nature* of psi, the hypothesis suggested by earlier experimental work as well as by the study of spontaneous psi experiences.

Procedure

A single subject, H. E. P., was tested for his ability to identify ESP test cards manipulated by the experimental assistant, J. G. P., in another building, part of the time at a distance of 100 yards and part of the time at a distance of more than 250 yards from the location of the subject. The experiment was designed to test for the clairvoyant type of ESP; and J. G. P., accordingly, did not know the card order in the test.

Aside from planning the experiment, J. B. R. participated only in the independent checking of results, except for Series D in which he participated with J. G. P. as the witness to the operation of the test.

There were, in all, four subseries, A, B, C, and D, totaling 74 runs through the pack of 25 cards; and the series extended from August, 1933, into March, 1934. The testing days were not consecutive, though within a given subseries they were more or less so. They were selected, however, at the mutual convenience of H. E. P. and J. G. P. Subseries C was begun in October, 1933, and four runs were added to it in March, 1934, with Subseries D following thereafter. Specific dates may be found in Table 1. Subseries A was done with the 100 yards distance, Subseries B at 250 yards, and the other two subseries back at 100 yards. The 74 runs represent all the ESP tests made with H. E. P. during this experiment under the condition of working with the subject and target cards in different buildings. It was, in fact, the only distance test involving different buildings done at the Duke Laboratory at the time.

Series A was set up with an advance commitment on termination point. It was agreed that 300 trials were to be given H. E. P. The following Subseries, B, was intended to be a duplication with only the additional distance involved, but the experimenters were interested in the big shift of scoring level from day to day which was shown at the longer distance. It was decided to allow H. E. P. to continue further so as to see what would happen. Subseries C was intended to be a repetition of Subseries A consisting of 300 trials designed to discover whether the lower scoring rate of Subseries B at the longer distance was a result of the altered situation or whether H. E. P. had declined in scoring ability. Subseries D, as has been stated, was intended as introducing a check on J. G. P., and its length was agreed upon in advance (150 trials, or six runs).

In actual operation the experiment proceeded as follows, regardless of which subseries was involved: At the time agreed upon, H. E. P. visited J. G. P. in his research room on the top floor of what is now the Social Science Building on the main Duke campus. The two men synchronized their watches and set an exact time for starting the test, allowing enough time for H. E. P. to cross the quadrangle to the Duke Library where he occupied a cubicle in the stacks at the back of the building. From his window J. G. P. could see H. E. P. enter the Library.

J. G. P. then selected a pack of ESP cards from several packs always available in the room. He gave this pack of cards a number of dovetail shuffles and a final cut, keeping them face-down throughout. He then placed the pack on the right-hand side of the table at which he was sitting. In the center of the table was a closed book on which it had been agreed with H. E. P. that the card for each trial would be placed. At the minute set for starting the test, J. G. P. lifted the top card from the inverted deck, placed it face-down on the book, and allowed it to remain there for approximately a full minute. At the beginning of the next minute this card was picked up with the left hand and laid, still face-down, on the left-hand side of the table, while with the right hand J. G. P. picked up the next card and put it on the book. At the end of the second minute, this card was placed on top of the one on the left and the next one was put on the book. In this way, at the rate of one card per minute, the entire pack of 25 cards went through the process of being isolated, one card at a time, on the book in the center of the table, where it was the target or stimulus object for that ESP trial.

In his cubicle in the Library, H. E. P. attempted to identify the target cards, minute by minute, and recorded his responses in pencil. At the end of the run, there was on most test days a rest period of five minutes before a second run followed in exactly the same way. H. E. P. made a duplicate of his call record, signed one copy, and sealed it in an envelope for J. B. R. Over in his room J. G. P. recorded the card order for the two decks used in the test as soon as the second run was finished. This record, too, was in duplicate, one copy of which was signed and sealed in an envelope for J. B. R. The two sealed records were delivered personally to J. B. R., most of the time before J. G. P. and H. E. P. compared their records and scored the number of successes. On the few occasions when J. G. P. and H. E. P. met and compared their unsealed duplicates before both of them had delivered their sealed records to J. B. R., the data could not have been changed without collusion, as J. G. P. kept the results from the unsealed records and any discrepancy between them and J. B. R.'s results would have been noticed. In Subseries D, J. B. R. was on hand to receive the duplicates as the two other men met immediately after each session for the checkup.

Thus, from day to day as the experiment proceeded, H. E. P. was kept informed, as he had been in all his earlier experiments, as to the rate of success achieved. The practice of expressing enthusiastic congratulations should be mentioned as a part of the procedure. If, as rarely happened, the scoring rate was low, favorable emphasis was placed on the overall performance, the general average maintained, and the high standing of the subject in the comparative scale of ESP subjects. Throughout the series the paramount objective of high-order performance was held before the subject with all the vigor and expectation that could be communicated.

Results

General Evaluation

Since they were one series of tests carried out under essentially the same conditions, the four subseries (totaling 74 runs, or 1850 trials) may be pooled. Mean chance expectation is 20%, or 370 hits. The total number of successes actually scored for the series is 558, which is better than 30%. The theoretical standard deviation derived on a conservative basis is 17.57. This total of 558 hits is 188 above the theoretical expectation and it gives a critical ratio of 10.70. The probability that a critical ratio so large as this would occur on the basis of random sampling in less than 10^{-22}. In the determination of the critical ratio given above, allowance is made for the slight correction applicable when, as in this experiment, the balanced ESP deck is used; that is, when there are five of each symbol in each pack. The variance of scores obtained with the 5 x 5 ESP deck depends upon the frequency with which the subject calls the different symbols. The largest variance results when the subject always calls exactly five of each symbol, and the SD of 17.57 was obtained on this assumption (2). However, the subject rarely called five of each symbol in a run, and the exact SD would therefore be smaller than the one used here, which makes the estimate of statistical significance a conservative one.

TABLE 1. Pearce-Pratt Distance Series: General Results

| Subseries | Dates | | Runs | Dev. | SD | CR | P |
	Start	End					
A........	8/25/33	9/ 1/33	12	+59	7.07	8.35	$<10^{-14}$
B........	9/ 2/33	9/30/33	44	+75	13.54	5.54	$<10^{-6}$
C........	10/18/33	3/10/34	12	+28	7.07	3.96	.000075
D.......	3/12/34	3/13/34	6	+26	5.00	5.20	$<10^{-6}$
Total. .	8/25/33	3/13/34	74	+188	17.57	10.70	$<10^{-22}$

Each of the four subseries is independently significant, as may be seen by reference to Table 1. The table shows for each subseries the date, number of runs, deviation, standard deviation, critical ratio, and the associated probability.[6] A complete record of the card order and calls for the series has been furnished from time to time to qualified workers who wish to make some special study of the material. This practice will continue.

Results of Further Studies and Analyses

Since this series was first reported, the data have been used by a number of research workers at the Parapsychology Laboratory for additional analyses. Some of the analyses bear upon the general question of whether the target order was sufficiently random to justify the assumptions underlying the statistical methods used in the evaluation of the results. Other analyses were aimed at trying to discover further psychological information relevant to questions of how ESP operates. The following review includes most of these analyses, though it does not cover all of the critical reviews and discussions.

Tests of Assumptions Underlying Statistical Methods. Greenwood and Stuart (3) did a cross-check in which the subject's calls were arbitrarily matched against the cards of the third run following, the calls for the first run being checked against the card sequence of the third run, the calls of the second against the cards of the fourth, etc. To make the cross-check series the same length as the experimental series, the calls of the last two runs were checked

---

[6] In the two reports, mentioned above, in which the run scores of the series were published, the scores of Subseries B and C were not given consecutively, and there were two other minor errors. It seems worth while, therefore, to list the complete run scores in chronological order here. The division between days or sessions is indicated by the use of semicolons.

Subseries A: 3; 8, 5; 9, 10; 12, 11; 11, 12; 13, 13, 12.

Subseries B: 1, 4; 4, 4; 7, 6; 5, 0; 6, 3; 11, 9; 0, 6; 8, 6; 9, 4; 10, 6; 11, 9; 5, 12; 7, 7; 12, 10; 6, 3; 10, 10; 6, 12; 2, 6; 12, 12; 4, 4; 3, 0; 13, 10.

Subseries C: 9, 8; 4, 9; 11, 9; 5, 4; 9, 11; 2, 7.

Subseries D: 12, 3; 10, 11; 10, 10. [J. B. R. and J. G. P.]

against the cards of the first and second runs respectively. The 74 cross-check runs give a total of 387 hits, a deviation of 17 above mean chance expectation, which is less than one standard deviation. . . .[7]

Analyses for Secondary ESP Effects. The data of this experiment were checked for displacement by Russell (9), who compared each call with the targets in the run for as many places away as the position of the call permitted. In the usual terminology this means that for backward displacement the data were checked for —1 through —24 displacement; and for forward displacement, for +1 through +24. No evidence of displacement was found.

The Pearce-Pratt Series was included by Pratt (5) among a number of high-scoring experiments, the results of which were studied to see whether the hits were clustered or whether, conversely, they were distributed as if they were in a random series. There was no evidence of grouping of hits in the Pearce-Pratt Series nor in any of the other ESP and PK data analyzed.

This experiment was also included among those surveyed by Pratt (4) in his analysis of ESP data to determine if there was any evidence that the subject interrupted or changed his habitual sequence of calling after making a hit. The Pearce-Pratt Series did not yield any evidence of change-of-call; that is, there was no difference between the frequency with which the subject followed a response that made a hit by the different ones of the five symbols in his next call and the frequency with which one of his calls that made a miss was followed by the various symbols.

Also, without giving the detailed figures, we can report here that there was no evidence that could be detected by a chi-square analysis to indicate that the subject interrupted his habitual sequences of symbol association at the point of making a hit. This is a ques-

---

[7] The cross-check score as originally reported was 385 hits. In the present paper the practice followed has been to report the corrected figure when any analysis previously published has been found to have an error. All of these corrections are trivial and none affects any interpretation of the findings. The student who notices any such discrepancies should give this review precedence over the earlier publications. [J. B. R. and J. G. P.]

tion that needs to be examined in longer series of high-scoring subjects where a weak effect would more likely be revealed by the statistical measures applied. If it is true that a subject scores well above the level attributable to chance without deviating from whatever habitual sequence preferences he may have, this fact might provide an important clue regarding the manner in which ESP impressions are brought to conscious expression.

In still another analysis of this series, Cadoret and Pratt (1) examined the misses in the subject's trials to see if there was any evidence of consistent wrong associations between responses and target symbols. No evidence of consistent missing in the Pearce-Pratt Series was found, though evidence in the results of other experiments led to the tentative conclusion that consistent missing was a genuine secondary effect.

All in all, the results of the analyses for secondary effects that have been made with the Pearce-Pratt data add up to a strong indication that H. E. P. was successful in achieving what he was attempting to do; namely, to direct his ESP calling upon the target for that trial, the card that was on the book at the moment the call was made. The single exception to this rule is one that was apparent while the series was still being done. That was the tendency in Subseries B for the subject to score below chance in some runs. That subseries produced a remarkable number of low scores, too many to be attributed to random fluctuation, though the above-chance scores still predominated to such an extent that the total score of the 44 runs of Subseries B is significantly above chance expectation. . . .

References

1. Cadoret, R., and Pratt, J. G. The consistent missing effect in ESP. *J. Parapsychol.*, 1950, 14, 244–56.
2. Greenwood, J. A. Variance of the ESP call series. *J. Parapsychol.*, 1938, 2, 60–65.
3. Greenwood, J. A., and Stuart, C. E. Mathematical techniques used in ESP research. *J. Parapsychol.*, 1937, 1, 206–26.

4. Pratt, J. G. Change of call in ESP tests. *J. Parapsychol.*, 1949, 13, 225–46.

5. ———. Trial-by-trial grouping of success and failure in psi tests. *J. Parapsychol.*, 1947, 11, 254–68.

6. Rhine, J. B. *Extrasensory Perception*. Boston: Boston Society for Psychic Research, 1934.

7. ———. Some basic experiments in extrasensory perception—a background. *J. Parapsychol.*, 1937, 1, 70–80.

8. ———. Some selected experiments in extrasensory perception. *J. abnorm. soc. Psychol.*, 1936, 31, 216–28.

9. Russell, W. Examination of ESP records for displacement effects. *J. Parapsychol.*, 1943, 7, 104–17.

10. Stuart, C. E. In reply to the Willoughby "critique." *J. abnorm. soc. Psychol.*, 1935, 30, 384–88.

ॐ

Here then are the results of one of the experiments which created the sensation in 1934, when Rhine published *Extrasensory Perception*. The reader has been promised an attempt at a variety of interpretations of the results. In general the minor or trivial objections will be considered before the major ones.

First it will be noted that the cards were shuffled and cut. It has been shown that shuffling does not produce perfect randomness and therefore is not ideally suited to the mathematical treatment used here, in which it is assumed that the chance of getting any given call right is one-fifth. Cards may stick together and there may be groups which are unbroken in the process of shuffling. Although the cut helps somewhat—in the sense that no matter how bad the shuffling, the shuffled deck could not, without collusion, then agree with any order which had been memorized or which was congenial to the preference pattern or calling order of Hubert Pearce—there is still a slight "headache" in the fact that the same cards were evidently used over and over again, and we have no information about the sticking of the cards or the adequacy of the cut to break up the patterns. It is hard to see how, without collusion, the shuffling and cutting could have played into Pearce's habits in such a way as to give the scores reported.

Since practically nothing about the habits of Mr. Pearce is known, is there not an outside chance that he may have used some of the various conjuring devices which are not altogether unfamiliar among students, such, for example, as the substitution of one set of materials for another? It is hard to see under the conditions described how he could have turned in his record to Dr. Rhine in such a way as to rule out all possibility of various substitution devices by which the first report is taken back and a second one, which has been faked, is used to replace it.

These, I think, are the more trivial and far-fetched possibilities. I will not discuss the abstract statistical issue whether results as extraordinarily improbable as these in terms of the theory of probability "could have been sheer coincidences." I have already discussed above why I think this statement is neither meaningful nor useful. I think then that we must move on to more serious problems.

The material was photostated, and long afterward Dr. B. F. Riess, Dr. Ernest Taves, and I looked up the photostats to see if there were the "recording" errors which are sometimes alleged to occur as a possible factor spuriously elevating the level of scores. We found in all this work just one error, and this was the omission of a hit; that is, the genuine score would appear to be one hit higher than what was reported.

Why could there not have been collusion between Pearce and Pratt? It is true that they turned in independent sealed reports to Rhine, but there is no way of knowing whether these were the actual records of the experiments. Those who know Pratt personally will be amused or enraged, depending on their temperament, at the suggestion that such a man could be guilty of such a thing, but amusement and rage are not effective safeguards, as the history of science shows, against an issue that cannot be settled by emotion. The same applies to the role of Rhine, both in the instances in which he received reports from subject and experimenter, and in those instances in Series B in which he was himself one of the experimenters. Indeed, Rhine could personally have engineered the entire result. This is true of a considerable number of the Duke University experiments. We must, in raising these questions, remind ourselves that no scientist claiming unusual results can ever ask for immunity from such charges. If independent repetition were available of most of the major effects, the difficulty would not arise. The fact is that experiments of the Pearce-Pratt type are among those which a number of people have tried to repeat, with occasional, but infrequent confirmation.[8]

We are left then with a typical human problem in probabilities: on the one hand, the enormous antecedent improbability of extrasensory phenomena; on the other hand, the extraordinary amount of certainty one must have in the supposedly established "laws of nature" to accuse serious human beings of rampant and egregious fraud.

This is simply one of a series from the Duke University Laboratory, some of which depend on Rhine's word, some of which do not, in an era in which a considerable number of other laboratories in American and other universities have gathered data dealing with the same general class of issues. In a certain sense we must use the "faggot" approach, rather than the "single stick" approach. To a certain extent everything throws light on everything else, and the credibility of the Pearce-Pratt results will depend partly upon the breadth of one's familiarity with other similar investigations. We shall leave the story at this point and come back to it when drawing certain general interpretative conclusions near the end of the book.

THE RELATION OF ATTITUDES TO ESP SCORING

One of the perennial questions of both laymen and professionals upon encountering such reports is whether certain kinds of people have a special gift for the paranormal; whether, aside from the specific physical or physiological conditions of the experiment (drugs, fatigue, etc.), there are certain personal idiosyncrasies, of a

[8] See J. G. Pratt, J. B. Rhine, *et al., Extrasensory Perception after Sixty Years,* New York, Henry Holt and Co., 1940.

psychological sort, which make results relatively likely to happen with some persons, unlikely to happen with others. This was the problem which took shape late in 1942 in the mind of Dr. Gertrude R. Schmeidler. The circumstances were as follows:

Harvard University had asked me in 1942 to offer in the Summer Session a course in psychical research; in large part it was because of the Centennial of William James, who had done so much for psychical research in the late nineteenth and early twentieth centuries. Among the nine students whom I guided through the literature of psychical research during that six-weeks period, Dr. Schmeidler was the one who, as a professional psychologist, saw an experimental attack on a live series of problems with which she might concern herself in the following academic year. Her husband was with the army, her three small children did not require absolutely 100 per cent of her time, and she began late in 1942, in correspondence with me (I was in New York, at City College), a series of experiments dealing with the basic attitudes of experimental subjects toward the task of succeeding in an ESP test. One preliminary cycle of experiments showed the general character of what was to be expected. Then began three years of work at Harvard, partly in the psychological laboratories in Emerson Hall, partly in the Psychological Clinic on Plympton Street. These experiments were followed up and expanded. In 1945 her husband returned and took up work in New York. She accepted a position in the Department of Psychology at City College. During the years since that time she has been one of the most active experimentalists in the field.

It will be noted that her work is reported not as it originally appeared in articles in professional journals, but in the form of a book by Schmeidler and R. A. McConnell. McConnell's role in the reporting of the Schmeidler experiments needs a few words of description. Becoming deeply interested in her work early in the 1950's and learning that she was preparing a volume for publication, he offered his services in the statistical evaluation and the whole quantitative approach to the material. As a biophysicist, familiar with the "hard" kind of science and, of course, well versed in mathematical ways of thinking, he had come to the conclusion that there were many fundamental statistical issues in the Schmeidler kind of material that needed to be worked through. Schmeidler agreed, and what began as a limited amount of statistical assistance grew more and more until he made this his major activity for over three years. Schmeidler had been engaged in experimental parapsychology since 1942, had gathered literally millions of ESP calls, had huge file cases full of material of many sorts, and if the job was to get the help of a "hard" scientist, this had to be done very thoroughly. He included, of course, among his labors, the sampling of the raw records themselves to satisfy himself that very few recording errors, errors of transcription and computational errors, had been made. Furthermore, he took the responsibility to see that all the major means and variances were thoroughly established. He satisfied himself that nothing that could have been done, either by the subject or by the experimenter, could have introduced any large error into the records which stood there waiting for his analysis. The rest of our commentary will wait till a summary of the main Schmeidler-McConnell data has been given.

The Initial Experiment: Separating the Sheep from the Goats[9]

. . . The first experiment was undertaken in 1942 almost as if it were a wager made [by G. R. S.] with herself: if extra-chance results were obtained from conditions which she knew at first hand to be impeccable, then she would resign her emotional opposition to the ESP hypothesis. And such results were obtained.

The arrangements for the first experimentation were as follows. . . .

Subjects. To be chosen "at random." In practice this meant asking acquaintances in the Harvard Psychology Department to act as

[9] Gertrude Raffel Schmeidler and R. A. McConnell, *ESP and Personality Patterns*, New Haven, Yale University Press, 1958, 21–27, 32–34, 42–45, 46–48.

subjects, and calling for volunteers from certain of the Harvard and Radcliffe elementary psychology classes.

Stimulus Material. The standard ESP cards, arranged in the usual decks of 25 were used because they facilitate comparison with the results of other workers. The decks were to be "open."[10] [See, however, page 98. G. M.] They were to be arranged in the following manner: A paid assistant would make a private and arbitrary list in which two digits would be assigned to each of the five ESP symbols. She would then enter at random a table of random numbers [Peatman and Schafer, 1942; Tippett, 1927]. She would note the point at which she entered the table, and would record lists of symbols by following the digits in the table according to some such system as reading down the columns, or reading across the rows from left to right, or reading up the columns. She was to treat each list of random numbers as circular, and when she returned to the starting point, continue according to some other system which she had not previously used. The lists of symbols were to be written on serially numbered sheets. Next, decks of cards, numbered to correspond with the sheets, were to be prepared following the same stimulus order. The cards were to be slipped into opaque containers, and the lists covered so that they were not in sight. The experimental room was to be kept locked both while she was making up the lists and after she left. The assistant was to tell no one, not even the experimenter, what the order of symbols was.

Experimenter. GRS was to act as the only experimenter.

Procedure. The assistant was not notified of what subjects were

---

[10] . . . In an open deck there can be from 0 to 25 of any one of the symbols, since each position is filled independently of the others. When a subject guesses the order of the symbols in a closed deck, or when two closed decks are matched against each other, the "mean chance expectation" of successful guesses or matches is 5, with a "standard deviation" of not more than 2.04. With open decks the expectation is still 5, but the standard deviation is exactly 2. The "mean chance expectation" is the simple arithmetical average of the card deck scores one would expect to get in a long series of experiments without ESP. The "standard deviation" is a measure of the scatter of those scores about their average value. [G. R. S. and R. A. M.]

to be tested, or of how many subjects were scheduled for any day, or of how many lists each subject would use, so that if she wished to give them advance information she would not be able to do so. (There was no evidence that such caution was necessary; but since the assistant evinced no interest in finding which subjects were to be tested, keeping the information from her was a part of the normal routine.)

Two rooms, separated from each other by intervening rooms and a corridor, were employed. The subject used one; the cards and target lists were in the other. The shortest distance from the subject's chair to the cards was 42 feet, on a line which passed through the walls of two other rooms and the corridor. The rooms were connected by an electric system which activated a buzzer or light in one room when a telegraph key was depressed in the other. This was used to signal the beginning or end of a test series.

The experimenter ushered the subject into the room in which he was to make his responses, explained something of the nature of the experiment to him, and gave instructions as to the procedure. The only information about the location of the cards was that they were "on top of the pile" in another room. The subject's comments and behavior were recorded. The experimenter then went to the other room, while the subject filled in the 25 blanks on a record sheet, numbered to correspond with the appropriate stimulus list. The experimenter remained there without having looked at the target. Thus, in the initial experiment, as in all of the later work except as specifically noted, the test was of an ostensibly clairvoyant type. The experimenter did not know the cards at the time they were guessed, although their order had been seen by someone when they were prepared.[11]

[11] From a logical point of view there are other possibilities beside the obvious one that information traveled directly from the cards to the brain of the subject (clairvoyance). To cite three examples, the information might have come from the thoughts of the assistant as he made up the card list (retrocognitive telepathy), from the memory traces of those thoughts (telepathy or clairvoyance, depending upon the definition), or from the future thoughts of the experimenter as she inspected the card list (precognitive

When, in this first standard procedure, the subject pushed the signal key, the experimenter took the target list to the subject's room and checked it against the subject's responses. If the subject was willing to make another run, the procedure was repeated with the next target list. There was a maximum of ten runs in each session, and the maximum length of each session was one hour. All responses were independently rescored later by the assistant, and discrepancies were checked.

The first few subjects that were tested scored slightly better on the hidden targets than the chance rate of one success out of five. . . .

•

This marked the end of the exploratory work. (These fragmentary, preliminary data are not tabulated in this book.) In beginning the first formal experiment, one basic modification was introduced into the procedure just described. During an initial chat, and before they had made their first ESP response, subjects were categorized as either accepting the possibility of ESP under the conditions of the experiment, or as rejecting any possibility of ESP under these conditions. What this amounted to, in practice, was that those whose expressed attitudes were favorable, or hopeful, or interested, or even hesitant were put into the former category; those who expressed themselves as being firmly convinced that there could be no paranormal success under the conditions of the experiment were put into the other. (It is to be noted that the hypothesis being tested by this two-class division of subjects was narrower than the one that had been first formulated.) [12]

---

telepathy). Although this kind of theorizing has occupied the attention of some parapsychologists, it need not, in view of our present experimental ignorance, concern us further here. [G. R. S. and R. A. M.]

[12] The subjects who accepted the possibility of ESP under the conditions of the experiment were called "sheep"; the others were called "goats." In retrospect, the problem of defining these terms seems less simple and more important than it did at the beginning of this research. In the early reports, which cover the individually tested subjects of this chapter and the next, the matter was discussed in a casual and possibly misleading fashion, particularly as regards the phrase "in the experimental situation." A ques-

Having thus "separated the sheep from the goats" according to whether or not they accepted the possibility of paranormal success in the present experiment, an attempt was made to sharpen the difference between the two groups by making the experimental conditions more agreeable for the former than for the latter. This involved minor procedural changes for each group. For the "sheep," the changes consisted of having cigarettes available for them throughout the session, of sometimes offering them candy, and sometimes, when the weather was warm, offering them a carbonated drink.

For the "goats," two changes of a different sort were introduced. The first was that the external surroundings were less pleasant. This was accomplished by reversing the two experimental rooms. Targets were placed in the airy corner room where the sheep made their responses, and each goat made his responses in the rather shabby and poorly lit darkroom where the sheep targets were kept. The pencil provided for making responses was only a stub; the surface of the table on which he wrote was battered. None of the goats commented on any of these points; and it was the experimenter's impression that they either did not notice them, or else took them

tion raised here by RAM is whether a subject who accepted the possibility of paranormal success under some conditions, but not under the conditions of the experiment, would have been classed (incorrectly) as a sheep.

To tie down the historical facts as objectively as possible, GRS has searched her interview notes of the earliest work. Those show that in the first of the three series reported in this chapter there was one subject who accepted the possibility of telepathy but not of clairvoyance and who was (correctly) classified as a goat. This fact and a critical reading of the published papers indicate that the restriction "in the experimental situation" was applied from the beginning of the research, to the extent that the informal questioning methods used with the individually tested subjects supplied the necessary information.

Another ramification not appreciated in the beginning was the possibility that a subject might believe that, although others could employ ESP in the given experimental situation, he himself could not. By definition, such a subject is a sheep. Examination of interview notes shows that all subjects who stated such beliefs were (correctly) classified as sheep.

The total number of subjects affected by these uncertainties would be small, and we judge that the resulting uncertainty in the operational meaning of the findings is negligible. . . . [G. R. S. and R. A. M.]

for granted as normal in any experiment.

The second change in procedure was that the goats were not permitted to see their scores at the completion of each run. This speeded up the experimental procedure so markedly that it was possible to set a maximum of fifty runs in the hour-long session. Since fifty separately numbered slips of paper might well have led to confusion, the goats were required to record their responses on large record sheets, each of which held eighteen columns. A further modification of the procedure followed on this one. After instructions were given, the experimenter went to the room in which the targets were kept and, without looking at the target list, pressed the telegraph key which sounded a buzzer in the subject's room. This was the signal that the subject was to begin his responses to the first list. When he completed them, he pressed a key which signaled in the experimenter's room. The experimenter then put aside the first deck, leaving the second deck on top of the pile, again without having examined it, and sounded the subject's buzzer as a signal to begin the second list. This was continued until fifty target decks—or symbol lists in lieu thereof—were completed, or until the hour was done.[13]

Although there were individual variations in scores, the over-all data of these first subjects were clearly in the direction suggested by the hypothesis. (See Table 2, Series 1, page 90.) When the difference between ESP scores of sheep and goats had reached the .03 probability level of significance,[14] it was decided to begin a second series of subjects.[15] The second series was to include, as nearly as

[13] Among all the individually tested subjects . . . two sheep (in the series designated as 2 and 3) requested that a testing procedure be used that would allow the experimenter to think of each card. This was done for 25 card guesses with each of these subjects, yielding in both cases a score of three correct guesses. For these cases the subject pushed the signal key after each guess, thereby telling the experimenter to look at the next card. [G. R. S. and R. A. M.]

[14] Approximate value using binomial theory with a card probability of one in five . . . [G. R. S. and R. A. M.]

[15] The termination of an experiment upon reaching a given level of significance is frowned upon by mathematicians who are concerned with the

possible, the same number of subjects and the same number of runs as the first series; and the subjects were to be tested under the same conditions. Their results were roughly similar to those of the first series. A third series was then instituted, and again the attempt was made to keep the experimental conditions, the number of runs and, so far as possible, the number of subjects, the same as in the other series. When this series, which also gave similar results, was completed, it was found that the pooled data of the three series showed a difference between average ESP scores of sheep and goats which was at the .005 level of significance. It therefore seemed wasteful to continue with further repetitions without modifying some of the variables.[16] These three series constituted the initial experiment. . . .

. . . the emphasis of the research shifted, after the first three series, from a contrast of sheep with goats to an analysis of personality factors involved in ESP scoring. There was no effort, in any later series, to make the goats less comfortable than the sheep. The procedure already described for testing the sheep was followed, in all essentials, for both sheep and goats of the four further series of individual tests. There were the following minor changes. All subjects were required to make nine runs. To save time, subjects were instructed to make three runs without interruption. After each series of three runs the responses were scored. There was a short break between successive sequences of three runs, which was filled with a short projective test, or with conversation, or both. A further change, necessitated by a removal from the Harvard Psychological Laboratory to the Harvard Psychological Clinic for the fourth, fifth, and sixth series,[17] and to the rooms of the American Society for Psychical Research for the seventh series, was that the target lists were kept in a closed closet or a closed drawer instead of in a

use of statistical method as a *logical* tool. This procedure is nevertheless frequently appropriate for the investigator to whom statistical method is an *experimental* tool. . . . [G. R. S. and R. A. M.]

[16] See the two notes just preceding. [G. M.]

[17] The distinction among the fourth to sixth series was primarily chronological. [G. R. S. and R. A. M.]

separate room. The experimenter stayed with the subject while he made his responses, busying herself with other work, and was ignorant of the stimuli in the target list until the subject's responses were completed. Some of the subjects in the seventh series were paid a small sum for taking part in the experiment.

The results for all individually tested subjects are shown in Table 2. The difference between sheep and goats for all series combined is

TABLE 2. ESP Scores of Subjects Who Were Tested Individually by Schmeidler. A Comparison of Subjects Who Accepted the Possibility of Paranormal Success Under the Conditions of the Experiment (Sheep) with Subjects Who Rejected This Possibility (Goats) †

ACCEPTANCE ESP OF	SERIES	NUMBER OF SUBJECTS	NUMBER OF RUNS (25 guesses)	DEVIATION FROM CHANCE EXPECTATION	MEAN HITS PER RUN ‡
Sheep	1	12	129	+ 56	5.43
	2	12	127	+ 33	5.26
	3	22	133	+ 31	5.23
	4	9	162	+ 34	5.21
	5	23	207	+ 45	5.22
	6	19	171	+ 27	5.16
	7	14	126	+ 16	5.13
	Total	111	1055	+242	5.23
Goats	1	4	200	− 10	4.95
	2	4	175	− 13	4.93
	3	4	199	− 11	4.94
	4	3	54	− 41	4.24
	5	3	27	− 23	4.15
	6	16	144	− 26	4.82
	7	6	54	+ 8	5.15
	Total	40	853	−116	4.86

† The procedure for series 1–3 is given in Chapter 3 and for series 4–7, in Chapter 4.
‡ Chance expected value is 5.00.

significant with a chance probability of .000,06. The scores from the later series are so similar to those of the earlier as to make it seem unlikely that the special conditions imposed upon the first twelve goats need be considered further. If anything, the goats showed a stronger avoidance of the target under the objectively pleasant conditions of Series 4–7 than under the objectively unpleasant ones of Series 1–3. The data suggest that the factor of belief or acceptance was somehow of crucial importance to the ESP scoring of these subjects. . . .

. . . In 1945 the classroom administration of ESP tests was begun with the hope of increasing research productivity. This work overlapped the last of the individual series and continued through the spring of 1951. The major part of the book is based upon the data of this period.

In the group testing, as in the individual tests already described, basic experimental safeguards were maintained: subjects had no normal method of observing or inferring the target order, the experimenter gave no clues as to this order, and the subjects were asked to designate themselves as sheep or goats before they knew their ESP scores.[18] However, the group sessions naturally differed in many respects from the sessions where a single subject was tested, and minor changes were introduced from one group session to the next. Some classes had been told about the general nature of the research and were, for the most part, eager to act as subjects; others were unprepared. The experimental room was sometimes uncomfortably stuffy. It was sometimes so large that it was difficult to hear the instructions. Some subjects were hurried (and in a few cases did not complete the assigned number of responses), whereas some who worked quickly had tedious delays. Some were permitted to check the results of the earlier runs before they made the later ones; others were not told their scores. It seems useless to itemize these and other similar minor differences for each of the 37 separate classroom administrations, for when so many conditions are casually or accidentally varied in the absence of a previously

[18] See, however, Appendix B, p. 125 [of the Schmeidler-McConnell book]. [G. R. S. and R. A. M.]

determined experimental design, it is unlikely that any can be sufficiently isolated for study. We shall therefore limit ourselves to describing one typical group session in some detail, and shall also discuss one condition that all the group administrations had in common: the fact that all members of a single class guessed at the same target lists.

Before this typical session the subjects had been told a little about the experiment and about psychic research. Perhaps the few absentees represented the students most hostile to ESP research or least interested in experimentation, but no attempt was made to check on this possibility. As they came into the room each subject was given two stapled sets of papers. One consisted of two identical pages, with carbon paper between. On the pages were mimeographed nine columns of twenty-five squares each. The top sheet and the carbon paper were cut between the third and fourth columns, and also between the sixth and seventh. Above the second, fifth and eighth columns a number was written which identified the subject. The other set of papers consisted of a blank sheet and another half-size sheet, numbered to correspond with the first set. On the half-sheet there was space for a name and the incomplete sentence, "I am a $\frac{sheep}{goat}$ because . . ." Below was mimeographed a three-inch horizontal line with the ends and center marked by short vertical slashes. At the left was written "Belief that guesses of this kind can be successful"; at the right was written "Complete disbelief."

The class was told that lists had been prepared which were made up of five symbols. (If they inquired about the location of the lists, they were shown a glimpse of the sealed, opaque envelopes, on the instructor's desk, which contained the lists.) [19] Sample ESP

[19] In certain cases this concealed-target procedure was modified to permit the possible operation of telepathy as well as clairvoyance. In the modified procedure the target symbols were looked at one at a time by a student or by the instructor while the class made their responses. When a student was to act as the "sender," he carried sealed targets and a synchronized timer into an adjacent room. When the instructor looked at the targets, she did so without speaking and with the targets screened from the class. She did not

cards representing these symbols were put in front of the class, leaning on the blackboard, where they remained for the rest of the period. The class was told, further, that the symbols had been arranged in random order, and thus might appear in any sequence; and that each symbol on a list might appear any number of times, from zero to twenty-five. Their task was to guess the order of symbols on the list, indicating that order by filling in the appropriate boxes on the sheets before them. They were to indicate the symbols by certain short-cuts (*W* for wavy lines, *S* for star, etc.), and the marks they were to use were written on the blackboard, each above the appropriate card. Before they made their responses, they were to write their names on the half-sheet of paper before them. The distinction between "sheep" and "goat" was explained. They were instructed to cross out the inappropriate word, and to give the reason for their choice by completing the sentence and adding others if necessary. They were then to indicate, on the line below, their position on the continuum extending from belief that guesses in this task could be successful, to disbelief in it, using the midpoint of the line to show uncertainty. These instructions were repeated in condensed form for latecomers; questions from the class were answered; and the subjects were instructed to make their guesses for the first three lists, using pencil or ballpoint pen. Pencils were distributed to students who needed them.

When almost all the subjects had completed their responses for the first three runs, the others were asked to hurry. When all were done, they were instructed to tear off and hand in the strip of paper on which they had written. They retained the carbon copy of the responses. After the strips had been collected, the top opaque envelope was opened. The three target lists which it contained were

---

wear eyeglasses (which in theory might reflect the target image). Less than 9 per cent of the data of Table 8 were gathered in this way and no significant difference was found between these and the remaining data. For the sheep, the observed-target and concealed-target run-score averages were 5.17 and 5.10 respectively. For the goats, the corresponding averages were 4.98 and 4.92. Data gathered in this exceptional fashion have been listed with the American Documentation Institute . . . [G. R. S. and R. A. M.]

read aloud, and the class was told to check correct responses. They were then told to draw a man on the sheet of blank paper before them. (Later cursory analysis revealed no obvious difference between drawings made by high scorers in ESP and by low scorers, and these data have not been reported.) While they were making the drawing, the experimenter fastened together and labeled the target lists and the material they had handed in. The class next filled in the fourth, fifth, and sixth columns on their record sheets, tore off and handed in the strips, and heard and checked the three corresponding target lists. Booklets for Rosenzweig's Picture-Frustration Study were distributed; the experimenter read the instructions; and the class filled out the booklets. While they were doing so, the experimenter fastened together and labeled the data for runs 4–6. On completing the booklets, the students made the last three ESP runs. The bell indicating the close of the period rang before these target lists could be read; the material was collected; and the session ended. . . .

In Table 3 are summarized the results for all sheep and all goats who have ever been tested by GRS in group experiments. The data are presented according to the academic semester in which the research was performed. Over all there is an unmistakable trend toward higher ESP scores for sheep than for goats. The difference between the two groups is statistically significant at the probability level of .000,03. When the results of the group and individual experiments are combined, the resulting chance probability of the sheep-goat difference is about .000,000,1. . . .

The fact that these differences between average ESP scores of sheep and goats are so small and so variable might give rise to the question of whether they are authentic, or whether they are due only to small, cumulative, autistic errors in scoring, which finally have made the results conform to the experimenter's bias. So many precautions were taken to prevent autistic errors as to rule out the possibility of their being of any importance in the final results. To list briefly the major precautions:

1. In the original analysis each of the runs was given two in-

TABLE 3. ESP Scores of All Sheep and Goats. Schmeidler's Group-Administered Experiments

ACADEMIC SEMESTER BEGINNING	SHEEP (accepting †ESP)				GOATS (rejecting †ESP)			
	Number of Sheep	Number of Runs (25 guesses)	Deviation from Chance Expectation ‡	Mean Hits per Run ‡	Number of Goats	Number of Runs	Deviation from Chance Expectation	Mean Hits per Run ‡
Feb. '45	35	319	+ 52	5.16	38	344	− 63	4.82
Sept. '45	14	125	+ 43	5.34	7	65	+ 2	5.03
Feb. '46	80	712	+ 39	5.05	69	620	− 31	4.95
July '46	52	467	+ 39	5.08	81	729	−119	4.84
Sept. '46	37	333	− 22	4.93	9	81	− 3	4.96
Feb. '47	52	466	+ 69	5.15	53	477	+ 67	5.14
Sept. '47	56	504	+180	5.26	30	270	− 31	4.89
Feb. '48	63	505	+ 68	5.13	29	240	+ 15	5.06
Sept. '48	75	675	− 5	4.99	11	99	− 35	4.65
Feb. '49	63	567	+ 6	5.01	31	279	− 46	4.84
Sept. '49	52	468	− 8	4.98	20	180	− 53	4.71
Feb. '50	48	334	+ 47	5.14	26	194	+ 47	5.24
Sept. '50	37	294	+ 37	5.13	20	156	− 7	4.96
Feb. '51	28	216	+119	5.55	41	316	− 44	4.86
Total	692	5985	+614	5.10	465	4050	−301	4.93

† The possibility of ESP under the conditions of the experiment.
‡ Chance expected value is 5.00.

dependent scorings to ascertain the number of hits. These scorings were usually made by two different individuals. Whenever possible, and in every case where the two scorings were made by the same individual, one check was taken from the original records and the other from a carbon copy of them. It is therefore unlikely that many scoring errors remain undiscovered.

2. The total number of responses that were correct in each run was independently recorded in two separate places.

3. Group totals were computed and checked in the usual way. They were then subjected to many cross-checks, as further analyses were made of the data.

4. After November 1946 in most cases the ESP response sheets were identified only by a number. (An occasional student disobeyed instructions and wrote his name.) On a separate sheet that number was associated with the name of the subject, the designation of sheep or goat, and other identifying material. This precaution against autistic scoring errors is a perhaps unnecessary supplement to the procedure of paragraph 1 above, for it is unlikely that the same error would occur on independent scorings.

5. Whenever a subject's classification of himself as sheep or goat was unclear, he was categorized by the experimenter or a consultant without knowledge[20] of his ESP score.

6. While re-analyzing the data for presentation in this book, RAM has done an independent recheck from original documents of a representative sample of the data, as described in Appendix B.

So much for procedural precautions. What are the results in detail? The analysis of variance of the data of Table 3 is given in Table 4. . . . The results follow closely the pattern found with the previous individually tested subjects. Using the pooled variance among subjects, we have tested the hypothesis that the sheep and goats are drawn from a common population. This hypothesis is evidently untenable ($P = .000,03$), as are likewise the suppositions that the

[20] Knowledge, that is, by any normal means. No precautions were taken against the experimenter or consultant being guided by ESP. [G. R. S. and R. A. M.]

TABLE 4. Analysis of Variance of ESP Run Scores. All Sheep and Goats in Schmeidler's Group Experiments. (Data of Table 3)

SOURCE OF VARIATION	SUM OF SQUARES	DEGREES OF FREEDOM	VARIANCE
Binomial theory	—	inf.	4.000
Within sheep	21,326.	5,293	4.029
Within goats	13,966.	3,585	3.896
Among sheep	2,844.	678	4.195
Among goats	1,925.	451	4.268
Sheep semesters	97.2	13	7.48
Goat semesters	77.6	13	5.97
Sheep vs. goats	75.6	1	75.6
Sheep vs. theory	—	(1)	63.0
Goats vs. theory	—	(1)	22.4
Total	40,311.4	10,034	—

SOURCE OF VARIATION	F	DEGREES OF FREEDOM	C.R. OR t	P
Within sheep vs. within goats	$\dfrac{4.029}{3.896}$	$\left(\begin{matrix}5293\\3585\end{matrix}\right)$	1.09	0.28
Among subjects vs. within subjects	$\dfrac{4.224}{3.975}$	$\left(\begin{matrix}1129\\8878\end{matrix}\right)$	1.38	0.08
Among semesters	$\dfrac{6.72}{4.224}$	$\left(\begin{matrix}26\\1129\end{matrix}\right)$	—	~0.03
Sheep vs. goats	$\dfrac{75.6}{4.281}$	$\left(\begin{matrix}1\\1155\end{matrix}\right)$	4.20	0.000,03
Sheep vs. theory	$\dfrac{63.0}{4.000}$	$\left(\begin{matrix}1\\\text{inf.}\end{matrix}\right)$	3.97	0.000,07
Goats vs. theory	$\dfrac{22.4}{4.000}$	$\left(\begin{matrix}1\\\text{inf.}\end{matrix}\right)$	2.37	0.018

sheep and goats separately are drawn from the theoretical binomial population for which p is one-fifth (P = .000,07 and .018, respectively). . . .

☙

Thus the sheep, over years of work, were scoring ahead of mean chance expectation; the goats were scoring at chance or a little below. The statistical significance of the difference, significant year by year, was, of course, hugely significant over the span of many years.

What are we to think of this? The possible role of recording errors, transcription errors, and computational errors had been greatly reduced. Since the Schmeidler procedure involved the preparation of the target material by assistants who placed the material in sealed envelopes (sometimes ESP cards and sometimes the sheer lists of them, run by run, for nine runs in the experimental hour), the possibility of a "leak" from her own activity or her own mind is apparently taken care of. It is hard to see how she could have hinted or given sensory cues as to what she did not know. The likelihood of confusion in the records and the likelihood of losses of considerable chunks of material were both apparently excluded by McConnell as a part of his survey of the work.

There are known to have been a few instances in which students, contrary to instruction, altered their report of their sheep-goat status after learning their scores.

Since the publication of the Schmeidler-McConnell book there has been some published[21] (and even more unpublished) discussion of the fact that many of the targets were not actually made up from random numbers. It is clear from the facts unearthed in this discussion (a) that some of those who prepared target decks did their job poorly, even at times making up "closed decks" (which contained five cards with each type of symbol) instead of "open" decks as requested by Schmeidler; (b) that relatively few sources of lists of random numbers were used, some of the lists being used repeatedly; (c) that records were not kept of the sources and exact pages of the random numbers used. Some readers of this material have concluded that the natural preference order of calling certain responses yielded "patterns" which might have coincided with the patterned order of the imperfectly randomized target lists. In reply, considerable study of these target lists fails to support the idea that

[21] *Journal of the Society for Psychical Research*, 1959, Vol. 40, 63–79.

the target lists contain any significant "patterning" with which a natural "patterning" of calls could coincide. It must be recognized that there is here a flaw in procedure. But that it is likely to have produced the results reported in the Schmeidler-McConnell book seems very improbable.

There has also been a considerable battle in the journals regarding statistical issues; cf. reviews, criticisms, replies, etc. in the journal *Contemporary Psychology*, October, 1958, July, 1959, October, 1959. Since my own feeling as editor is that knockdown proof is not available by any statistical method, no matter how refined, and that the main problem is to get experimental ideas in a form to permit ultimate repeatability, I do not feel impelled to present all these debatable issues.

If anyone believes that telepathy from the assistant rather than clairvoyance for the cards themselves was at work, he might be able to push this point.

Noting the flaws in these and in other experiments, two ideas are occasionally expressed by intelligent persons and must in all fairness be included. The first might be phrased in this way: "People can be so muddle-headed that all sorts of things can happen. Through the history of science, as in all other human affairs, unreal things have been reported over and over again. It is a very common thing in the physics laboratory to have artifacts perpetuated for years or for decades. There is no absolute certainty even that one sees correctly with one's own eyes. We don't know about the competence of these people; we do know about the inherent improbability of the kinds of things of which they are talking. We do know, moreover, that there are quite serious motives that lead many people to make the most of such happenings; they have a fascination, and in many cases become absolutely overpowering, overmastering. When the results are impartially repeated by good scientists in many different laboratories, we shall come to the point of being willing to admit that phenomena as marvelous as these might occur. In the meantime, let us take a simpler position, namely, that we cannot claim to know just what happened, but we do know that it's awfully improbable that ESP did happen."

The second point of view is an extension of the first: "After all, is it not rather odd that after nearly a century of claims in this field there is no person anywhere that can say to a scientific individual or to a scientific body, 'Come, look, here is the thing I am talking about; here is an ocular demonstration!' " There is no place at Duke University, or City College, or Harvard, or the Society for Psychical Research in London, where time and place can be set for a demonstration in which scientists can find all their difficulties openly, simply and fully met. Hand in hand with this is the fact that the investigator cannot describe in full the conditions under which he himself would certainly obtain such results in his own laboratory. The inquiring scientist is told that something wonderful has happened and been observed by people whom he does not know. He is not in the habit of believing on this basis, especially when the results run counter to his major assumptions about reality.

These are some of the possibilities. The reader, either now or before he gets to the end of this book, will have to come to terms with these and other possibilities and make some sort of a decision.

Two features of the Schmeidler investigations call for special notice: First, the exploration of the area of the subject's attitude toward his task; second, the attempt to define the psychology of the situation in such a manner that successful repetitions of the experiment, with confirmation of the results, can be achieved. In the first matter we appear to have here the operation of a releasing mechanism similar to what operates in all perception. We perceive, to some degree, in terms of our readiness to perceive, and we manage to exclude in terms of our determination to exclude. "There are none so blind as those who will not see." This principle, so well established in the experimental psychology of recent years, would appear to apply to extrasensory phenomena in about the same way that it applies to normal perception. This, of course, does not explain the nature of the paranormal act, but it means that whatever can facilitate or interfere with the attitude of making contact with the environment can operate whether we are dealing with normal or with paranormal perception. If the principle is sound, it should permit successful repetition of such experiments in which it is diligently incorporated into the design. Since 1942, Schmeidler has published a dozen experiments in which this attitude factor has been stressed, and apparently has succeeded in most of these instances.[22] It is not quite so easy to say how many people have successfully replicated her procedure, but it would appear that among other investigators who have tried a method more or less like that of Schmeidler the majority have obtained results in the direction anticipated by her.[23]

Quite similar in spirit and in outcome are many series of experiments in classroom situations in which the attitudes of children toward their teacher, and of teachers toward the children, are investigated in relation to extrasensory perception. These studies were first launched in 1950–1951 by J. G. van Busschbach, inspector of schools in Amsterdam, the Netherlands, and soon thereafter by Margaret Anderson and Rhea White in the United States. The van Busschbach experiments relating to Dutch children began to appear in the *Journal of Parapsychology* in 1953 and thereafter, the various Dutch studies being followed by studies comparable in outcome in American schools in several states. In general, children of an age which we would call pre-adolescent (fifth and sixth graders in our system) appear to have yielded consistent results both in the Netherlands and in the United States: Children succeeded in successfully guessing prepared target material set up and looked at by their own teacher who sat in a little booth, shielded from outside observation but within the structure of the classroom situation. Considerably younger children, however, did not yield such results, and there was room for considerable speculation as to whether the results depended upon age or upon classroom atmosphere.

There seemed to be a need for a more direct study of the attitudes

[22] Gordon L. Mangan, A Review of published research on the relationship of some personality variables to ESP scoring level, *Parapsychological Monographs*, No. 1, New York, Parapsychology Foundation, Inc. 1958, 30.

[23] Gordon L. Mangan, *op. cit.*, 31–36.

obtaining between children and teachers. Attention to these factors —together with various other improvements and elaborations—are included in the Anderson-White studies which follow. These latter studies, now extending to some ten series of experiments, focus not on the factor of age of the children, but on the matter of the attitude of the child toward the teacher and the attitude of the teacher toward the child. It will be seen in what follows that large quantities of data under uniform conditions have been gathered to permit the prediction that children who indicate liking and disliking certain teachers will, in fact, when the data are independently scored, show a tendency to make significantly higher scores when experimenting with those teachers whom they like than with those whom they do not like so well. Parallel with this is an equally impressive mass of data indicating that those children who are regarded by their teachers as suitable members of an "ideal" classroom do better than those not so regarded. Finally the two factors are combined, the liking of the child for the teacher and the liking of the teacher for the child. We find that when both of these conditions are realized, the scores are substantially better than those under conditions in which neither child nor teacher reaches out toward the other.

The reader will have to satisfy himself as to the strictness of the experimental control. The point stressed here is the repeatability of the procedure. Of all the many attempts in recent years to get results which will meet the scientist's demand for repeatability thoroughly built in and permitting unequivocal positive results to be reported, those of Anderson and White should receive special attention. (Even here, we note, as we go to press, three unsuccessful attempts at repetition. See p. 122, fn.) There are other "repeatable" experiments in the sense that several investigators have gotten results similar to those first published by a pioneer among them. True repeatability, however, is rare. The original investigator himself may often fail to achieve adequate confirmation in later work, and in the majority of instances a successful experiment has not been rigorously and extensively followed through by other investigators. This very important step toward the establishment of a science of parapsychology is only very slowly being taken.

❦

A Further Investigation of Teacher-Pupil Attitudes and Clairvoyance Test Results[24]

In an earlier paper (2),[25] we reported an experimental study of the relation between ESP test performance by high school students and the attitudes (liking or disliking) of the students and their teachers toward each other. It was part of a larger inquiry into the conditions affecting the functioning of psi capacity, with special concern for the subtle interpersonal influences that may help or hinder psi.

In a review of the relevant literature in that article, we drew attention to specific attempts to pair up, as subjects and agents in GESP tests, persons who liked each other, were closely related, were engaged or married, etc. A few attempts have also been made to rate the attitudes of subject and experimenter toward each other and to correlate them with the level of ESP scoring. Although these experiments were undertaken with the expectation that high scoring would be associated with warm, friendly, and favorable attitudes, this was not always the case. However, in most of the experiments, not enough runs were done to yield satisfactory conclusions. One might question whether the conflicting results of these earlier tests may not have been due to the experimenters who, while taking the interpersonal relationship into account, did not conduct their tests in situations where the relationship might have been functioning as an everyday occurrence.

[24] Margaret Anderson and Rhea White, *Journal of Parapsychology,* 1957, Vol. 21, 81–97. [The authors were supported in the work reported here by grants from the Parapsychology Foundation, Inc., of New York City, and both hold Ralph Drake Perry Fellowships in the Parapsychology Laboratory of Duke University. They wish to express their appreciation for the cooperation given by the seven teachers and their students—[M. A. and R. W.]
[25] The numbers in parentheses refer to the references appearing at the end of this section. [G. M.]

Unlike earlier experimenters, J. G. van Busschbach (3, 4, 5) conducted his tests in a classroom where interpersonal relations were already established and operating prior to the ESP test. Using a GESP[26] test on fifth- and sixth-grade children in Holland and in America, he obtained highly significant results when the teacher served as "sender," but the same test gave insignificant results when the sender was an adult other than the regular teacher or was a pupil in the class. These tests were conducted and administered by test leaders who were not the children's teachers. From this work it becomes clear that when the test was inserted into the classroom situation, significantly positive ESP scoring occurred. No effort was made to determine the nature of the teacher-pupil relationship, and it is possible that negative attitudes may have been present which diluted the over-all positive deviation. Also, further research is needed to determine the role the test leader may play in the operation of ESP in the van Busschbach tests.

In the first Anderson-White experiment (A-W 1), the authors, with the cooperation of seven high school teachers, carried out clairvoyance tests on students in seven academic classes. The teacher administered the test. The objective was to discover whether any effect on scoring rate in the test might be associated with the attitude of the teacher toward the individual pupil or the liking of the pupil for the teacher, but primarily the combination of the two. There were 28,500 trials, carried out by 228 subjects. Teacher and pupils filled out questionnaires designed to reveal their attitudes toward each other.

It was found that the students preferred by the teacher scored above the chance mean in the ESP tests while those not preferred scored below the mean. The difference was statistically significant and was consistent. When the total results were divided according to whether the student was highly positive, moderately positive, or negative in his attitude toward the teacher, the first group gave

[26] GESP, General Extrasensory Perception; i.e., a task which permits the operation of either telepathy or clairvoyance or both—as when an experimenter looks at prepared material, and the subject succeeds in perceiving it. [G. M.]

significant positive results; the second, chance results; and the third, significant negative results.

When the teacher and pupil attitudes were combined, it was found that along with positive attitudes on the part of the teacher and pupil toward each other went ESP results with a highly significant positive deviation. On the other hand, the combination of negative attitudes gave results with a significant negative deviation. In addition, a chi-square test of consistency applied to the combination of attitudes on the part of the teacher and pupil gave a highly significant result.

In November, 1956, an opportunity was provided for one of the authors to extend the teacher-pupil attitudes and clairvoyance test research to the fifth and sixth grades (1). Four classes were tested in the same school in a suburb of Chicago. The test was similar to A-W 1 except that fewer trials were made and the student questionnaire was adapted to fit the fifth-sixth grade level.

This series consisted of 446 runs of ESP trials by 113 subjects, and the data were analyzed, as in the previous study, in relation to teacher and student attitudes. The teacher's attitude toward the students was related to the ESP scoring rate in the same direction as in the A-W 1 experiment and with approximately the same difference in average scores. With the smaller number of runs in this second experiment, this difference, unlike A-W 1, was not significant, but the pupils the teacher liked gave an average above the mean chance expectation and those whom the teacher disliked averaged below mean chance expectation. As in the earlier study, the student's attitude toward the teacher divided the ESP scores to a significant extent, with those who liked the teacher averaging above chance and those who disliked him averaging below. When the two attitudes were combined, it was found that the scores of the subjects who liked and were liked by the teacher were positive, and those of the students who disliked and were disliked by the teacher were negative. The difference between the two opposing groups was significant, with P = .0006. It should be emphasized that this second experiment yielded the same type of relations to a significant degree with only half as many subjects as the first.

The purpose of the present experiment, conducted in November, 1956, was to extend further the investigation of the relationship between teacher-pupil attitudes and clairvoyance test results in the high school classroom indicated by A-W 1. The only change between this experiment and A-W 1 was the introduction of seven different high school teachers of academic subjects (English, mathematics, history, psychology, chemistry, and biology) and in six different states.

PROCEDURE

Seven academic high school teachers were asked to participate in this experiment. Six of them were known directly or indirectly by one or both experimenters. The seventh one was recommended by a friend of M. A. When the request was made, the teachers were told that they would have to: (1) distribute the student test envelopes; (2) allow their students to answer a questionnaire concerning the teacher (a copy of the questionnaire was sent to the teacher at this time); and (3) indicate their attitude toward each student participating in the test. All seven teachers promptly replied that they would be willing to cooperate.

The teachers were asked to select a class of their choice for the experiment. Each teacher received a standard sheet of instructions (see A-W 1) with which he was asked to familiarize himself before administering the test. When the test was given, the teachers were asked to "tell," not "read," it to the class. As in A-W 1, no reward was offered. The teacher expressed his request and desire that the student do his best both for the student's own self, but even more, for the teacher.

At the beginning of the test, each student received an envelope containing a standard ESP record sheet on which were written five runs of ESP symbols, twenty-five trials to each run. These target sheets had been made up at the Parapsychology Laboratory from *Tables of Random Sampling Numbers* by M. G. Kendall and B. Babington Smith, 1954. A different target order was used for each sheet; the sheets were numbered, and a carbon copy of each was kept on file at the Parapsychology Laboratory in R. W.'s possession. Each target sheet was placed between three sheets of opaque paper —two on top and one underneath—and enclosed in a manila envelope. Two blank ESP record sheets for the subject's calls were then stapled to the outside of every envelope, serving as the means also of sealing the envelope. There was a piece of carbon paper between these two outside sheets so that a copy of each subject's ESP calls could be obtained. The carbon copies were used for an independent check.

Each student was asked to write on the topmost outer record sheet the symbols that he thought were written on the target sheet enclosed within the envelope. The students were allowed to make their calls in their own way and at their own rate of speed.

A small white envelope was stapled on the back of the manila test envelope. It contained a questionnaire regarding the student's opinion of the teacher. (See Appendix in A-W 1.) After the ESP test was completed, the teacher asked the students to answer the questionnaires and then to replace them in the white envelopes and seal them. He emphasized that the students should answer honestly and he assured them that he would not see their answers.

Finally, the teacher completed a statement of his own regarding his acceptance or rejection of each individual student in his class. The question, to which a *yes* or *no* answer was requested, was: "If you could form your ideal group for this class, would you include this student?" It was thought that a question stated in this manner, although it did not directly ask whether or not the teacher liked the student, would nevertheless get at this fact indirectly. The teacher, it was assumed, would probably have to consider all of the various factors making up his attitude toward the student in order to answer this question.

When the tests had been completed, the teacher mailed all of the material, unopened, to M. A. at the Parapsychology Laboratory. The sheet on which the teacher had recorded his attitude toward each student provided an alphabetical listing of the names of all the students in the class. From this sheet, M. A. and R. W. independently transferred the students' names and teacher attitudes so that each had in her possession a master copy of the subjects.

Next the two experimenters jointly removed each questionnaire from the white outside envelope and copied on it the name of the student, which had been written on the topmost outer record sheet. (In order to encourage frank answers, the students had not been requested to put their names on the questionnaires.) The questionnaires were then divided in half, and M. A. in her office totaled the attitude rating for her half of the students, recording the classification on her master list. R. W. took the other half to her office and independently rated and recorded the attitudes in the same manner. The attitude sheets were then exchanged and the last half of the independent classification and recording by each experimenter was completed. At this point, the two experimenters checked their master sheets to see if there was agreement on the number and names of the students, the ratings on the student attitudes, and the teacher ratings. If a discrepancy was found, each experimenter independently re-examined the original sheet and the two then agreed as to the correct rating.

Next, both authors unsealed and opened the ESP envelopes. The name which each student had written on the outer record sheet was then written on the inner target record sheet and on the carbon copy of the target sheet which had been in R. W.'s keeping at the Laboratory. R. W. checked the calls on the student's original call sheet against the carbon copy of the target sheet, while M. A. checked the carbon copy of the student's call sheet against the original target sheet. These duplicate scores were independently recorded on the master sheet of each experimenter, and they were then checked run-by-run for agreement. Later on, Mrs. Stober of the Parapsychology Laboratory checked the scores call-by-call to insure against the possibility that both experimenters might have overlooked a hit in the same run. In this way, independent tabulations were made on each checker's master sheet for each student on the basis of his ESP score, acceptance or rejection of him by his teacher, and his own classification of the teacher into one of the ten possible attitude scores.

RESULTS

The data were collected by seven secondary school teachers from 205 students (distributed in grades 9–12), who were given a total of 1025 runs or 25,625 trials. In keeping with the purpose and design of the experiment, these results, as in the two previous reports, were analyzed in relation to student and teacher attitudes.

The extent to which ESP scoring is related to the direction of the teacher's feeling toward the student is shown in Table 5. Where the teacher is positive in feeling toward 121 subjects, the average run

TABLE 5. ESP Results as Related to Teacher's Attitude Toward Student

Teacher's Attitude Toward Student	No. of Subjects	No. of Runs	Av. Run Score	Deviation	CR	P
Positive........... . ..	121	605	5.26	+160	3.25	.001
Negative......	84	420	4.85	− 61	1.49	
Total..........	205	1025	5.10	+ 99	1.55	. ..

$$CR_d \text{ (Pos. attitude—Neg. attitude)} = 3.20$$
$$P = .001$$

score is 5.26, and the CR = 3.25. The 84 subjects to whom the teacher is negative in feeling give an average run score of 4.85. The CR of the difference between the two groups is 3.20 (P = .001).

The evaluation of the difference between the total trials and hits of two groups by means of the CR based on the binomial hypothesis is, of course, only a statistical test of the chance hypothesis and it is therefore strictly relevant only to the question of evidence for ESP. Some other method for evaluating the difference between groups in a way that makes due allowance for the possible variation introduced by ESP itself must be used if one is to draw any conclusion regarding the effect of the difference in conditions (e.g., positive and negative teacher attitudes) upon the ESP process. In this paper, as in the previous two studies, we have used for this purpose the chi-square test of the proportions of students above and at-or-below mean chance expectation in ESP scores under the two attitude groups in question.

In order to evaluate in this way the consistency of the students' ESP scoring when the teacher was positive or negative in feeling, the results were arranged in a two-by-two contingency table. The number of subjects whose total score was above mean chance expectation (M.C.E.), and the number of subjects whose scores were at or below M.C.E., divided according to the teacher's feelings, are given in Table 6. The results of this analysis of individual scoring

TABLE 6. Student ESP Score in Relation
to Teacher's Attitude Toward Student

	Teacher Positive	Teacher Negative	Total
Students with ESP Scores Above M. C. E.	67	32	99
Students with ESP Scores at or Below M. C. E.	54	52	106
Total	121	84	205

$$\chi^2 = 5.93 \text{ (1 d.f.)}$$
$$P = .015$$

trends in relation to teacher attitudes is significant (P = .015).

Another aspect of the experiment dealt with the direction of the student's feeling for the teacher in relation to his rate of scoring in ESP. The 84 students most favorable to the teacher (10–9 level) give an average run score of 5.16. At the other end of the scale, 55 subjects with a negative attitude toward the teacher obtained an average run score of 4.73. The CR of the difference between these two groups is 2.77. The 66 subjects who are in the average-to-positive classification of feeling for the teacher (8–7 level) give an average run score of 5.33, CR = 2.97. (See Table 7.)

TABLE 7.   ESP Results for the Three Levels of Student's Attitude Toward
Teacher

Rating of Teacher by Student	No. of Subjects	No. of Runs	Av. Run Score	Deviation	CR
10-9 (Positive)............	84	420	5.16	+ 66	1.61
8-7 (Positive)............	66	330	5.33	+108	2.97
Total Positive Ratings......	150	750	5.23	+174	3.18
6-0 (Negative)..........	55	275	4.73	− 75	2.26

CR_d (Total pos. rating—Total neg. rating) = 3.57
P = .0004

Combining all of those who are average-to-positive in feeling, the
10–7 level, 150 subjects give an average run score of 5.23. The CR
of the difference between these positive 150 subjects and the 55
negative-reaction subjects is 3.57 with P = .0004.

A chi-square test of consistency was made of the distribution of
ESP hits and misses in relation to the three levels of the student's
attitude toward the teacher. The chi square of the three-by-two
table is 13.98 (2 d.f.) with P = .0009. (See Table 8.)

TABLE 8.   Chi-Square Distribution of ESP Scores in Relation to Student's
Attitude Toward Teacher

ESP Results	STUDENT'S RATING OF TEACHER			Total
	10 - 9 Level	8 - 7 Level	6 - 0 Level	
Observed Hits..............	2166	1758	1300	5224
Expected Hits..............	2141	1682	1402	
Observed Misses.............	8334	6492	5575	20401
Expected Misses.............	8359	6568	5473	
Total..............	10500	8250	6875	25625

$x^2 = 13.98$ (2 d.f.)
P = .0009

In order to determine the consistency of the scoring obtained when the student was positive or negative in feeling, the results were arranged in a two-by-two contingency table. (See Table 9.) All subjects whose ratings were positive (both the 10–9 and 8–7 levels)

TABLE 9. Student ESP Score Level in Relation to Student's Attitude Toward Teacher

	Students with Positive Attitude	Students with Negative Attitude	Total
Students with ESP Scores Above M. C. E.	80	19	99
Students with ESP Scores at or Below M. C. E.	70	36	106
Total	150	55	205

$$\chi^2 = 5.69 \ (1 \text{ d.f.})$$
$$P = .017$$

are included in the positive group in the table. The chi square is 5.69 (1 d.f.) with P = .017.

The results of the ESP scoring when the teacher and the student are both favorably disposed to each other are given in Table 10. Sixty-one subjects who rate their teacher 10–9 were also given positive ratings by their teachers. The average run score is 5.28. At the other end of the scale, 35 subjects experiencing a mutually unfavorable relationship with the teacher give an average run score of 4.53. The CR of the difference between these two conditions is 3.96 (P = .00007). Combining the highly positive (10–9 level) and the average-to-positive (8–7 level) students when the teacher is positive gives an average run score of 5.30. The CR of the difference between this group and the mutually negative group is 4.38 (P = .00001).

Here again a two-by-two contingency table was made to ascertain the consistency of scoring when the teacher and the student were mutually positive and when the teacher and the student were mutually negative. (See Table 11.) The resulting chi square is 9.82 (1 d.f.) with P = .002.

TABLE 10.   ESP Results as Related to Attitude of Teacher and Student Toward Each Other

Rating of Teacher by Student	TEACHER'S ATTITUDE POSITIVE					TEACHER'S ATTITUDE NEGATIVE				
	No. of Subjects	No. of Runs	Av. Run Score	Dev.	CR	No. of Subjects	No. of Runs	Av. Run Score	Dev.	CR
10-9 (Positive)........	61	305	5.28	+ 86	2 46	23	115	4.83	−20	
8-7 (Positive)........	40	200	5.33	+ 66	2.33	26	130	5.32	+42	1.84
Total Positive Ratings........	101	505	5.30	+152	3.38	49	245	5.09	+22	
6-0 (Negative)........	20	100	5.08	+ 8		35	175	4 53	−83	3.14

CR_d (Total Pos. rating—Total Neg. rating) = 4.38
P = .00001

TABLE 11.   Student ESP Score Level When Student and Teacher Had Same Attitude Toward Each Other

	Teacher and Student Positive	Teacher and Student Negative	Total
Students with ESP Scores Above M. C. E.	57	9	66
Students with ESP Scores at or Below M. C. E.	44	26	70
Total	101	35	136

x^2 = 9.82 (1 d.f.)
P = .002

Comparative Results of the Three Studies

The significance of the present report may be better viewed in comparison with the two preceding experiments (1, 2). The three studies (A-W 1, M.A. 1, and A-W 2) involve 14 high school teachers of 9 different academic subjects in 9 states testing 433 students, and two fifth- and two sixth-grade teachers testing 113 students. It should be pointed out that while the high-school students did five runs apiece at one session, the elementary school children did two runs in two sessions for a total of four runs. Among the elementary grade pupils, three children were absent for the second session. This accounts for the seeming discrepancies in the following tables where the number of runs is given as 446 when the total would normally have been 452. The data, therefore, concern 18 teachers and 546 students, the latter of whom were given 2611 runs or 65,275 trials. The total results of the three series are shown in Table 12 for whatever incidental interest they may have for the reader. (See Table 12.)

Table 12.   Total ESP Results of Three Studies

Experiment	Number Teachers	Number Subjects	Number Runs	Av. Run Score	CR
A-W 1.....................	7	228	1140	5.07	1.15
M. A. 1.....................	4	113	446	4.99	. ..
A-W 2.....................	7	205	1025	5.10	1.55
Total.............	18	546	2611	5.07	1.67

The next analysis deals with ESP scoring as related to the direction of the teacher's feeling toward the student. Three hundred and thirty-three subjects liked by the teacher give an average run score of 5.21 on 1581 runs, CR = 4.20 (P = .00003). Where the teacher is negative in feeling toward 213 subjects, the average run score is 4.84 on 1030 runs, CR = 2.54 (P = .01). The CR of the difference between the positive and the negative groups is 4.63 (P = 4 x 10^{-6}). (See Table 13.) In order to evaluate the consistency of the

TABLE 13. ESP Results as Related to Teacher's Attitude Toward Student

Experiment	TEACHER POSITIVE			TEACHER NEGATIVE			P of CR$_d$ (Pos.-Neg. Ratings)	P of x^2 Consistency
	No. Runs	Av. Run Score	CR	No. Runs	Av. Run Score	CR		
A-W 1....	660	5.22	2.80	480	4.86	1.51	.003	.09
M. A. 1...	316	5.09	....	130	4.72	...	.08	.048
A-W 2....	605	5.26	3.25	420	4.85	1.49	.001	.015
Total...	1581	5.21	4.20	1030	4.84	2.54	4 x 10^{-6}	.0009

scoring obtained when the teacher was positive or negative in feeling, the results were arranged in a two-by-two contingency table (not shown in the paper). This analysis of individual scoring trends in relation to teacher attitude gives a chi square of 11.01 (1 d.f.) with P = .0009 as shown in Table 13.

A third aspect of the study deals with the relation of the student's feeling for the teacher to his rate of ESP scoring. The 230 subjects most favorable in feeling toward the teacher (the 10–9 level) give an average run score of 5.26 on 1103 runs, CR = 4.26 (P = .00002). The 149 subjects with a negative attitude toward the teacher give an average run score of 4.64 on 708 runs, CR = 4.74 (P = 2 x 10^{-6}). The CR of the difference between these two groups is 6.46 (P = 1 x 10^{-9}). (See Table 14.)

Combining all those who are average-to-positive in feeling, the 10–7 classification, the 397 subjects give an average run score of 5.22 on 1903 runs, CR = 4.80 (P = 2 x 10^{-6}). The CR of the difference between this group and the 149 subjects who are negative in feeling toward the teacher is 6.59 (P = 1 x 10^{-9}). (See Table 14.)

In order to determine the consistency of the scoring obtained when the student was positive (rating 10–7) or negative in feeling, the results were arranged in a two-by-two contingency table. The chi-square is 20.18 (1 d.f.) with P = .00001. (See Table 14.)

TABLE 14.   ESP Results for the Three Levels of Student's Attitude Toward Teacher

Experiment	10 - 9 (Positive)		8 - 7 (Positive)		10 - 7 (Positive)		CR Total Pos. Rat- ings	6 - 0 (Negative)		CR Total Neg. Rat- ings	P of CRd (Pos.- Neg. Rat- ings)	P of χ^2 Con- sist- ency
	No. of Runs	Av. Run Score	No. of Runs	Av. Run Score	No. of Runs	Av. Run Score		No. of Runs	Av. Run Score			
A-W 1..........	515	5.35	330	5.09	845	5.25	3.58	295	4.56	3.78	6x10⁻⁷	.0003
M. A. 1....	168	5.23	140	4.99	308	5.12	1.05	138	4.66	2.00	.025	.14
A-W 2....... ...	420	5.16	330	5.33	750	5.23	3.18	275	4.73	2.26	.0004	.017
Total.......	1103	5.26	800	5.17	1903	5.22	4.80	708	4.64	4.74	1x10⁻⁹	.00001

The most important aspect of the three studies concerns the interaction of the teacher's and the student's feeling for each other. The results of the ESP scoring when the direction of the teacher's and student's feeling is mutual are presented in Table 15. The 269 students who share mutually positive feeling with the teacher give an average run score of 5.31 on 1285 runs, CR = 5.54 (P = 4 x 10^{-8}). The 85 subjects who experience a mutually negative feeling with the teacher give an average run score of 4.54 on 412 runs, CR = 4.66 (P = 3 x 10^{-6}). The CR of the difference between the mutually positive and the mutually negative groups is 6.80 (P = 3 x 10^{-12}).

A two-by-two contingency table was again made to determine the consistency of scoring when the teacher and student were mutually positive and mutually negative. The resulting chi square is 23.08 (1 d.f.) with P < .00001. (See Table 15.)

DISCUSSION

The present study may be about as near to a replication of an experiment as the psychological sciences will allow. It is not, how-

TABLE 15. ESP Results as Related to Attitude of Teacher and Student Toward Each Other

Experi-ment	TOTAL MUTUALLY POSITIVE			MUTUALLY NEGATIVE			P of CR_d (Pos.-Neg. Ratings)	P of χ^2 Consist-ency
	No. of Runs	Av. Run Score	CR	No. of Runs	Av. Run Score	CR		
A-W 1....	550	5.37	4.39	185	4.63	2.50	$< 1 \times 10^{-6}$	$< .005$
M. A. 1...	230	5.17	1.29	52	4.27	2.64	.003	.006
A-W 2....	505	5.30	3.38	175	4.53	3.14	.00001	.002
Total...	1285	5.31	5.54	412	4.54	4.66	3×10^{-12}	$< .00001$

ever, the purpose of this paper to probe the question of the repeatability of psi experiments. Divergent meanings and interpretations leave the issue confused, and experimental results rather than armchair philosophizing will have to put the question in its proper perspective. It does appear, however, that one of the most basic and fundamental aspects regarding an ESP test is frequently overlooked; namely, the psychological factors involved. While this point is so obvious as to seem irrelevant to a discussion, the appreciation of it often appears lacking. While psychological factors exclude the possibility of repetition in the strict sense of the word, they do allow extension to similar situations, and, actually, it is by extension, with a view to finding regularity, that science proceeds. The main contention of the reported research here, showing the outstanding order of consistency that it does, is that it is a successful extension.

The A-W 1 experiment was extended to new participants with no alteration of procedure. Naturally there were differences: there were different teachers, students, degrees of interest, academic subject matter, schools, and geographic location. But as far as possible the two sets of participants were similar. Accordingly, the importance of the closely similar results is considerably greater in the display of underlying lawful relations in the ESP effects produced.

The three questions involved in this research have been directed at the teacher's attitude toward the student, the student's attitude toward the teacher, and the interaction of these attitudes as related to the direction of ESP scoring. The comparative results indicate an increased sign of consistency from A-W 1 to A-W 2 on the teacher attitude. (See Table 13.) On the other hand, a lower level of consistency occurs from A-W 1 to A-W 2 on the student attitude. (See Table 14.) However, it appears that the student attitude is more significant than that of the teachers. The most important aspect of the research has been the interaction of mutual attitudes, and it is here that the most striking similarities, showing a remarkable order of consistency, are evident. (See Table 15.) The scoring level differences, discernible from the tables, are hardly worth mentioning since they are negligible, even the CR's of the difference, but there are proportionate shifts noticeable in the column showing the consistency of the results which suggest the fluidity of the situation.

An interesting aside came out of the A-W 1 experiment. When the teacher was positive toward the student, but the student's feeling was negative toward the teacher, the 22 subjects gave a negative CR of 2.96. Thus there appeared a similarity in the two conditions of teacher positive, student negative; and teacher negative, student negative. This was puzzling and posed the question of how important the teacher's attitude is if the student is negative in his feeling. In the M.A. project, the 22 corresponding subjects gave an average run score of 4.90 on 86 runs, while in the A-W 2 experiment, the 20 corresponding subjects, doing 100 runs, gave an average run score of 5.08. We can only say that this does not bear out the A-W 1 results on this point and it may, therefore, be taken less seriously.

The most significant aspect of the research is the appearance of a lawful operation evidenced by the high level of consistency in the relationship between ESP scoring and the attitudes registered. It is apparent from the van Busschbach work and the experiments reported here that ESP does operate in the classroom. It remains for patient research to seek out the variables in the situation which

ultimately may lead to an understanding of the lawfulness underlying these phenomena.

References

1. Anderson, M. Clairvoyance and teacher-pupil attitudes in fifth
   and sixth grades. *J. Parapsychol.*, 1957, 21, 1–11.
2. Anderson, M., and White, R. Teacher-pupil attitudes and clairvoyance test results. *J. Parapsychol.*, 1956, 20, 141–57.
3. Van Busschbach, J. G. An investigation of extrasensory perception in school children. *J. Parapsychol.*, 1953, 17, 210–14.
4. ————. A further report on an investigation of ESP in school
   children. *J. Parapsychol.*, 1955, 19, 73–81.
5. ————. An investigation of ESP between teacher and pupils in
   American schools. *J. Parapsychol.*, 1956, 20, 71–80.

Under certain conditions, Anderson and White[27] report, this
effect of attitude is not observed. This prompted me to write the
following for publication in the *Journal of Parapsychology*[28]:

I have just been reading your article: "A Survey of Work on
ESP and Teacher-Pupil Attitudes," in the *Journal of Parapsychology*, December, 1958.

I need considerable enlightenment in understanding where this
study leaves us. I have been completely convinced by the earlier
studies that you had real ESP by the tail, and that you had two
very powerful factors: teacher attitude, pupil attitude, and indeed
the interactions of these as two parameters, giving rise to ESP. It
is not clear to me in what sense the present group of investigations
are "exploratory," in what sense the others are not exploratory, and
it is not clear to me how these studies differ psychologically from

[27] Margaret Anderson and Rhea White, A Survey of Work on ESP and
Teacher-Pupil Attitudes, *Journal of Parapsychology*, 1958, Vol. 22, 246–268.
[28] 1959, Vol. 23, 133–134.

those which gave such dramatic positive results. On the one hand, there is emphasis in the present paper on the "experimental variations introduced from our original design," but lower on the same page (247) one learns that "the method of testing used in all the experiments summarized here is essentially the same as that used in our original work." Apparently there were various factors of attitude in the broad sense, which were held to be different in the significant and the nonsignificant series. If this were foreseen, you would expect that the hypotheses written down in advance would be quoted here. If the differences were not foreseen, it is not clear in what sense these studies can be called exploratory and handled in a second category. While it is true that many of these studies give results in the expected direction, the differences are usually slight and some are in the unexpected direction, and no one could possibly regard this block of studies as randomly selected from the same master population of studies which yielded the more successful ones already published. It becomes, therefore, imperative *to know what the psychological distinction is,* other than the sheer statistical fact that one group brought in the gravy and the other didn't. It is also important to know what the plans might be for cross-validation, to see if any hunches about the rather unsuccessful results obtained here will be borne out by independent work involving no selection of data.

I don't personally believe that the significance level or the psychological meaning of the earlier successful studies is going to be much affected, but I think you have to protect yourself by a fuller statement as to the logic of the separation of the earlier studies from the present ones. Can you set me right on this?

Sincerely,
(Signed) GARDNER MURPHY

This was Miss Anderson's reply: [29]

Dear Dr. Murphy:

Our first school experiment was designed to test the teacher-pupil attitude factor in relation to ESP scoring in academic classes of the public high schools. On the basis of the results from the first study, we set out to *confirm* our findings, which we did in the following two series. In each of these three series, all of the aspects of the test were the same (to the extent that the word is ever justified).

Having these studies behind us and being rather well convinced by them, as well as by those of others, that psi does occur in the classroom, we wanted, and thought it would be valuable, to do some *exploring*. We discussed our plans with colleagues here in the Laboratory and, with their added thoughts and suggestions, proceeded with our research.

We should have amplified our statements that these new experiments were "divergent in design from our original research" (p. 246) and that "the method of testing used . . . is essentially the same" (p. 247). We wrongly assumed that our meaning would become evident to the reader as he considered each of the studies presented. Your pointing out of this lack of clarity on our part gives us the opportunity to explain more fully. The experiments were "divergent in design" in that each of the studies was carried out under conditions which differed contextually from the original series. We (1) tested for precognition in two of the series; we (2) presented the test to nonacademic students and students in a reform school; we (3) utilized teachers who had taken part in the school experiments before and who were, therefore, familiar with the school work; we (4) had two teachers test several classes rather than just one; and we (5) placed the experiment in two studies in the hands of someone connected with the school who in turn carried out the study.

While we could not say that we *knew* these variations from our original theme would reveal various factors of attitude in the broad sense which would be different from our confirmatory work, we certainly did anticipate this. That this was not so stated is unfortunate.

There are plans now for further studies with, for example, non-academic students. Our usual test for clairvoyance can be used, but we feel that if we would direct the test to the nonacademic classes in terms of the "play" aspect or less academic nature of the situation, we might find results in accord with our first three series. You may recall that van Busschbach found that his test worked at the fifth- and sixth-grade level but not with seventh- and eighth-grade pupils, who thought the whole thing "silly." It appears that an ESP test to be effective must *fit* the classroom situation from every standpoint. Cross-validation of these exploratory studies may be expected to furnish more answers than are now available.

Sincerely yours,

(Signed) MARGARET ANDERSON

It would appear that the Anderson-White studies offer a pretty good promise of repeatability. Professor James C. Crumbaugh of MacMurray College, who has outspokenly and challengingly insisted on repeatability, has recently enlisted two of his graduate students in this endeavor, each of them writing his M.A. thesis in the form of an experiment partially identical in design with that of Anderson and White. One of them, working with high-school students, has been successful. The other, working with grade-school students, has not. (Arnon Desguisne, Gerald Goldstone, and James C. Crumbaugh, Two Repetitions of the Anderson-White Investigation of Teacher-Pupil Attitudes and Clairvoyance Test Results, *Journal of Parapsychology,* 1959, 23, 196–214.)[30]

Broadly conceived, the Schmeidler studies, the van Busschbach studies, and the Anderson-White studies have pointed to the importance of attitude in extrasensory perception. They seem to make a cumulative case for the importance of letting oneself go, with belief in the task and the wish to succeed, as contrasted with blocking out

---

[30] As proof is read, it must be noted that three other unsuccessful attempts at replication have come to my attention. [G. M.]

the impulse or turning unhappily from the assignment imposed by the experimenter. If this is, in fact, the interpretation of this block of studies, it would bring such investigations very closely into line with a movement in experimental psychology in recent years in which the readiness to perceive, the "set" to perceive, or even at times the will to perceive, has been used as an experimental variable related to success in perceiving, and in which great ingenuity has been spent in devising situations in which the experimental subject does not wish to perceive, in which he "defends himself" against perceiving. Under conditions of a favorable attitude one would expect for example that the threshold—the amount of stimulation required to elicit a perceptual response—would be low when the attitude is favorable, high when it is unfavorable. Studies of "perceptual defense" indicate, for the most part, the elevation of thresholds when a stimulus has been associated with electric shock, social disapproval by the experimenter or other persons in the laboratory situation, or in which words or symbols have been used which elicit some rejection response, as in the case of "taboo" words, or in which pictures have been used toward which there is an aversion.

If this line of reasoning is sound, it would suggest, as in fact many other sources of evidence suggest, that extrasensory perception is not really a fundamentally different kind of perception, subject to laws different from those which appear in normal perception. Indeed, if we did not properly control the extrasensory aspect of the stimulation, we could say that we were just dealing with ordinary cases of perceptual response. One view to which the student of perceptual phenomena may come is that extrasensory perception is just ordinary perception under conditions in which the external energies of the physical stimulus are inoperative. How such stimulation of the organism could arise without stimulation of the sense organ is itself, of course, a grave psychological, physiological, or philosophical problem. But the central issue of the nature of the extrasensory response must be separated from the question of the nature of the act of perceiving, which appears to be the same whether it is sensory or extrasensory.

Even this last point, speculative as it may seem, is itself easy to attack if one wishes to point out that extrasensory responses are often lacking in the subjective experience of actual perceiving. Often a subject says that when he calls his squares or waves he sees them in the mind's eye as if they were memory images, not percepts. Or he may simply have an impulse to call a square or wave so that the whole matter is motor and verbal, and in no way sensory. Or finally, he may have sheer knowledge, sheer cognition that it is a square or wave that he wants to call, everything else coming later and being derivative from this cognition. He may begin to see the square and the wave in the mind's eye *after* he has known that it is a square or wave that he wants to call, and the impulse to give a name to the cognized object may come a considerable length of time after cognition occurs. Some people have preferred the broad term *psi* for all psychical phenomena, including all the phenomena just described, and some others to be described later. This has the advantage that one does not wrangle about subclassifications, as for example between "psi cognition" and "extrasensory perception." Of course it loses in specificity what it has gained in comprehensiveness. It may be worth while to ask whether the experimental work done by Schmeidler, van Busschbach, Anderson-White, and others, relating to the role of attitude, would apply likewise to other psi processes as it does to extrasensory perception as such. The reader who goes beyond the sheer adequacy of experimental techniques and clarity of experimental findings to ask more pressing questions about the psychological character of the phenomena which actually occur, will find much ground that has not been spaded up. In many cases where the sheer fact that an experiment seems to be sound has been established, it is only the beginning of broad psychological research as to the actual character of the phenomena observed.

V.

Precognition

IF AN impression can be conveyed from A's mind to B's mind without use of the sense organs, this would be called *telepathy;* if B can perceive an objective event by means other than his senses this would be called *clairvoyance.* In the spontaneous cases already cited, we may have cases of telepathy—there may be contact between two minds—or they may all be cases of clairvoyance—direct perception of distant events (cf. pp. 65–66). But there are still other possibilities. If B can get correct impressions of *future* events by means other than inference from present evidence, this would be called precognition (cf. page 43). Precognition of an objective event that could not be rationally inferred from present evidence would be *precognitive clairvoyance;* precognition of another person's mental state, not inferable from present evidence, would be *precognitive telepathy.*

As we turn from reports of *spontaneous* cases of the precognitive type to reports of *experimental* studies, we find the usual insistence on gathering extensive data under uniform or *systematically varied* conditions, and the run of standard statistics to assess the differences, if any, that may exist between the level of success achieved and the levels to be expected by sheer guesswork or "chance." For the most part the methods already described in connection with experimental telepathy and clairvoyance might be used, but with the difference that one compares a subject's impression with a physical or psychological event which is still in the future. Outstanding here are the experiments of S. G. Soal and his collaborators with the subject Basil Shackleton.

❦

The New Experiments of Basil Shackleton[1]

In December 1940 . . . S. G. S. sought out Basil Shackleton with a view to further experiments. He was now in London again, after having been discharged from the Army owing to ill-health . . . and carried on his business as a photographer. S. G. S. thought it advisable to tell Shackleton something about the interesting effects[2] that had been discovered [in his earlier data], but did not enter into much detail as Shackleton was quite willing to try some fresh experiments. . . .

After one or two preliminary trials, S. G. S. decided to ask Mrs. K. M. Goldney (K. M. G.), a fellow member of the Society for Psychical Research, to assist him with the investigation. . . .

No one who knows K. M. G. will question either her great ability or her integrity or the meticulous accuracy of all her work. Not only did she play a leading part in the present experiments with Shackleton, but she also rendered valuable assistance with the Report on them which appeared in the *Proceedings of the S.P.R.* for December 1943 (Vol. 47, Part 167). . . .

There were two main types of experiment. In the first, the card to be looked at by the agent was determined by means of a list of random numbers (1 to 5) prepared beforehand by S. G. S., or in

[1] S. G. Soal and F. Bateman, *Modern Experiments in Telepathy,* New Haven, Yale University Press, 1954, 132–167.

[2] In 1936 Shackleton had carried out 800 trials in a telepathy experiment, with apparently chance results, i.e., he did not succeed to a significant degree in identifying the card at which the agent was looking at the time. At the suggestion of W. Whately Carington, however, Soal re-examined the data and found that Shackleton had succeeded to a highly significant degree in identifying (a) the card which had *just been looked at* by the agent and (b) the card *about to be looked at by the agent.* A hit on the actual target card is called an (0) hit; one on the immediately preceding card a (−1) hit; and one on the card following the target card a (+1) hit. A hit on the card *two* places behind the target is called a (−2) hit, while a hit on the card *two* places ahead of the target is called a (+2) hit. The present report deals with these "displacement" effects. [G. M.]

a few cases by some other person. This type of experiment will be referred to as a PRN (Prepared Random Numbers) experiment. In the second type of experiment, the card to be looked at was determined by a counter selected by touch by one of the experimenters from a bag or bowl which contained equal numbers of counters in five different colours. This type of test will be called a COUNTERS experiment.

We shall begin with a description of the PRN experiments. The technique which we shall describe was for all practical purposes standardized by 7th March, 1941, in the seventh sitting of the series. A screen was in use on the card table from Sitting No. 1 on 24th January 1941, but the additional precaution of the enclosing and screening of the five cards inside a box was adopted on and after 7th March 1941. The introduction of a second experimenter whose function was to control Shackleton first took place on 7th February 1941, at Sitting No. 3. . . .

In general, four persons took part in the experiments. They were (1) the guesser or percipient Basil Shackleton referred to as (P); (2) the sender or agent referred to as (A); (3) the experimenter controlling the agent referred to as (EA); (4) the experimenter controlling the percipient referred to as (EP).

In addition, on most occasions a fifth person was present, who acted as an observer; he is referred to as (0).

From January 1941, till June 1941, the role of (EA) was assumed by S. G. S., and that of (EP) by K. M. G. and various other persons. On and after 14th August 1941, K. M. G. usually played the part of (EA), while S. G. S. acted as (EP). This change-over gave to each experimenter experience of the different roles.

The experiments were conducted in Shackleton's studio. This is below the level of the street, and none of the rooms has any windows. The rooms consist in the main of a large studio and an ante-room. There are, in addition, some small private apartments, which are reached from the ante-room through a curtained archway and from the studio through the door D_3. (See Fig. 9.) The ordinary entrance to the studio from the ante-room is by the

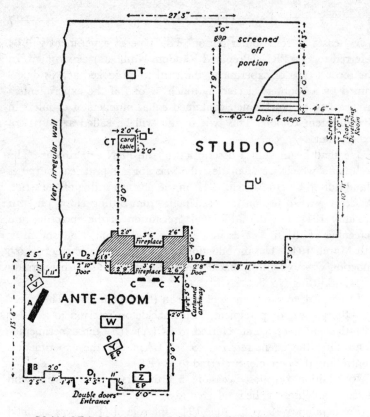

PLAN OF ROOMS IN THE SHACKLETON EXPERIMENTS

A=Sofa
B=Worktable and stool
C=Chairs before fireplace
X=Seat of photographer's assistant
Z=Table showing position of (P) and (EP) on 14th and 25th August 1941
Y=Position of table on 24th September 1941
W=Position of table on 21st November, 4th and 21st December 1941
V=Desk where B.S. sat from 15th May 1942 to 26th August 1942
T=Position of card table till 21st February 1941
CT=Position of card table on and after 21st February 1941
L=Photographer's lamp
U=Position of R.E. on 5th June 1942
D₁
D₂ =Doors
D₃

Fig. 9

door D_2. The folding entrance doors, D_1 lead to a short passage from which stairs ascend to the outer door of the building, which opens on the street. The shaded area in the plan between ante-room and studio is intra-mural and hollow, and the walls are not solid but built-up with plywood, plaster-covered, as are also the doors. The screened-off portion shown in the right hand corner of the studio is a temporary plywood platform used for photographic purposes.

. . . The card table (size 24 inches square and 25 inches high) was situated in the studio at a distance of about 9 feet from the dividing wall between studio and ante-room. It was lighted by a powerful photographer's lamp, L. Standing on this card table was a plywood screen (size 31 inches wide by 26 inches high) with an aperture (3 inches square) in its centre. The plane of the screen was about parallel to that of the dividing wall. The agent was seated on that side of the screen remote from the ante-room, and the experimenter (EA) sat or stood on the side nearer to the ante-room. Resting on the table on the agent's side of the screen was a rectangular box with its open face towards the agent. . . . Inside this, on the floor of the box and entirely screened by it, were five cards with backs like those of playing cards and bearing on their faces pictures of the five animals.

Elephant (E)
Giraffe (G)
Lion (L)
Pelican (P)
Zebra (Z)

The pictures were in appropriate colours.

On the table in front of (EA) were five cards on which were printed in large, bold type the numbers 1, 2, 3, 4, 5.

. . . The percipient, Shackleton, sat in the ante-room while he was guessing the cards, in one of the following positions. For the first 18 sittings, between 24th January 1941 and 13th June 1941, he sat on one of the chairs (C), with the experimenter (EP) beside him in front of the fireplace. On and after 14th August 1941, and until 21st December 1941, Shackleton and (EP) sat at a small table towards the far end of the ante-room. On and after 15th May 1942, Shackleton and (EP) sat at a desk (V). . . .

. . . S. G. S. brought to each sitting scoring sheets (see Fig. 10), foolscap size, each designed to accommodate two columns. For each column there were two divisions: the one on the left was headed G (for guesses), and the one on the right A (for actual cards). The two divisions were divided into 25 rectangular cells, and, for convenience, these cells were numbered at intervals of five. The left hand column with its two divisions of 25 cells will be referred to as the (a) column, and the right hand one with its two divisions of 25 cells as the (b) column. Thus sheet 4(a) means the left hand column (with its two divisions of 25 cells) on the fourth sheet; sheet 4(b) the right hand column (with its two divisions of 25 cells) on the fourth sheet. Before coming to the sitting, S. G. S. filled in the A-divisions of all the sheets to be used by (EA) with a random sequence of the digits 1, 2, 3, 4, 5. In general, S. G. S. prepared these lists from the last digits of the seven-figure logarithms of numbers selected at intervals of 100 from Chambers's Tables. . . . In some cases, however, Tippett's[3] random numbers were used. These lists were compiled by S. G. S. at his lodgings in Cambridge, with no one present but himself, and they were kept under lock and key until the day of the sitting. They were then brought to London in a suitcase which was never out of S. G. S.'s sight till the experiment was about to start. At the last moment S. G. S. took the suitcase into the studio, extracted the compiled lists, and handed them to (EA). (P), therefore, who never entered the studio till the experiments were finished, had no opportunity of seeing these sheets before his guesses had been recorded.

S. G. S. also handed Shackleton (P) some empty scoring sheets similar to those in the possession of (EA), and both (EA) and (P)

[3] Tippett's tables were used on the dates 7th November 1941, 14th November 1941, and 21st November 1941. The total score was 124 in 480 (+1) trials. This corresponds to a CR of 3.2 (odds about 700 to 1). [S. G. S. and F. B.]

SCORING SHEET : NAME B.S.

SHEET 1 DATE 14 November '41

Totals (+1)(0)(-1) Totals
6/7/3 5/5/5

(+2) = 3 (+2) = 1
(-2) = 5 (-2) = 7

(CO+1) = 6 (CO+1)=3

G	A
2	5
3	1
4 ⟷ 4	
1	3
1	1
3	2
5	5
4	3
2	2
3	2
5	5
3	4
4	3
2	2
2	5
3	1
5	3
5	1
4	4
3	2
5	3
1	2
4	1
1	5
1	4

direct hit

5

10

(+1) precognitive hit

15

20

(-1) postcognitive hit. 25

TO BE FILLED IN BEFORE LEAVING THE LABORATORY.

Experimenter's Name.

Witness's Name.

Guesser's Name.

Remarks or Suggestions:

[Continue overleaf]

CODE
Z P G E L
1 2 3 4 5

Time
Not timed.

Time
58 secs.

G	A
4	3
5	2
4	5
3	2
4	1
2	4
4	2
3	3
3	4
5	4
1	5
4	4
5	3
3	3
1	4
4	2
1	5
2	1
3	3
4	5
3	5
5	2
4	4
2	1
3	1

5

10

15

20

25

TOTAL CORRECT =...............

This independent record has been checked with
the duplicate and found to agree..........................
Signature of Experimenter...................................
Signature of Witness.....................................

TOTAL CORRECT =...............

This independent record has been checked with
the duplicate and found to agree..........................
Signature of Experimenter...................................
Signature of Witness.....................................

FIG. 10

numbered the sheets they were about to use '1', '2', '3', etc. (P) recorded his guesses in the G-divisions on each sheet.

The lists of random numbers were made out in blue-black ink, but (P) found it more convenient to use a pencil in recording his guesses. (P) and (EP) now seated themselves in the ante-room. The door D₃ was kept closed. In the earlier experiments, till Sitting No. 10, the door D₂ was completely closed also. After Sitting No. 9, however, it was left an inch or two ajar in order to facilitate hearing. From where he sat, Shackleton was quite unable to see either (EA) or the screen, even had the door D₂ been wide open. Still less was he able to see the box on the far side of the screen or the agent (A). The purpose of the box was to screen the five cards from the view of any person who might conceivably be concealed in the studio or who might be gazing down into the studio through some hypothetical hole in the ceiling. In fact, with the cards inside the box, no one could see them unless he was standing directly behind (A), in which case his presence would be apparent at once.

The five cards were now shuffled by either the agent (A) or the observer (O) if an observer was present. Throughout the experiments S. G. S. and K. M. G. adopted as a cardinal principle the rule that neither (EA) nor (EP) should shuffle the five cards or witness the shuffling. Hence, since (EA) did not know the order of the cards inside the box, he could give nothing away to Shackleton by any inflections of the voice when he gave the vocal signal for Shackleton to write down his guess. Furthermore, since (EP), who sat beside Shackleton, was also unaware of the order, he could not help (P) in any way when the latter recorded his guess. If (EA) looked through the square aperture in the screen, he could see only (A) and the top of the box.

. . . At the beginning of the experiment the agent (A) and sometimes the observer (O) shuffled the cards out of sight of the experimenters (EA) and (EP) and laid them faces downward in a row on the floor of the box. (EA) then called to Shackleton in the next room 'Are you ready?' and on receiving the answer 'yes' from the experimenter (EP) in the ante-room, lifted to the aperture in the screen the printed card bearing the number in the first cell of the A-division of the (a) column of the first sheet. (EA) paused for about half a second and then called 'one'. On seeing, say, the number 4 at the aperture, (A) lifted up the fourth card counting from left to right, just far enough for him to see the picture on its face. He then let the card fall back face downwards on the floor of the box, without, of course, disturbing the order of the five cards. On hearing the word 'One', Shackleton wrote down in the first cell of the G-division of the (a) column of his scoring sheet the initial letter of one of the animals E, G, L, P or Z. The momentary pause by the experimenter (EA) was to ensure that the agent (A) had lifted the card by the time Shackleton had received the signal. (EP) verified that Shackleton synchronized his recording with (EA)'s calls. While the guessing was in progress, (A) remained absolutely silent. To summarize: (A) or (O), the only persons who knew the order of the five cards, never spoke at all; (EA), the only person who spoke, did not know the order of the cards. The possibility of a code being conveyed by the voice was therefore precluded.

Until Sitting No. 9 (21st March 1941), Shackleton used to shout 'Right' immediately he had recorded his guess; but, after a time, this became unnecessary, since he got into the habit of writing down his guess at the instant he heard (EA)'s serial call, or at an interval scarcely ever exceeding two-fifths of a second after the call. (This was timed by S. G. S. with a stop-watch.)

(EA) now showed the next random number at the hole in the screen, and called 'Two' after a pause of half a second. On seeing the number card at the aperture, (A) lifted the appropriate animal card, looked at it, and let it fall back into its place in the row. Shackleton, on hearing 'Two' immediately recorded his guess in the second cell of his G-division; and so the guessing continued. (EA) called the numbers 1, 2, 3, 4, up to 25 at a rhythmical rate, keeping the intervals as constant as possible. At guess number one (EA) started a stop-clock which he stopped at guess number twenty-five. When the (a) or left hand column of 25 guesses was complete, there was a pause of at least six or seven seconds, after which (EA) shouted 'next column,' and, on hearing (EP)'s 'Right,' began again with 'One,' 'Two,' 'Three,' etc., until the right hand, or (b) column of the sheet was run through. The average time taken for a column of 25 guesses worked out at 62.33 seconds, which corresponds to an average interval of 2.6 seconds between successive calls. The actual time for a column of 25 calls varied between limits of about 50 and 80 seconds. This was found to be a comfortable rate of guessing, and we referred to it as the 'normal rate.'

When the sheet of 50 calls (2 columns) was completed, there was a break of perhaps a couple of minutes for the recording of the code. The experimenter (EA) went round to the other side of the screen, and, watched by the observer (O), or by the agent (A), turned the five cards faces upward without disturbing their order. He then recorded the code at the bottom of the scoring sheet thus. . . .

G	E	Z	L	P
1	2	3	4	5

This represented the order of the five cards as seen and lifted by the agent, counting from left to right. Shackleton in the meantime remained with (EP) in the ante-room.

Before a start was made on the second sheet, which both (EA) and (P) numbered '2,' the five cards in the box were shuffled by (A) or (O), out of sight of both (EA) and (EP), and this was done each time before a new sheet was begun.

. . . The decoding and counting of successful hits was carried out by (EA), (EP), and (O) with (A) looking on.

(EA) first brought the random number sheets into the ante-room (or Shackleton's sheets into the studio), and laid sheet No. 1 on a table by the side of (P)'s guess-sheet No. 1. One of the experimenters read aloud (P)'s guesses, and, as he did so, (O) or the other experimenter copied down in the appropriate cell of (EA)'s G-column the code number for each of (P)'s letters, which he obtained by referring to the code at the bottom of (EA)'s sheet. As this number was entered, either (O) or the other experimenter checked it, while (A) checked the letter read out by the first experimenter. Thus, each member of the *active* pair was checked by a looker-on. All the decoded numbers were entered in ink. When a column of 25 guesses was filled in on (EA)'s sheet, the numbers of successes were counted in the order

(a) direct hits (0),[4]
(b) precognitive (+1) hits,
(c) post-cognitive (—1) hits,

with, as a rule, at least three persons checking the counts. These numbers were then entered in ink at the top of (EA)'s sheet thus:

$$(+1) \Big/ (0) \Big/ (-1)$$
$$\quad 6 \qquad 4 \qquad 3$$

Ticks were made against the direct hits. The checking was usually done immediately after the last experiment of the day was completed, though in some of the earlier sittings it was done at the end of each sheet, and later on at the end of three sheets. The two experimenters as well as (O) signed their names at the bottom of each scoring sheet.

In the earlier sittings Shackleton often watched the decoding and checking as a passive observer, but after June 1941 he was seldom present at the checking, having left the studio. He would usually return after we had finished, but, as a rule, he was (after June 1941) not told his exact scores. After a successful sitting the experimenters would remark to him 'The results were first-rate today', or something of that sort. If the results were poor, he would be told 'Not so good today'. . . .

In connection with the above method of decoding and checking, it must be understood that many variations and changes of personnel were made in order to discount the criticism that the same two persons, playing the same roles, might be in collusion to falsify the records. All the independent observers without exception were satis-

---

[4] See footnote 2, p. 126. [G. M.]

fied that the task of checking was performed in a straightforward manner, and many testified to this in writing. The experimenters frequently asked the observer whether he would like to re-check independently some of the higher scores. Professor H. Habberley Price . . . for instance, himself selected three columns of high scores, and re-checked independently both the decoding and the counting of hits. No errors were found. . . .

On 14th August 1941, and on several subsequent occasions, Shackleton did not record his own guesses in writing. On these occasions at his own request, five cards bearing the pictures of the five animals were laid on the table in front of him, and, instead of Shackleton writing down his own guess, he merely touched one of the five pictures with a pencil, and the choice was recorded by S. G. S. acting as (EP). S. G. S. noticed that Shackleton always touched the card from two-fifths to four-fifths of a second after the call. We used this method only at Shackleton's request. He said he felt it involved less conscious effort, and was more automatic. The method has the slight draw-back that errors might occasionally arise, through inaccurate recording by (EP) of Shackleton's choice, but S. G. S. is confident that such was not the case. . . . [discussion of further precautions regarding records]

In all the original scoring sheets so checked over the total period of the experiments fewer than a dozen isolated errors were found, *none of these being in the precognitive groups*. These few errors almost cancelled one another out, and were of no significance whatsoever. . . .

Throughout this investigation no attempt was made to count beyond (—2) and (+2) displacements. The scores on (—2), (—1), (0), (+1) and (+2) trials only were considered. As the card sequence was a random one, the expectations on these five types of score are theoretically independent of each other, though the variances . . . are not independent. As we have stated previously, throughout this work the odds against chance corresponding to any deviation x from mean expectation is understood to mean the odds against there being a deviation which lies outside the range —x to $+x$. In other words we estimate our odds on the assumption that we are just as interested in negative deviations as in positive deviations.

Two methods of evaluation were employed.

(a) In a series of N trials the mean expectation of successes is $N/5$, and the standard deviation is $0.4\sqrt{N}$. These formulae apply when we are dealing individually with any of the five types (-2), (-1), (0), $(+1)$ or $(+2)$.

(b) The expectation and variance were calculated for each set of, say, 24 $(+1)$ trials or 24 (-1) trials by formulae due to Mr. W. L. Stevens . . . and the results were summed for all sets. This is perhaps a slightly more accurate method than that described in (a). The scoring of large batches of trials by both methods showed that the standard deviations obtained by Stevens's method were, almost without exception, very slightly less than those given by the formula $0.4\sqrt{N}$. We are, therefore, on the safe side in using $0.4\sqrt{N}$ for the standard deviation instead of the value given by Stevens's formula, which is tedious to evaluate. But the expectations were found from Stevens's formula. . . .

The experimenters were most interested in the $(+1)$ scores, and for this type a 'cross-check' was made by the scoring of the (a) G-column of each sheet against the (b) A-column of the same sheet, and the (b) G-column against the (a) A-column. That is the 'guesses' in the left hand 25 trials of the sheet were compared with the 'target' presentations of the right hand 25 trials and *vice versa*.

Thus in a total of 3,789 $(+1)$ trials at telepathy, working with prepared random numbers at 'normal' rate, with Miss Elliott as agent, the 'cross-check' gave 798 hits which number is not significantly different from the Stevens expectation of 775.8. The actual number of hits made by Shackleton on these 3,789 $(+1)$ trials was 1,101 which exceeds the chance level by 13.2 standard deviations.

. . . Shackleton started on the new experiments with animal cards on 24th January 1941. The 'sender' was Miss Rita Elliott, who remained the principal agent for a whole year. K. M. G. was not present at the first two sittings, and S. G. S. was the only experimenter. He acted as (EA), and also checked the results with the agent and Shackleton looking on. At the first sitting there were no fewer than 67 hits on 192 (+1) trials compared with a Stevens expectation of 39.7. This is a highly significant result but on the 'actual' or 'target' card there were only 40 hits in 200 trials, the exact number which chance might be expected to produce. The score on 192 post-cognitive (—1) trials was 41, which again is a chance result.

At the conclusion of this first experiment on 24th January, S. G. S. asked Shackleton to keep on reminding himself during the following week that at the next sitting on 31st January he was going to score *direct* (0) hits, and not precognitive hits. Each day during the week S. G. S. kept repeating aloud 'Shackleton will score *direct* hits next Friday.' The suggestions seem to have taken effect, for on 31st January he scored 76 *direct* hits on 200 trials—an excess over chance expectation of 36 and corresponding to odds of more than ten million to one. But on the 192 (+1) trials the score was only 30, which is below expectation.

At the end of the sitting on 31st January S. G. S. asked Shackleton to concentrate during the following week on the idea of scoring (+1) precognitive hits, and S. G. S. also repeated aloud several times a day 'Shackleton will score precognitive hits next week.'

The results of these suggestions were disappointing, but this may have been due to the presence of K. M. G. and Mr. H. Chibbett, both of whom were meeting Shackleton for the first time. It has been noted by Rhine, Tyrrell and others that the effect of the arrival of a fresh personality on the scene is sometimes a temporary lowering of the score. At the third sitting on 7th February Shackleton obtained 39 (+1) hits in 144 trials, which corresponds to odds of about 30 to 1. But, contrary to the suggestion given, he scored 43 hits on the 'target' card in 150 direct trials, a result which is better than the precognitive score, the odds in this case being about 120 to 1.

After this sitting no more suggestions were given, and during the succeeding weeks, in which there was an influx of fresh visitors, the interest of everyone became centred on the remarkable precognitive (+1) scores which Shackleton now continued to produce week after week. The experimenters and visitors talked to Shackleton only of 'precognition'. The effect of all this may have been to direct his extra-sensory faculty into the precognitive channel, from which it scarcely ever strayed for a whole year.

Between 24th January 1941 and 21st December 1941, Miss Rita Elliott acted as agent at nineteen sittings in which prepared lists of random numbers were used to decide which card in the box was to be looked at by the agent. Except on the dates 14th and 25th August 1941, the material for telepathic transmission consisted of pictures of the five animals. On the dates mentioned, however, experiments with the animal pictures were alternated with experiments in which cards inscribed with the associated words TRUNK, NECK, MANE, BEAK and STRIPES were substituted for the corresponding animal pictures. These latter experiments . . . are here included in the grand total of 3,789 (+1) trials. These yielded 1,101 (+1) hits as compared with a Stevens expectation of 775.82. We have therefore an excess of (+1) hits which amounts to 325.18 and corresponds to 13.2 standard deviations. It follows that the odds against the occurrence of a positive or negative deviation of this magnitude are greater than 10^{35} to 1. Since, however, the (+1) score was picked out as the best score of the five categories (—2), (—1), (0), (+1) and (+2), the above odds should be divided by five, but this hardly affects their colossal significance. With the exception of the tremendous score on (+1) trials none of the scores has the least significance but for completeness we give them in Table 16.

In Table 16 the results are all given to the nearest whole number. With the exception of that on (+1) all the deviations are less than twice the corresponding standard deviations. The experiments were all conducted at 'normal' rate. That is, the *average* time for 25 guesses was 62.33 seconds, which corresponds to an average interval of 2.6 seconds between successive calls. Significant

TABLE 16.   Prepared Random Numbers. Telepathy. Normal Rate.
Agent: Miss Rita Elliott

Category	(−2)	(−1)	(0)	(+1)	(+2)
Trials	3,630	3,788	3,946	3,789	3,632
Expected hits	726	758	789	776	726
Actual hits	714	768	829	1,101	703
Deviation	−12	+10	+40	+325	−23
Standard deviation	24	25	25	25	24

successes in (+1) trials were obtained at almost all rates between 50 and 80 seconds for a column of 25 calls. These extremes represent the lower and upper limits for the 'normal' rate. . . .

It is interesting to compare the 'telepathy' scores in this second series with the alternated 'clairvoyance' scores on the precognitive (+1) trials. On 864 (+1) 'telepathy' trials Shackleton obtained 243 hits, compared with a chance expectation of 174.4 (Stevens), and this corresponds to a critical ratio of 5.84. But on the 768 alternated clairvoyance trials he scored only 160 (+1) hits which exceeds the expected number (156.64) by fewer than 4.

In other words, the 'telepathy' experiments show odds against chance of at least ten million to one, whereas the 'clairvoyance' experiments give results entirely consistent with chance.

Shackleton's failure to succeed in the 'clairvoyance' tests was certainly not due to any lack of confidence. At no time did he so much as hint that he anticipated or feared failure in experiments when the agent did not look at the cards. . . .

The clairvoyance experiments described above made it highly probable that Shackleton succeeded only when the agent knew the order of the five pictures in the box. The next step was to discover whether the experiment would succeed if, instead of using lists of random numbers prepared before the experiment began, the experimenter (EA) determined the agent's selection of cards by drawing counters from a bag or bowl at random. With this method the choice of cards would be determined during the progress of the experiment by the colours of the counters drawn instead of by a series of numbers already in existence at the start of the tests.

For this purpose 200 bone counters of the same make and size, but in five different colours, were thoroughly mixed inside a cloth bag, there being equal numbers of each colour. It was agreed with the agent, Miss Elliott, that the five colours stood for the digits 1–5 in the following order: white = 1; yellow = 2; green = 3; red = 4; and blue = 5.

In order to assist the agent, five counters with colours in the above order from left to right were placed in a row on top of the box containing the cards, so that, when the experimenter (EA) showed, say, a red counter at the aperture in the screen, (A) would merely have to lift up the card directly beneath the red counter before her. In actual practice the association between the card positions and colours is rapidly memorized, so that the appearance of a colour at the aperture results in the agent's almost automatic selection of the correct card. After an abortive effort by S. G. S., who proved to be far too slow in extracting the counters at the required speed, this task was allotted to K. M. G., who was much more successful in presenting the counters at a uniform and 'normal' rate. The recording of the counters in the A-column of a scoring sheet as they appeared was, as a rule, entrusted to S. G. S., who translated them mentally into the corresponding digits.

On 14th March 1941, however, in K. M. G.'s absence, Miss Ina Jephson selected the counters. In the first two experiments, on 7th March and March 14th, (EA) drew the counters from a cloth bag, replacing each counter in the bag after it had been exposed at the aperture in the screen. After the sitting on March 7th, K. M. G. wrote a short description of her method of extracting the counters. She said:

'I arranged the bag so that the counters were easily accessible. I then dipped each hand in alternately and showed a counter at the screen-aperture with one hand while the other hand was already delving in the bag for the next counter. At intervals I hesitated just long enough to give the bag a quick shake and always picked out counters from all corners, and above and below, in order to avoid picking the same counters up twice as far as possible.'

On and after March 21st K. M. G. found it more practicable to place all the counters in an open bowl. In order to avoid conscious selection, which would destroy the desired random character of the presentation, she stood up, looking straight over the top of the screen and selected the counters with each hand alternately by touch alone and without looking at the bowl. After presenting each counter at the aperture she let it fall back into the bowl. Now, although this method of selection appears to give approximately equal numbers of each of the five colours when the extraction is done at 'normal' speed, this is certainly no longer the case when the speed of calling is doubled, as it subsequently was. Even at a comfortable 'normal' rate it is doubtful whether the distribution is strictly 'random' in the sense that it would satisfy all the theoretical criteria for randomness. But when the rate of selection of the counters is increased to, say, 35 seconds for a run of 25 from the usual time of 62 seconds, the numbers of the different colours chosen become very unequal. This is probably due to the fact that at the increased speed there is not sufficient time for the experimenter's hand to delve into all parts of the bowl as described in K. M. G.'s note quoted above. If, therefore, there happens to be, say, an excess of white counters on the surface of the bowl, white counters may be picked up more frequently than those of the other colours. However, there is some compensation for this in the fact that Stevens's method of working out the expectation of hits, which we have used throughout, takes into account the unequal distribution of the five symbols in a run of 25 calls. . . .

As K. M. G. showed the counters at the hole in the screen, S. G. S. recorded the corresponding digits 1–5 in the appropriate cell of the A-column of his scoring sheet. During the first four sittings with the counters, S. G. S., while recording, sat by the side of the box in such a position that he could not see the five cards. But in subsequent sittings at which counters were used he sat behind the agent in such a position that he could not only record the counters, but was able, at the same time, to observe whether the agent lifted the correct card. As in all the experiments, the only person to speak a single word was (EA), who did not know, and could not possibly see, the order of the cards. While K. M. G. and S. G. S. were occupied with the counters in the studio, an observer acted as (EP), sitting beside Shackleton in the ante-room.

Apparently the new method by which the experiment was conducted with counters instead of with lists of numbers prepared beforehand had no effect whatever on the nature of the results or on the degree of success. With Miss Elliott acting as agent, Shackleton still continued to score on precognitive $(+1)$ presentations at the same high rate of success. Between 7th March 1941 and 3rd January 1942, Miss Elliott acted as agent on eight occasions on which counters were shown at 'normal' rate. On 1,578 $(+1)$ trials Shackleton scored 439 hits, compared with a Stevens expectation of 321 . . . 'cross-check' . . . gave a total of 327 $(+1)$ hits which is in excellent agreement with the Stevens expectation.

It will be noticed that the total number of $(+1)$ trials, 1,578, is not an exact multiple of 24. The reason is that on 18th April 1941, Dr. Wiesner, who was acting as (EP) on this occasion, noticed that in one column Shackleton hesitated at call No. 20 and got completely out of step. The last six $(+1)$ trials, therefore were not taken into account. The scores on the other four categories (-2), (-1), (0) and $(+2)$ were all close to chance expectation and call for no comment.

. . . On 21st March 1941, when Mr. Kenneth Richmond . . . (then editor of the *Journal* of the Society for Psychical Research) acted as (EP), an important discovery was made. After Shackleton had completed three sheets of guesses at the 'normal' speed, with an average interval between successive calls of 2.8 seconds, someone suggested that the experiment with the counters should be speeded up, so as to reduce the interval to about half its previous value, if this proved to be practicable. In order to facilitate this rapid rate of presentation, K. M. G., who had been drawing counters from the cloth bag, emptied them into the bowl, and drew them out with alternate hands as described on p. 142.

Mr. Richmond sat beside Shackleton to see that he kept in step, noting hesitations and gaps, if any, and using a stop-watch. S. G. S. sat next to the agent by the side of the box, so that he could not see the cards, and recorded the counters. It was impressed on Shackleton that he must keep in step at all costs. If, on hearing the call to write down the initial letter in a certain cell, he found his response was not quick enough for him to write down the letter in time, he was instructed to leave that cell a blank, so that he would be ready to fill in the next cell when its serial number was called.

The new experiment was a strain on all concerned. After three sheets of guesses were completed, the experimenters stopped, and checked the results. Everybody expected the experiment would be a failure, and, indeed, we found only chance scores on the categories (—1), (0) and (+1), although the preceding experiments on the same day at 'normal' speed had yielded a significant score on pre-cognitive (+1) trials. Then it was suggested that a count should be made on the (+2) precognitive trials. When this was done, it was at once obvious that Shackleton had been scoring significantly above chance expectation on (+2) instead of on (+1) presentations. In other words, when the speed of calling was approximately doubled, his 'precognitive' faculty shifted from the (+1) card and fastened upon the one which immediately followed it.

In order to make sure of their discovery, the experimenters did three more sheets of guesses at the same rapid speed (after giving Shackleton fifteen minutes' rest). The results confirmed the previous observations.

For the six sheets at 'rapid' rate the average interval between successive calls was 1.44 seconds—equivalent to an average time of 34.6 seconds for 25 calls. In the last three sheets Shackleton left a few blank spaces here and there. On the 280 (+1) trials done on this first occasion the number of hits was 57, compared with a Stevens expectation of 56.4. But on the 265 (+2) trials there were no fewer than 84 hits, compared with the Stevens expectation of

53.6. This gives a critical ratio of $+4.67$, and corresponds to odds of more than 50,000 to 1 when the score is selected as the best in the five categories considered.

The experiments with counters at 'rapid' rate with Miss Elliott as agent were continued for four sittings. In all, a total of 794 ($+2$) trials gave 236 hits, while the Stevens expectation was only 159.4. The corresponding odds against chance amount to more than a hundred million to one. On the other hand, the total of 831 ($+1$) trials at rapid rate on the above occasions yielded only 154 hits, compared with a Stevens expectation of 167. . . .

The scores on the categories (-2), (-1) and (0) were all close to the chance expectations. . . .

Now that Shackleton had re-established post-cognitive (-1) scoring, a characteristic which had been absent from his guessing for a whole year, an interesting question presented itself. When the rate of calling was speeded up to about double the 'normal' rate, would there be a displacement of the post-cognitive (-1) hits corresponding to the displacement of precognitive ($+1$) hits which took place with Miss Elliott as agent? The results show that this is what actually happened. On the three occasions (22nd May 1942, 5th June 1942 and 6th January 1943) experiments were carried out at 'rapid' rate, lists of random numbers being used instead of counters. As before, cards bearing the initial letters of the five animals were employed. The modified procedure on all three occasions was as follows:

The screen, which normally stood on the card-table, was removed, and the five cards which bore the numerals 1–5 were arranged in order on the *top* of the box, which was in its ordinary place on the table. The agent, Mr. Aldred, sat in the usual position, and laid his five letter cards in a row faces downward inside the box out of sight of (EA) and (EP). (EP) sat with Shackleton at his desk in the ante-room and the latter had before him five 'letter' cards similar to those in front of the agent. (EA) stood facing Aldred on the near side of the box, with his prepared lists of random numbers. He called 1, 2, 3, etc., up to 25 at a rapid rate, and, as he called each serial number, he touched with a pencil the number card on top of the box corresponding to the figure on his prepared list. As Aldred saw the numeral touched with (EA)'s pencil, he instantly jerked up the corresponding card inside the box, looked at it and dropped it into its place again. As Shackleton heard the serial number of the call, he instantly touched with a pencil one of the five letters E, G, L, P, Z in front of him. (EP) recorded the letter in the appropriate cell of the G-column on the scoring sheet.

The experiment went without a hitch on all three occasions; there were no gaps, and Shackleton was never out of step. As Aldred was new to the 'rapid' technique, on each of the first two occasions the actual experiment was preceded by a rehearsal in which (EA) and Aldred took part, using the previous week's lists of random numbers. During this trial run S. G. S. sat by the box to verify that Aldred was able to synchronize the lifting of the cards with (EA)'s calls at the required rapid rate.

The average intervals between successive calls on the three occasions were 1.37 seconds, 1.39 seconds and 1.44 seconds. The results are given in Tables 17 and 18 below.

TABLE 17.

(+1) and (−1) scores (rapid rate)

Precognitive			Post-cognitive		
Trials	Hits	Expected	Trials	Hits	Expected
552	126	111	552	112	110

TABLE 18.

(+2) and (−2) scores (rapid rate)

Precognitive			Post-cognitive		
Trials	Hits	Expected	Trials	Hits	Expected
529	149	106·5	529	151	103
Critical ratio = 4·62			Critical ratio = 5·21		

A glance at these tables shows that, at the 'rapid' rate of calling, the (+1) and (−1) hits are quite without significance, and have been replaced respectively by (+2) and (−2) hits. . . . This, how-

ever, is an over-simplification. The fact is that, on the first occasion
the two effects did appear to proceed simultaneously, and there
were moderately significant scores on both (+2) and (—2) trials.
On the second occasion, however, there was a very significant score
on (+2), but only a chance score on (—2). And finally, on the
last occasion, there was a chance score on (+2), but a tremendous
score (critical ratio = 6.23) on (—2). But on no occasion was
either the (+1) or the (—1) score significant.

The violent switch over to (—2) on the last occasion is very remarkable. There was, however, an interval of seventeen weeks between the second and third occasions, during which Shackleton had
had a good rest.

The fact that Shackleton's *psi* faculty could still flare up to a
peak represented by 6.23 standard deviations on only 184 (—2)
trials, two years after the beginning of the experiments, testifies to
the strength of his paranormal ability.[5]

Mr. Rozelaar took away with him a list of the total scores in each
of the five categories (—2), (—1), (0), (+1) and (+2). He also
compared each original scoring sheet carefully with the corresponding duplicate, and himself posted the duplicates to Professor Broad.

. . . If lists of random numbers were in existence at the start of
an experiment, it would be unnecessary to assume that Shackleton
was predicting a future event when he scored significantly on the
(+1) card. It would be possible for him to succeed by employing
either telepathy or clairvoyance to ascertain certain facts existing
in the present. By telepathy from (EA)'s mind, or by clairvoyance,
he could learn what was the next number on the list. And by
telepathy from the agent, or by clairvoyance, he could obtain knowledge of the order of the five cards in the box. By combining these
two bits of information he would be able to say what animal picture

[5] On this occasion Mr. L. A. Rozelaar, M.A. (Senior Lecturer in French
at Queen Mary College, London University), who acted as (EA), wrote:
"I carried out every step of decoding and checking with S. G. Soal checking
every step of the process. The agent did not speak during the guessing, nor
did I notice any signs of his signalling by shuffling of feet, coughing or in
any other manner. I inspected and recorded the code at the end of every
50 guesses." [S. G. S. and F. B.]

the agent would look at next. When, however, coloured counters are drawn by touch from a bag or bowl the problem is more complicated. Since, however, in most of the experiments with counters K. M. G. drew them out of a bowl with alternate hands, it might still be possible to explain away the apparent prediction of a future event .by supposing that Shackleton exercised clairvoyance or a combination of clairvoyance and telepathy upon an existing situation. For, at the instant when Shackleton wrote down his guess, and K. M. G.'s right hand was holding a counter to the hole in the screen, her left hand might already have selected the next counter. Shackleton would know by clairvoyance the colour of the counter which would be shown next at the aperture, and by clairvoyance or telepathy from the agent he would know the order of the cards in the box. He could, therefore, deduce the $(+1)$ card from the facts belonging to the existing situation. One difficulty in the way of this hypothesis is that Shackleton never at any time showed that he possessed the gift of clairvoyance. We might perhaps dispense with the assumption of clairvoyance on the part of Shackleton or K. M. G. by supposing that the latter was able to recognize certain colours subconsciously by *touch*. That is the various pigments might possess a slightly different feel. In the experiments especially designed to test clairvoyance he failed completely.

But when we try to explain the $(+2)$ displacement in the experiments with counters at 'rapid' rate, the hypothesis seems to break down completely. For, when Shackleton makes his guess at, say, the instant when K. M. G.'s right hand is holding a counter to the aperture, and her left hand is delving in the bowl for the $(+1)$ counter, the $(+2)$ counter is not known until the right hand has returned to the bowl and made a selection.

It is not easy, therefore, to see how Shackleton could have deduced the $(+2)$ symbol from existing data.

A more recondite possibility, however, suggests itself. Having obtained by telepathy from the agent the order of the cards in the box, could Shackleton, as he recorded his guess, have influenced the subconscious mind of K. M. G. in such a way that the *next* counter she drew tallied with the symbol Shackleton had just written down? In the case where the counters were taken from a closed bag, we might have to suppose, in addition, that K. M. G. herself used clairvoyance in selecting the colour implanted in her subconscious mind by Shackleton. When the counters were in an open bowl, she might, in spite of the fact that she looked steadily over the top of the screen, know enough about the positions of various counters to be able to select the right colour without using clairvoyance. It is true, of course, that K. M. G. was blissfully unaware of any influence from Shackleton, but in everyday life it may well be that we often imagine that we are exercising free choice when, in reality, we are acting under unconscious compulsions of various kinds.

The experimenters thought it advisable, in view of the above suggestion, to carry out two special tests in order to discover whether Shackleton could influence K. M. G.'s selection by touch of counters from a bowl. In these experiments the ordinary agent was absent, and the box with the five cards was not in use.

The first such experiment on 9th May 1941, was conducted as follows:

Dr. Wiesner (EP) sat in the ante-room with Shackleton, who had in front of him the five differently coloured counters. He was also given a number of scoring sheets whose A-columns had been previously filled in by S. G. S. with random digits 1–5. Dr. Wiesner shuffled the five counters so that they stood in a row in any haphazard order, the order being changed after the completion of each sheet of fifty calls. Shackleton touched the counter whose position in the row corresponded to the random number on his sheet. He was checked by Dr. Wiesner. As he touched each counter, Shackleton called out 'Right'. On hearing this signal, K. M. G. in the studio immediately chose a counter from the bowl while looking straight over the top of the screen, just as she did on ordinary occasions in the counter experiments. K. M. G. let the counters drop back one by one into the bowl, the contents of which she stirred up at frequent intervals as usual. S. G. S., seated on the other side of the screen in the place normally occupied by (A), recorded the *numbers* standing for the five colours as the counters appeared at the aperture. After four sheets had been completed, the sheets of random numbers were decoded into colours according to the code records for each sheet kept by Dr. Wiesner. The sheets filled in by S. G. S. during the experiment were similarly decoded into colours, and the number of successes in each of the five categories (—2), (—1), (0), (+1) and (+2) was counted. In every category the number of hits agreed closely with the chance expectation. For instance, in 192 (+1) trials K. M. G. scored 41 hits, as compared with 38.4, the expected number, and in 184 (+2) trials she scored 32 hits, compared with an expectation of 36.8. There was, in fact, not the slightest sign that Shackleton had influenced K. M. G. in her choice of the counters. The calls were made at about the 'normal' rate.

Perhaps the chief objection to this control experiment is that Shackleton was not exercising free choice, as he presumably did when he wrote down his animal symbols in an ordinary experiment. The colour he tried to make K. M. G. select was rigidly determined by the number on the list. Shackleton, therefore, may not have been acting with his usual spontaneity. Moreover, he was *consciously* trying to influence K. M. G. The psychological conditions undoubtedly were very different from those which obtained in an ordinary 'precognitive' experiment.

In the second test on 7th August 1942, no lists of random numbers were employed.

Shackleton sat at his desk in the ante-room with five coloured counters in front of him arranged in the order

W, Y, G, R, B,

the capitals denoting the initials of the five colours. Shackleton touched the counters one by one with a pencil at 'normal' speed, and, as he did so, called aloud the serial numbers 1, 2, 3, up to 25. S. G. S. sat opposite him, and recorded the numerical position of each counter in the row as it was touched, counting from Shackleton's left to right. K. M. G. sat in the studio at the card-table with a friend, Mrs. Wykeham-Martin. In front of K. M. G. was a bowl containing 245 counters, there being equal numbers of each of the five colours. On hearing the serial number of the call, K. M. G., who sat throughout with her eyes closed, drew out a counter, letting it fall back in the bowl. The corresponding number (in the order W, Y, G, R, B) was recorded in the A-column of a scoring sheet by Mrs. Wykeham-Martin. At the end of each column of 25 calls, there was a pause of from 30 seconds to a minute, during which K. M. G. thoroughly reshuffled the counters in the bowl. Then the work was resumed until ten sheets were completed.

The sequence of 500 counters drawn by K. M. G. appears to satisfy the usual tests . . . of a random distribution, but Shackleton's selections were very far from being a random set.

Except in the category $(+2)$ all the scores achieved by K. M. G. were in good agreement with chance expectation. But in 460 $(+2)$ trials there were 112 hits, compared with 92, the number to be expected. There is, thus, a positive deviation equivalent to 2.33 standard deviations, but this cannot be regarded as significant since the $(+2)$ score is chosen as the best score in the five categories. Hence the odds against chance have to be divided by five, and amount to no more than 10 to 1. Thus the experiment affords no conclusive evidence that Shackleton could influence K. M. G.'s selection of counters from the bowl. But here again this second control experiment is not really satisfactory, since Shackleton knew that he was attempting an entirely different feat from that which he performed in his ordinary routine. It would perhaps have been better if he had been led to believe that he was *guessing* the counters shown by K. M. G. in the other room instead of trying to influence her.

On the other hand, the theory that Shackleton scored his $(+1)$ or $(+2)$ hits by being influenced by a future event, i.e. the image which was to enter the agent's mind in about three seconds' time, has much to support it. It affords a satisfactory explanation of the conversion of $(+1)$ hits into $(+2)$ hits at the 'rapid' rate of calling. We must suppose that Shacketon possesses a span of telepathic precognition which ranges between 2 and $3\frac{1}{2}$ seconds into the future, or possibly between 2 and 4 seconds. If the object of presentation is closer to his 'present instant' than, say, two seconds, it is perhaps too near in time for him to perceive it, and so he cognizes the next object which is within his span. We cannot, of course, attempt to fix too accurately the upper and lower limits of this supposed span of precognition, but the fact that Shackleton invariably failed to cognize telepathic presentations five seconds ahead of his 'present instant' strongly suggests that the upper limit is about $3\frac{1}{2}$–4 seconds. All that it is permissible to affirm is the probable existence of an optimum span of prehension.

It is an interesting hypothesis to suppose that our percipient developed a fixed precognitive time-*habit,* engendered originally by the 'normal' rate of calling, to which he had become accustomed during the earlier experiments. If his prehensive span into the future remained fixed when the rate of calling was doubled, his successes would then fall on the $(+2)$ trials instead of on the $(+1)$.

It seems highly probable that whatever theory is invoked to explain the apparent precognitive effect in the 'counters' experiments must account also for the same effect observed when prepared lists of random numbers were used, for there appears to be little or no difference in the degree of success obtained by the two methods. . . .

That the personality of the agent plays a part in the process is clear from the fact that, except for a single occasion, Shackleton obtained only precognitive successes when working with Miss Elliott, while with Aldred both precognitive and post-cognitive effects were produced. With a third agent, Mrs. Albert, who came on only two occasions, Shackleton obtained $(+1)$ successes only, as in the case of Miss Elliott. In fact, on 432 $(+1)$ trials with Mrs. Albert as agent he scored 139 hits, compared with a Stevens expectation of 88.6. This gives a positive deviation which exceeds 6 standard deviations, and corresponds to odds of more than a hundred millions to one. In none of the other categories was the score anywhere near significance. There were no experiments at 'rapid' rate with this agent, and prepared random numbers were in use throughout.

In addition to the three successful agents, Miss R. Elliott, Mrs. G. Albert and Mr. J. Aldred, eight other persons acted as agent, but Shackleton had no success with them. . . .

In all, 1,152 (+1) trials at 'normal' rate were made with the eight agents but these yielded only 222 hits which is only slightly below the Stevens expectation of 233.5. Among the unsuccessful agents were Mrs. Basil Shackleton, K. M. G., Dr. Wiesner and S. G. S.

As regards K. M. G., there was an earlier occasion (21st February 1941) on which she was apparently a successful agent. On this date, after Miss Elliott had acted as agent for four sheets of guesses, K. M. G. took her place, while Miss Elliott watched K. M. G. Miss Elliott sat about three feet away, but in a position where she could certainly have seen the cards in the box if she had chosen to do so. It is quite possible, therefore, that Miss Elliott was, all unwittingly, the agent on this occasion, though she reported that she was watching K. M. G. the whole time and did not look at the cards. There is, however, an interesting difference between results scored with K. M. G. as agent and those previously obtained earlier in the sitting with Miss Elliott as agent. In fact, on the 192 (+1) trials with Miss Elliott as agent the score was not significant (CR = +1.84), but the score on 200 trials on the actual or target card was just significant (the odds are about 40 to 1 when it is regarded as the best score in the five categories).

But when K. M. G. took Miss Elliott's place at the box, there was a score of 61 in 192 (+1) trials, and a chance score on the target card. The odds against getting this (+1) score by chance, when it is regarded as the best score out of five categories, amount to 2,000 to 1.

It may be that, even if Miss Elliott was the unconscious agent in this case, K. M. G. did perhaps have some influence on the result, although on a later occasion (25th April 1941) when K. M. G. was again the agent, Miss Elliott being absent, there were no significant scores of any kind. We cannot, of course, draw conclusions from such a limited number of guesses.

If the reader finds himself temperamentally or philosophically ill at ease with the phenomena of precognition, he may find some comfort in the fact that the same is true of most modern readers. Whether there is a sound philosophical basis for finding telepathy easier to accept than clairvoyance may well depend upon some vague feeling that telepathy is more likely to be understood sometime in terms of physics; and telepathy and clairvoyance together are *certainly* easier to cope with than precognition, since the time dimension is involved in the latter. To make contact with that which does not yet exist is, for many, a contradiction in terms, a philosophical paradox, an outrage; or even may be held to come under the category of "impossibility" in a way which is not quite true of telepathy or clairvoyance. I can only state the position to which my own mind has been worn smooth, like a stone worn smooth by the waters over many decades, namely to the effect that where evidence groups itself according to some inner logic of its own, the organized resistance of philosophical rejection is somehow gradually worn down. The question is to let nature group data for us as she likes, however absurd the conclusions in terms of the thought patterns of a given era. I do not say that this is a *"valid"* or "correct" way of working, but that it is the way in which some minds work—including the mind that makes the initial mistake, if it be such, to expose itself to these classes of materials.

In addition to this sheer psychological fact about the readers of such reports, and waiving the ultimate question of the soundness or intellectual respectability of this approach, there are additional considerations to be cited here, which are likely, when grasped, to have some effect upon the credibility of the material. As in the case of the clairvoyance material given above, the credibility of the data depends to some degree upon their orderly psychological character, that is, their reflection of general psychological laws which are known on other grounds to have some cogency. In the case of clairvoyance we seemed to find various positive and negative attitude factors operative to enable clairvoyance to occur or preventing it from occurring (p. 100), and these factors are closely related to factors of motivation, boredom, fatigue, health, and disease which are well known in the general experimental psychology of perception. Here, too, in the case of the precognition research, we find psychological variables which are not strange to us, appearing as context in which precognition may apparently occur. This does not explain how one might cut through the future into a situation not yet existent, but that would remain a problem for philosophy or indeed for the physics of the future, and would give the psychologist a relatively easy time. The psychologist would be dealing, in the case of precognition, with psychological laws which he already knows from other studies. But philosophical difficulties remain, and the experimental evidence can certainly not be regarded as settling the issue conclusively.

VI.

Psychokinesis

IT MIGHT be easier to maintain good contact with my readers if I refrained altogether from a consideration of the claims offered for the reality of "physical phenomena"; the reported influence of psychological processes, such as the will, upon *physical* events, without utilization of the nervous and muscular systems. Of course we experience incessantly the conversion of ideas into acts when our muscles are involved; but the notion that an idea could move a speck of dust as it dances in the sunlight, or that it could alter the gravitational fields in which we live, would be even more abhorrent to common sense than is the claim for telepathy, or clairvoyance, or precognition. In a recent survey of research characterizing modern parapsychology,[1] I decided at first to review some twenty experimental studies of extrasensory perception and to include at the end a few studies of "psychokinesis," or the reported influence of mind upon matter. At the last moment, however, I decided that I had a sufficiently difficult task on my hands; I must slight the precognition problem and postpone the endeavor to cope with psychokinesis. Yet in the present setting I cannot carry through any such determination. There are difficult or indeed "outrageous" observations that have to be dealt with in one way or another. The point of view of this volume has consistently been to ask what the thoughtful modern reader might reasonably conclude about various assertions made in the field of parapsychology. We must adhere to this principle.

[1] Gardner Murphy, Trends in the study of extrasensory perception, *American Psychologist*, 1958, Vol. 13, 69–76.

Throughout the history of man's concern with paranormal interactions between himself and his environment, and through the long history of early religion and the more evolved religions, there has loomed the question whether thought could influence the material environment. It will not disturb the reverent reader to recall Jesus' turning water into wine, nor the effort of Peter to walk upon the sea, as did his Lord, failing only because faith was insufficient. Often in the history of Christianity it was conceived to be a diabolical, rather than a divine, agency which caused objects to move or caused a missile to reach or to swing wide of its mark. Here again, the Hydesville rappings were said to be accompanied by a shower of "physical phenomena," and early spiritualist mediums were often accompanied by musical instruments which were reported to play without physical agency. I do not know how to provide "criteria of credibility." Reports are numerous but published records with a serious attempt at authentication are rare.

The most celebrated of all early experimental efforts in this field was that of Sir William Crookes,[2] who reported at length on his own experiments, including the physical phenomena associated with a "materialized" woman, and in the same era various witnesses stated that D. D. Home floated from a window into another window, dealt with red hot coals which did not burn his fingers, and satisfied many that he had a "power." Yet investigations of "physical mediums" from the 1870's until the 1930's were in general rather discouraging.

THE DUKE UNIVERSITY EXPERIMENTS

A completely new attack on this problem of movement without known physical agency, however, was launched by J. B. Rhine shortly after his early experiments in extrasensory perception. He described simple procedures by which dice sliding down a runway, tossed about by baffles, and coming to rest on a table top would show the effect of the will, in the sense that those die faces called for in a particular experiment and willed for by the subject would,

[2] *Researches in the Phenomena of Spiritualism*, London, J. Burns, 1874.

in fact, come up in a proportion significantly above that which was to be attributed to chance. In addition to reporting several successful experiments along these lines, Rhine reported that many other experiments which did not seem to give an over-all success nevertheless showed a strange tendency to produce strings of successes whenever the subject started a new task, the successes rapidly beginning to fail, in the form of a "decline curve," as the subject went on. Not only at the beginning of new experiments, but whenever the subject turned from one page to another or even from one sharply defined half page to the next half page, etc., his scores would go up, only to go down again as he completed the specified unit of work. Decline curves of this sort were likewise found by L. A. Dale at the American Society for Psychical Research (shown below) and by R. A. McConnell and his collaborators[3] at the University of Pittsburgh, using an automatic die-throwing machine and automatic photography of the dice after each throw. We shall use here two PK experiments, one by L. A. Dale, the other by Forwald and Pratt.

The Psychokinetic Effect:
The First A.S.P.R. Experiment[4]

. . . It was against this wide background of already existing PK research that we decided in September of 1945 to perform our own experiment. In planning the research an effort was made to meet certain criticisms which have been raised in relation to some of the already existing PK research . . . and to anticipate criticisms which might later be raised by other writers. The purpose of the research was to obtain answers to two major questions . . . (1) Does PK occur in the new experimental situation?[5] and (2) if it

---

[3] R. A. McConnell, R. J. Snowden, and K. F. Powell, Wishing with dice, *Journal of Experimental Psychology*, 1955, Vol. 50, 269–275.

[4] L. A. Dale, *Journal of the American Society for Psychical Research*, 1946, Vol. 40, 123–151.

[5] It is necessary, of course, in any parapsychological investigation, to ask

does, what is the bearing (if any) of the subjects' expressed attitude toward the possibility of PK on their scoring ability? Minor questions concerned the possibility of consistently demonstrating PK through the work of a large number of subjects, and the influence of sex upon scoring ability.

Methodology and Procedure

Subjects: The subjects were 54 college students, principally from Hunter, Columbia, and the City College of New York. There were 29 women and 25 men. . . . They were paid at the rate of a dollar an hour. None of them had previously taken part in PK experiments, but some had been subjects in ESP research. Experimentation began in January, 1946, and was completed by the end of March.

Experimental equipment and materials: The dice used were four ordinary commercial dice, red with scooped-out white spots. They were $\frac{5}{8}$ inches on a side. (Our original plan called for the use of "good" professional dice, with inlaid faces—so-called "perfect" dice true to $\frac{1}{1000}$ of an inch—but such dice were not obtainable at the time we started the experiment. In any case, this was not important. Even if "perfect" dice (which through wear and tear would soon cease to be "perfect") had been available and used, we would have had to depend on the experimental set-up and statistical controls to rule out the hypothesis of faulty dice. (This point will be further discussed under the heading of "Results.")

Figure 11 shows the randomizing chute down which the dice were thrown. . . . The photograph is taken from above to show the baffles over which the dice had to bounce before landing in the dice-box. The chute itself (B) is three feet six inches long, five inches wide, and four inches deep. It is covered over by a glass strip. There are 55 baffles. The inner measurements of the dice-

---

a bedrock question concerning the occurrence in the experiment of the paranormal phenomenon hypothesized. Without evidence that the phenomenon (in this case, PK) is present, questions concerning its nature are irrelevant. [L. A. D.]

box (C) are eighteen and one half inches by twelve inches. It is lined with a padded material, and illuminated by bulbs set along the edges. The cover is shown closed in the photograph, but it was kept open during the experimental session. The dice were shaken in a dice cup and then poured into the open mouth (A) of the chute, finally coming to rest in the dice-box. The type of record sheet used throughout the experiment is shown in Figure 12.

Method of acquiring data: Each of the fifty-four subjects was used for one sitting only. After determining and recording his attitude (see below under "conduct of the sitting"), the subject was asked to throw four runs[6] for each die face as target, thus in all filling six record sheets (see Figure 12), one for each target face. Four dice were thrown simultaneously from a regular dice cup down the chute; therefore six throws of these four dice completed the run. The order of the target faces thrown for was rotated in the following manner: The first group of nine subjects filled out their first page trying for *ones,* the second page trying for *twos,* and so on up to *sixes.* The second group of nine subjects started out on their first page trying for *twos,* then for *threes,* and ended up on their last page trying for *ones.* The third group started with *threes* and ended with *twos,* and so on with this method of rotation until the last group of nine subjects, who had for their first target the *six* face. Thus each die face was not only thrown for an equal number of times in the whole experiment, but was also represented with equal frequency at first, second . . . or last target in the session. The need for this rotation of faces will become clear when decline effects and other statistical analyses are discussed below.

Both the subject and the experimenter kept a complete record of every die face that turned up, the experimenter keeping her record in ink. At the end of each run, subject and experimenter

---

[6] The Duke work has standardized a "run" in PK as 24 single die readings, thus approximating the standard run of 25 guesses in ESP card tests. It should be remembered that 24 die readings constitute the run no matter whether, for instance, all 24 dice are thrown at once, whether one die is thrown 24 times, or whether, as in the present experiment, four dice are thrown six times. [L. A. D.]

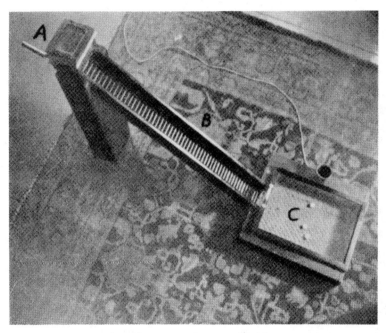

FIG. 11   Randomizing chute down which dice were thrown.

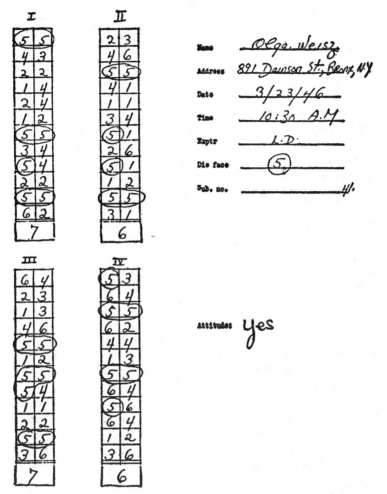

FIG. 12 Subject number 41's first record sheet. The five-face is the target for the whole page. The hits are circled. A score of four in each column is expected by chance. Thus subject number 41 was plus 10 on this page.

both counted the number of hits appearing in the column, then went on to the next run on the page. (When the data were checked and analysed at the end of the experiment, all discrepancies in respect of hits between subjects' and experimenter's recording were carefully noted, and the *lower score* was in every case taken as a basis for statistical analyses.)

To summarize, then, 1296 runs (31,104 single die readings) were completed by the subjects, each die face having been thrown for an equal number of times, and suitably rotated in regard to its order of appearance as target on the series of six record sheets.

Conduct of the sitting: Each of the 54 subjects made an individual appointment for a session and, as stated above, was used in one session only. The session lasted anywhere from fifty minutes to and hour and a half, depending upon the rate of speed at which the subject worked, how many questions he (or she) felt like asking, and so on. No attempt was ever made to rush the subject through the working period; on the other hand, if he obviously wanted to finish quickly and with a minimum of conversation, the experimenter kept things moving rapidly. In spite of a rather highly routinized experimental plan, every effort was made to create an informal atmosphere within the framework of this plan. Cigarettes and gum were offered, and time out was taken for casual conversation at the completion of each page in the series of six record sheets. Appreciation was expressed when the dice seemed to be turning up well. Most of the subjects volunteered the information that they enjoyed the session, asked that a report of the experiment be sent to them, and offered to take part without remuneration in future dice-throwing experiments. . . .

A dozen of the sessions were witnessed, either in whole or in part, by Dr. Ernest Taves, by Dr. J. L. Woodruff, or by friends of the subjects.

Results . . .

Since hypotheses alternative to PK, such as chance, faulty dice, etc., can only be ruled out in the light of a number of interlocking analyses which were performed on the data, we present in this section with a minimum of discussion the results of these analyses, and in the next section go on to a fuller consideration of them.

As stated, 1296 runs of 24 die throws were performed. The number of hits obtained beyond chance expectation was 171, and the average score per run[7] was 4.13. This positive deviation of 171 gives a CR of 2.60, and a P-value of .005. Thus, only five times in a thousand similar large-scale experiments would such a deviation be expected on a chance basis. Our results in terms of total deviation are summarized in Table 19.

TABLE 19. Results of PK Experiment in Terms of Total Deviation from Chance Expectation

N (in single die-throws)	31104
Hits obtained	5355
Hits expected	5184
Deviation	+171
Mean score (per run)	4.132
SD	±65.727
CR	2.60
P	.005

The way in which the hits were distributed on the six faces of the dice is shown in Table 20.

TABLE 20. Number of Hits and Deviation from Chance Expectation on All Faces of the Dice as Targets

	One-face	Two-face	Three-face	Four-face	Five-face	Six-face	Total
No. of hits	826	909	837	879	939	965	5355
Deviation	—38	+45	—27	+15	+75	+101	+171

[7] If 24 dice are thrown with a specified face as target, one sixth of them should by chance turn up with that specified face. Therefore the average score per run (of 24 die readings) expected by chance is 4.00. [L. A. D.]

To what degree the concentration of hits on the five-face and the six-face shown in Table 20 is a matter of mechanical bias of the dice and to what degree it may be due to some *psychological* factor favoring the higher faces (the six-face seems to be preferred by nearly all subjects) can only be determined by extensive control data. Such control data are now being gathered and will be reported at a later date. But, in any case, the hypothesis of mechanically biased dice is irrelevant in connection with the extra-chance deviation obtained. Since each die face was thrown for as target an equal number of times, the effect of mechanical bias would cancel out. It is impossible, that is, for dice "loaded" to favor, say, the three higher faces not to *disfavor to approximately the same degree* the three lower faces. In this case, of course, there could be no significant total deviation from chance expectation.

Next we wish to dispose of the question whether the subjects' attitude toward the possibility of PK was a variable of any importance in this experiment. . . .

TABLE 21.   Comparison of Scores Obtained by Subjects Who Accepted and Subjects Who Rejected the Possibility of PK

	Ss who accepted the possibility of PK (41)	Ss who rejected the possibility of PK (13)	Total (54)
N (in runs)	984	312	1296
Hits obtained	4052	1303	5355
Hits expected	3936	1248	5184
Deviation	+116	+55	+171
Mean Score	4.117	4.176	4.132
SD	±57.271	±32.249	±65.727
CR	2.03	1.71	2.60
P	.02	.04	.005

CR/d ("accepted"-"rejected") negligible

Because of the homogeneous nature of the data under consideration, we were able to make use of what is known as the "split-half" method of estimating their reliability. This method is often used in psychological testing, but as far as we know it has seldom been applied in parapsychological testing. A word on the use of the method in psychological testing may be helpful. Suppose that a "general information" test consisting of twenty true-or-false statements is given to a group of subjects; we may then wish to know something about the *consistency* with which this test measures the ability of these subjects. If the subjects were retested and scored at more or less the same level as on the first occasion, we would conclude that the test had some reliability; but if there were wide discrepancies in the scores obtained on the two occasions, we would say that the test was unstable, or lacking in reliability. Now, for a variety of reasons it is not always feasible to retest the subjects, or to use a parallel form of the test. But the test can be divided into two equal parts, and the scores on these two parts can be examined to see if there is any correlation between them. If there is found to be a significant correlation between the two sections of the test, then we may conclude that the scores are not chance artifacts, and that the test has a useful degree of reliability, providing a rough measure of the ability of the subjects. If the subjects in a hypothetical "information test" merely answered the twenty true-or-false statements at random, getting some correct by chance and missing others, we should not expect to find a significant correlation between the results on the two comparable halves—even-numbered and odd-numbered questions, for instance.

Briefly, then, we pooled the scores that the subjects in the PK test obtained on their odd-numbered record sheets, and compared, or correlated, these with the scores deriving from their even-numbered sheets. The amount of positive correlation found between these two sets of scores was clearly significant.[8] Those subjects who

---

[8] The self-correlation of the half-test was .30; application of the Spearman-Brown formula indicates that the reliability coefficient of the whole test is .46, which is between six and seven times its *PE*. Thus the subjects' scores on half their runs provide a significant predictability regarding the

scored high on odd-numbered sheets tended to a significant degree to score high on even-numbered sheets; conversely, subjects scoring poorly on odd-numbered sheets tended to do equally poorly on even-numbered sheets. (Since each die face was thrown for an equal number of times, and was systematically rotated from page to page, no bias of the dice can have any bearing on this significant correlation.) The results of this statistical test on our PK data have two strong implications. The first bears on the question of chance, and the second on the dynamics of PK itself. With a chance distribution of hits, there would be no expectation of a significant correlation between scores on odd-numbered and even-numbered pages. Thus the test reinforces the significance of the CR of 2.60 obtained in respect of the total positive deviation of the experiment. But the fundamental implication of the "split-half" finding would appear to be that the psychokinetic effect is not chaotically distributed throughout the work of the subjects, but rather that it varies in degree from one individual to another. There seems to be, in other words, a psychokinetic "gift"—either a gift inhering in individual subjects, or a gift of the experimenter . . . which is liberated in the presence of some subjects more freely than in the presence of others. This does not mean that we have accurately measured each individual's PK ability (or the ability of the experimenter on different occasions), which would require a much higher correlation. But, to sum up, it *does* mean that a non-chance factor runs through the data—a factor partly responsible for the individual differences in the scores.

For some years interest has focused on "decline effects" which have in various ways manifested themselves in ESP research. . . . Many ESP series have been marked by a deterioration of scoring rate within the run, or across the page, or from the beginning of an experimental series to the end. Quite naturally, therefore, the Duke University research group was interested in examining their PK data for evidence of comparable decline effects. Reference to

---

scores on the remainder of the task. This finding, of course, is independent of the significant positive deviation which was obtained in the whole experiment. [L. A. D.]

the papers listed in the Bibliography [omitted for reasons of space] will show that they found decline phenomena in abundance in their large mass of PK data. Almost every paper has a section devoted to analyses for position effects, and some of the best evidence for PK derives from these analyses. Decline effects were also found in the data from our own experiment, and analyses of these will be presented next.

From the data of Table 22 we see an orderly decline in rate of scoring from Run I to Run IV on the record page. If we pool the

TABLE 22. Comparison of Scores Obtained on Runs I, II, III, and IV (of Each of the Six Record Sheets)

	Run I	Run II	Run III	Run IV	Total
N (in runs)	324	324	324	324	1296
Hits obtained	1396	1351	1308	1300	5355
Hits expected	1296	1296	1296	1296	5184
Deviation	+100	+55	+12	+4	+171
Mean score	4.309	4.170	4.037	4.012	4.132
SD	±32.863	±32.863	±32.863	±32.863	±65.727
CR	3.04	1.67	.37	.12	2.60
P	.001	.05	.36	.45	.005

CR/d (I-IV) 2.07

number of hits obtained on the upper half of the record page (Runs I and II) and compare this number with the hits obtained on the lower half of the page (Runs III and IV), we get the result tabulated in Table 23.

The psychokinetic effect is thus seen to be most highly concentrated when subjects start work on the record sheet. They score high on the first half of the sheet, then peter out to almost nothing as they progress to the lower half, then go high again at the top of the next sheet. The greatest concentration of hits occurs in the first run of all. Therefore, quite naturally, it is of interest to ask

TABLE 23. Comparison of Scores Obtained on First Half of Record Sheet with Scores Obtained on the Second Half

	First half	*Second half*
N (in runs)	648	648
Hits obtained	2747	2608
Hits expected	2592	2592
Deviation	+155	+16
Mean score	4.23	4.025
SD	± 46.476	±46.476
CR	3.34	.34
P	.0004	.37
CR/d (1st half-2nd half) 2.11		

where the hits occur within the individual runs. One might reasonably predict that the greatest concentration of all will occur in the *first half of the first run*. Table 24 shows that this is just what did occur.

TABLE 24. Location of Hits in First Half of the Run Versus the Second Half of the Run

	Run I	*Run II*	*Run III*	*Run IV*
Hits and deviation in first half	727 +79	668 +20	656 +8	630 —18
Hits and deviation in second half	669 +21	683 +35	652 +4	670 +22
Total first half: 2681				
Total second half: 2674				
Difference: 7				
CR/d negligible				

From the data of Table 24 it is apparent that many more successes were recorded in the *first half of the first run* than in any other subdivision of the record sheet containing the same amount of material. This concentration of hits in the first half of the first run results in a deviation from chance expectation which is statistically significant,[9] but the tendency to do well at the beginning of the run is not maintained in the other runs. Pooling *all* runs and comparing the hits obtained on the first half of the run with hits obtained on the second half of the run, we see that there is no significant difference. But the fact remains that more than one-third of the entire positive deviation obtained in the whole experiment comes from the first half of the first run (on each record sheet), the *second* half of the first run showing a rather striking falling-off effect. . . .

Table 25 shows that the women obtain scores which are independently significant, while the men score only very slightly above chance.

TABLE 25. Comparison of Scores Obtained by Male and Female Subjects

	Female Ss (29)	Male Ss (25)	Total (54)
N (in runs)	696	600	1296
Hits obtained	2923	2432	5355
Hits expected	2784	2400	5184
Deviation	+139	+32	+171
Mean Score	4.200	4.053	4.132
SD	±48.166	±44.721	±65.727
CR	2.89	.72	2.60
P	.002	.24	.005

CR/d (F-M) 1.63

[9] Since the cell containing the positive deviation of 79, derived from the first half of the first run, is one cell selected from eight, the CR representing its deviation from chance expectation is to be taken with a grain of salt; but for those interested in its exact value (as pointing to a problem worthy of study in future research), the CR is 3.40, and P is .0003. [L. A. D.]

In Table 23 we showed that the psychokinetic effect was most highly concentrated in the first half of the record sheet. We therefore thought it would be of interest to examine the distribution of hits obtained by female and male subjects in respect of position on the record sheet. Table 26 compares, in terms of deviation, the scores obtained by women and men on the first and second halves of the record sheet.

TABLE 26.   Comparison of Scores Obtained by Male and Female Subjects on First and Second Halves of the Record Sheet

	Female, first half	Female, second half	Male first half	Male second half
N (in runs)	348	348	300	300
Deviation	+101	+38	+54	—22

The women obtained 51.0% of their hits on the first half of the record sheet (Runs I and II), and the men 51.6%. Thus we see that both women and men subjects declined at approximately the same rate as they progressed from the first half to the second half of the record sheet.

This completes the presentation of the major analyses performed on the data. Two minor analyses, however, remain to be discussed. The first concerns the grouping of hits, and the second recording discrepancies.

It will be remembered that four dice were thrown at a time. Special attention was focused during the session on the turning-up of doubletons, tripletons, and (especially) quadruplets of the desired face. Analysis showed that, given a positive deviation of 171, the grouping of hits was *not* significantly different from chance expectation; there was no measurable tendency, that is, for the PK effect to act in an "all or none" fashion upon the four dice which were simultaneously thrown.

As stated before, in every sitting a duplicate record was kept by the subject, the experimenter keeping the official record in ink. All die faces were recorded by both subject and experimenter. In spite of the greatest care, 21 discrepancies (in respect of hits) were found between the subjects' and the experimenter's recording. In twelve instances subjects recorded one hit fewer in a run than the experimenter; in nine instances the subject recorded one hit more than the experimenter. In every case the *lower* score was taken as official.

Discussion

Hypotheses alternative to PK:

Before we can interpret our results as confirming the hypothesis that mind can act volitionally upon the falling dice, certain counter-hypotheses must be considered.

The hypothesis of chance is untenable in view of the CR of 2.60, derived from the total deviation, the significant result deriving from the application of the "split-half" method of self-correlation, and the orderly decline effects observed in the data. The experiment was especially designed to rule out the hypothesis of faulty dice. It is true that the dice favored the higher faces (Table 20); but, in view of the fact that each die face was thrown for as target an equal number of times, this cannot account for the positive deviation. The decline effects and the self-correlation result clinch the case, so to speak, both from the point of view of chance and from the point of view of faulty dice. It is equally far-fetched to suppose that "skilled throwing" could have contributed to the results. The dice were shaken in a dice cup, and then thrown down a chute more than three feet long. No "expert," as far as we know, will attempt to control dice except when he is allowed to throw them by hand along a smooth surface. The theory of optional stopping (the hypothesis that an experiment is arbitrarily stopped at a favorable point) is irrelevant since the exact amount of data to be collected in the experiment was determined in advance. Recording errors did occur, since there were discrepancies between subjects' and experimenter's tabulation of hits; but the lower score was always taken as official, and it is hence extremely unlikely that recording errors led to a spuriously high deviation. Quite to the contrary, it is probable that the experiment was penalized by this method. Computing errors are equally unlikely. Dr. Taves and the present writer worked together on all the analyses, checking on each other, and then the whole material was rechecked by Mr. Cook. Only one error was found by Mr. Cook, a very minor one. The correction of this raised the CR of the difference between scores obtained on the first half of the record sheet versus scores on the second half from 2.08 to 2.11 (Table 23).

All these counterhypotheses, then, are insufficient to account for the positive results, and the only alternative to PK is bad faith on the part of the experimenter, with collusion on the part of at least some of the subjects. The original data are open to the inspection of any interested person. . . .

Summary: Data from the first PK experiment performed at the A.S.P.R. have been presented, counterhypotheses to PK have been considered, and the conclusion has been reached that the hypothesis of "mind over matter" is the only one adequate to account for the results obtained. This conclusion is based on the total positive deviation of the series, on certain "lawful" decline effects, and on the findings from the split-half method of estimating reliability. Finally, it is of interest to note that the PK effect was apparently sturdy enough to manifest itself within the framework of a rather highly routinized experimental procedure.

The reader is asked to consider four aspects of the Dale experiment, aside from the sheer fact that the results were positive: (1) it was itself a repetition of the Duke University studies in which dice were used on an inclined plane; (2) it required the subjects to "will" for specific dice at specific times, on a predetermined basis, thus ruling out the possibility that the subject simply scored well on the die faces that he preferred, or which he tended most frequently to call; (3) it obtained well-defined decline curves similar to those obtained at Duke; (4) it gave significant individual differences, as shown by the odd-even reliability figures. It is not maintained that *all* experimenters obtain such results; indeed, Dale herself was not able to achieve a successful repetition.[10] The results of the experiment reported, as analyzed above, do not at all suggest a sheer fluke. The field of PK, however, has not yielded very much in the domain of clearly repeatable experiments.

The studies described hitherto relate to the hypothetical action of the mind or will upon the dice as they tumble—affecting their centers of gravity, perhaps, or altering their constitution. It was thought desirable to do two additional kinds of experiments: First, to conduct more exact measurements of the forces involved, so that it would be possible to calculate the energy which acts upon the dice to make them come to rest in the desired position; secondly, in facilitating such calculations, to draw a mid-line down the table on which the dice were to be thrown and to will them at certain specified times to move to the right of this line, and at other specified times to move to the left of it. Measurements could then be made on the actual positions at which the dice come to rest and thus indicate something about the magnitude of the physical forces involved. Both types of experiments just described have actually been performed repeatedly by Haakon Forwald, a Swedish engineer who has for many years made the experimental study of psychokinesis his specialty. His recent visit to Duke University made it possible for him to give a series of demonstrations of the phenomena in the presence of various witnesses. It is from one of these recent experiments that the following data are drawn. In a certain sense we still encounter here the decline curves already described. It is when switching to a new task that Forwald makes his high scores. It is the difference between what happens when he tries to push the dice to the *right* and what happens when he tries to push them to the *left,* in the *first* series of such efforts, that constitutes the focus of the problem.

[10] *Journal of the American Society for Psychical Research,* 1947, Vol. 41, 65–82.

CONFIRMATION OF THE PK PLACEMENT EFFECT[11]

. . . This paper is a report of PK placement tests carried out in the Parapsychology Laboratory of Duke University in October and November, 1957, during a visit by one of the authors, H. F. Over a long period of time, working alone in Sweden with himself as subject, H. F. had obtained highly significant and remarkably consistent PK placement results. The purpose of his visit to Duke was to try to confirm his findings with the assurances against error provided by a second observer and by independent records of the results. . . .

All of his work has been concerned with the use of PK to influence the placement of falling cubes. The objects have been released electrically at the top of an incline so that they fell under the force of gravity and spread out upon a horizontal throwing surface. This surface was divided by a center line into equal right-hand and left-hand areas, designated *A* and *B*. The two sides were used equally often as target areas. . . .

The general procedure was to throw five times for one target area, followed by five throws for the other. The evidence for PK was derived not only from the total scores but also from the *distribution* of scoring within the five successive releases made for one side as target. When the five-throw sequences were pooled, the highest rate of success was found on the first and last trials. . . .

In 1954 H. F. published his first results using a new method of recording, the "scaled placement" test. In these tests he recorded to the nearest centimeter the lateral position in which each cube came to rest on the table. Success thus became measurable in terms of the degree to which the cubes were influenced to go toward the target side of the table. . . .

From the beginning of the scaled tests, it became apparent that the significance of the results was primarily due to the outstanding success of the first throw for the *A*-side as target, and to a marked degree also to the first throw for the *B*-side. Since the comparison

[11] J. G. Pratt and H. Forwald, *Journal of Parapsychology*, 1958, Vol. 22, 1–19.

of *both* targets is required as a control against any possible bias in the apparatus, this beginning salience in the five-throw sequence within the set was stated in terms of the *B-A* difference[12] in averages for Throw 1. The Throw 1 effect persisted in H. F.'s own placement work (but was generally not present on the few occasions when he used other people as subjects) right up to the time his research in Sweden was interrupted by his visit to the Laboratory. . . .

. . . During his Duke visit, therefore, the first important objective was to find out whether the Throw 1 effect would hold up in his results. If it did, then further tests would be designed with the plan of selecting those data for separate evaluation. . . .

Apparatus

A PK placement test apparatus was constructed by H. F. after his arrival at the Laboratory. Since this is essentially a duplication of the set-up which was used in Sweden, a general description will suffice in the present report.

A release mechanism is mounted above an incline which curves downward and joins one end of a horizontal throwing surface. Before being released, the cubes lie in a row starting at the back end of a wooden V-shaped channel which is held in a horizontal position. The cubes are released by pressing a control button attached to an electro-magnetic release mechanism at the end of a long, slack cable, part of which lies on the floor. When the button is pressed, the end of the V-channel toward the incline drops and the cubes fall and spread out over the horizontal surface. A low wooden wall on the three sides of the table away from the incline prevents

[12] The centimeter lines were numbered from 0 on the *A*-side to 80 on the *B*-side, with the center line 40. Thus, a *positive B-A* difference is in the desired direction. In all the preceding reports and throughout the present one the *B-A* difference has been obtained by getting the average position of the cubes when the *A*-side was target and the average when the *B*-side was target and then subtracting the former from the latter. Thus any given *B-A* difference is the average difference in placement per cube-pair. [J. G. P. and H. F.]

any of the cubes from falling off onto the floor.

The surface of the table is made of thin, transparent plastic stretched over a layer of plate glass. Under the glass there is a sheet of lined co-ordinate paper with numbered centimeter intervals. The longitudinal lines are numbered from 0 at the right-hand (A) edge of the table to 100 at the left-hand (B) edge. This is the scale by which the lateral position of the cubes is recorded. . . .

The cubes in the Duke experiment measured ⅝ of an inch on each edge and were made of seasoned beechwood. They had sharp corners and smooth surfaces, and the same six cubes were used throughout the experiment. In the first series, D1, the surfaces were covered with squares of silver, 48 mm. thick, but in all the other series they were uncovered.

Procedure

Two main aspects of the experimental procedure need to be distinguished. The first is the general strategy by which the research was guided toward the objective of getting a confirmation of H. F.'s PK effects. The second is the tactical one: the details of how the tests were conducted.

General Plan of the Experiment

For H. F., shifting the scene of his operations from the basement of his own home, where he had worked previously, to the Parapsychology Laboratory involved a big change in the psychological conditions. It was necessary to try to minimize the effects of this shift. The best approach seemed to be to proceed cautiously, allowing the plan to develop from the results themselves. To reduce the risk that H. F. might become self-conscious and inhibited in the new situation, he was not invited to share in the discussions regarding the general experimental approach. H. F. co-operated wholeheartedly under this limitation, even though he was sometimes asked to take part in a test which he would not himself have chosen to do at that particular time.

Since it was not possible to say in advance what the effect on the results would be of having a second person present to observe and record them, it was necessary to carry out exploratory tests to find the right conditions for success. Only after that had been accomplished would it be possible to set up a confirmatory experiment. It did not matter how much time and how many trials went into the exploratory stage of the work. What did matter was that this stage should provide a clear-cut basis of prediction regarding the effects anticipated in the confirmatory series. Only statistically significant *predicted* results in the confirmatory tests could fully meet the objectives of the research. . . .

The tests are divided into four exploratory sections, A through D, and one confirmatory section, E. The sections were introduced in the research in alphabetical order, but the tests of one section were not always completed before the next was begun.

Section A. H. F. worked alone, as he had done in Sweden. The object was to see if he could duplicate his earlier success under conditions similar to those he had used previously.

Section B. H. F. was the subject, and a laboratory staff member was present as a passive observer and independent recorder of the results.

Section C. H. F. continued to act as the principal subject and to release the dice, and a staff member was once more present as an observer and independent recorder. This staff member, however, had an additional part in the experiment: he consciously attempted to help H. F. influence the dice.

Section D. Someone other than H. F. was the principal subject and releaser. H. F., and a third person when there was one, also consciously attempted to help the subject. H. F. acted as the only recorder, witnessed by the other one or two persons present.

Section E. The confirmatory section comprised tests made with H. F. as subject and P. M., the one observer with whom H. F. had worked successfully in Section C, as co-subject. Both recorded independently.

Detailed Test Procedure

Before each release of the six cubes, the release mechanism was reset by lifting it with one finger until it was automatically caught and held by the anchor of the release magnet. The cubes were swept together on the table and, held in a row by the pressure of two fingers, were lifted and placed so that the back cube was even with the back end of the V-channel. This left approximately two inches of clear space at the front end of the channel. Care was taken to see that all of the cubes were resting securely on the bottom of the channel so that they were touching on both sides. The resetting of the release mechanism and the placing of the cubes was always done by H. F. and was observed by others present.

Each person taking part in a test chose his own position, but no one was in contact with the apparatus or the table on which it rested when the cubes were released. H. F. stood on the right-hand or A-side of the table, as he was in the habit of doing from his earlier work. The other person or persons generally stood on the opposite side. No change of position occurred when the shift of target was made from the A- to the B-side.

The cubes were released by pressing the control button. As soon as the cubes had come to rest, their positions were observed and recorded. This was always done by H. F., and in some sections of the tests, as already explained, by a second person as well. In making the two records, each observer worked alone and completed his recording without taking any notice of the other. When both were finished, the two records were compared; and in case any discrepancy was found, each observer rechecked the cube or cubes involved, and agreement was reached as to which of the two records was accurate. The infrequency of discrepancies showed that H. F. had higher than 99% accuracy in his recording; and as the second observer became more experienced at the task, he soon approached the same level. In almost every instance when an error occurred, it was only when the cubes were difficult to judge for two adjacent centimeter lines, and not as a result of mistakes in reading the centimeter scale. In those few cases in which the cubes were so nearly balanced between two lines as to make a judgment impossible, the results were recorded so as to disfavor the target side.

The trials were made in *sets* of 10 throws, 5 for the *A*-side as target, followed by 5 for the *B*-side. Once a set was begun it was finished without interruption, and generally only one set was done at one experimental session. Five sets under a given experimental condition constituted a *series*. Since six cubes were released at a time, a set thus consisted of 60 trials; and a series, of 300 trials.

Results

. . . The confirmatory tests consist of the two series of Section E. The first set of Series D13 was done on November 12 and the last set of D14 on November 21. Thus the work was carried out at the average rate of more than one set per day—faster than the usual rate for H. F. in Sweden. The experiment was terminated after Series D14 because H. F. had to return to Sweden at that time.

As previously decided, Throw 1 was again selected for separate evaluation. In Series D13, the *B-A* difference on Throw 1 was +21.47. This is the largest difference obtained in the work at Duke University and it was not equalled by any of H. F.'s previous results. The t_d is 3.79, with P = .00015. In Series D14 the *B-A* difference in Throw 1 was +8.80, for which $t_d = 1.68$ and P = .093. When the two probabilities are combined by Fisher's method, the result is: $X^2 = 22.36$ (4 d.f.); P = .0002. The results (shown in the last section of Table 27) confirmed the prediction made on the basis of Series D5, and thus they constitute a general confirmation of H. F.'s PK placement effect under laboratory conditions safeguarded by independent observation and duplicate recording of the results. . . .

Discussion

. . . Is it conceivable that there was some bias in the apparatus which produced the Throw 1 effect? This would have had to be a

TABLE 27. Total Results

Section*	Series	Subjects	Throw 1				All Throws			
			B−A diff.	SD$_d$	t$_d$	P	B−A diff.	SD$_d$	t$_d$	P
A. (Exploratory)	D 1	H. F. alone	+ 7.67	2.85	2.69	.0071	+2.36	1.35	1.75	.080
	D 2	H. F. alone	+ 9.63	4.04	2.38	.017	+1.25	1.89	.66	.51
B. (Exploratory)	D 3	H. F.	+ 2.73	5.17	.53	.60	− .51	2.40	.21	.83
	D 4	H. F.	− 3.43	4.86	.71	.48	+ .75	2.48	.30	.76
C. (Exploratory)	D 5	H. F. & P. M.	+15.47	5.62	2.75	.006	+6.53	2.53	2.58	.010
	D 8	H. F. & J. G. P.	− 2.00	4.62	.43	.67	−1.99	2.19	.91	.36
	D 12	H. F. & F. G.	− 4.13	5.22	.79	.43	− .27	4.42	.06	.95
D. (Exploratory)	D 6	L. L., A. F., & J. F.	− 2.53	5.05	.50	.62	+4.43	2.14	2.07	.038
	D 7	J. F. & H. F.	+ .63	4.69	.13	.90	+4.18	2.13	1.96	.050
	D 9	M. J., H. F., & W. S.	+ 9.87	5.70	1.73	.084	+2.09	2.29	.91	.36
	D 10	C. B., H. F., & J. F.	+12.23	5.13	2.38	.017	+3.49	2.27	1.54	.12
	D 11	A. L., H. F., & J. F	+ 5.17	4.99	1.04	.30	+3.81	2.17	1.76	.078
E. (Confirmatory)	D 13	H. F. & P. M.	+21.47	5.66	3.79	.00015	+4.01	2.58	1.55	.12
	D 14	H. F. & P. M.	+ 8.80	5.25	1.68	.093	+3.91	2.32	1.69	.091

†Combination of P-values by Fisher's method
$$\chi^2 = 22.36 \text{ (4 d.f.)}$$
$$P = .0002$$

*Conditions for different sections:
A: H. F. working alone in dual role of experimenter and subject.
B: H. F. acting as subject and recorder; P. M., as passive observer and second recorder.
C: H. F. as main subject; a staff member as a co-subject; both recording independently.
D: Someone brought in as a new subject for each series; H. F. present only as co-subject and he alone recorded.
E: H. F. as main subject; P. M. as co-subject; both recording independently. This section was set up as a confirmation of Series D 5.

systematically shifting bias. The sturdy construction of the apparatus and the very slight effort required in resetting the release mechanism make it seem most unlikely that any effect of the sort required to produce the result could have been brought about either consciously or unconsciously. The cubes were handled in a uniform manner in placing them in the release mechanism. They almost always settled snugly into the release channel under the force of gravity. These observations argue compellingly against the possibility that the manner in which the cubes were handled could have caused the results. If additional argument on this point is needed, it can be found in the fact that there were no significant results in other parts of the investigations when H. F. gave every sign of very much wanting to succeed. In Section B, for example, he was very highly motivated to get results since he had just been successful alone (Section A) and for the first time he was under pressure to produce evidence with an observer present. His lack of success there is reasonably explained on *psychological* grounds, but not on the grounds that a normally faulty apparatus suddenly lost its bias—only to regain it as a later stage. Furthermore, it is difficult to explain why the results should be restricted to Throw 1 if there was any sort of bias in the apparatus. As far as it could be observed, the releasing was done in the same manner throughout the set; and if there was any bias favoring the *A*-side on the first throw for that target, it should have favored the *A*-side for the other four throws as well, and similarly for the five throws for the B-target. . . .

The material selected here from Pratt and Forwald is representative of the more serious efforts at getting an experimental and quantitative definition of a physical force of a sort unknown to physics.

It may be that we are demanding too much, but it has become evident that the repeatable PK experiment is even harder to find than is the repeatable ESP experiment. One reason why we have used the Pratt-Forwald study above is that it is an experiment repeating the earlier work done by Forwald alone, both in Sweden and in the United States. It does constitute, therefore, a serious effort in the direction of repeatability of psychokinesis, and deserves emphasis.

Opinions will differ as to whether psychokinesis is actually more incredible than extrasensory perception. This will be partly a matter of personal metaphysics. Opinions will also differ as to whether the empirical data described are sufficient to warrant the attention given them. It is proper to inform the reader that many of the psychokinesis experiments are rough-and-ready affairs with very little control as to the critical physical and psychological considerations which produced the results—a serious point, since a very considerable number of psychokinesis experiments have yielded no positive results either in total deviation from chance expectation or in terms of decline curve. In a good many psychokinesis experiments there is just one die face for which the subject tries. In view of the unknown imperfections in dice, we cannot say how much is due to the imperfections *unless* the subject tries all six faces at different times on a random basis, that is, now trying for twos, now for fives, etc., and unless, under these conditions, the dice turn up with a five, when he tries for fives, etc. It is, of course, necessary that we use the same dice as we try now for one, now another face, following a set of random instructions which tell us when to try for one, when for another. Any gradual insidious factor causing uneven wear on the dice would presumably be independent of the fluctuations inherent in a random method of determining targets.

It appears to be no longer a defensible gesture to say: let us wait and see if there is anything here, as would have been the case when Rhine first approached his audience with this material in the *Journal of Parapsychology* in 1943. Independent experimental lines of work, all well safeguarded, tend to support his conclusions. I do not say that the conclusions are established; indeed, this is a word I do not use. I say that the thoughtful modern reader can no longer slam the door on psychokinesis.

VII.

Survival

THE BELIEF that soul and body are distinct and separable things, that beyond the period of their temporary union in this life there may be prolonged or even eternal existence of a soul freed from the body, is a belief often intimately associated with belief in paranormal events of the sorts with which our volume has been concerned. For many people the existence and meaning of telepathy, clairvoyance, precognition, psychokinesis lie in the reality of spiritual forces. For some, every telepathic event is ultimately a transaction in which unseen spiritual entities assist in the communion between the living. For others, while refraining from such a conception of intervention by unseen entities, the very fact that such things as telepathy can exist is held to mean the reality of a spiritual order, an order which provides a place for discarnate as well as incarnate entities. Both for preliterate man with his medicine men and for the spiritualist with his gifted medium, there are those whose powers of perceiving the invisible and predicting the unpredictable are simply gifts bespeaking the continuous presence of a spiritual world.

In general, modern psychical research has taken the position that all of the claims for the paranormal must be investigated whether they made any assumptions about the deceased or not. There must be investigation of telepathy and clairvoyance, precognition, and psychokinesis in their own right; there must also be investigation of those special sensitives who are called mediums, who offer themselves as mediators between incarnate and discarnate personalities; and an unflinching attempt to ascertain objectively whether the

deceased actually do play a part in the phenomena so often attributed to them. If there is a poltergeist ("troubling spirit") as
represented in the unexplained hurling of objects, the breaking of
windows, the pulling of hair, anything paranormal which is reported to have happened must be investigated;[1] and then if there
is any reason to believe that the phenomena are associated with
the death of some person in the house or room in which the events
occur, the arduous job arises of finding out whether there is anything really to connect the event with the deceased person. If in
addition to such strange occurrences there are repeated appearances
of humanlike forms which resemble deceased persons, we find ourselves in the realm of apparitions and ghosts[2] and have the additional responsibility of finding out whether there are any special
acts of these apparitions or ghosts which, upon investigation, turn
out to be the sorts of things which deceased persons liked to do, or
were in the habit of doing, or planned to do. Very rarely, but
nevertheless occasionally, such inquiries lead from the question of
the nature of the apparition to the nature of any possible evidence
that the apparition may present for the continuation of a deceased
personality. From this point onward again, if we should find that
an apparition, not expected at the time, appears in a form so well
defined that we can infer the nature of the cause of death, or of
some event associated with death, and can independently establish
that this is veridical, we are in the region pointed out below on
pp. 186 ff., in which a spontaneous paranormal occurrence may lead
us willy-nilly into the problem of "survival evidence."

Most survival evidence from the psychical research of the West-
ern world, however, is a more organized kind of evidence, a kind
of evidence associated with the cult of mediumship. Certain individuals are found in many preliterate and in many advanced societies who act as if "possessed," as if conveying messages from the
deceased. Sometimes they protest; sometimes they gladly accept

[1] J. G. Pratt and W. G. Roll, The Seaford disturbances, *Journal of
Parapsychology*, 1958, Vol. 22, 79–124.
[2] G. N. M. Tyrrell, *Apparitions*. London, Society for Psychical Research,
1942.

this function assigned to them. In a large proportion of cases they train themselves or are trained by sponsors or mentors who develop them as mediums. Whether surrounded by utter credulity or by a hard-bitten skepticism, their task is to convey information from the deceased which will give comfort and aid to the living. Sometimes they take the form of proving to the living by an appropriate reference to secret past events that it is actually the deceased that are communicating. Sometimes it is a question of giving practical advice in matters of war, love, finance, or politics. In view of the very widespread belief in the reality of mediumistic communication and the very large amount of investigation which has been carried on in this field, no serious book could possibly by-pass this kind of investigation.

But there are special reasons why modern psychical research made a heavy investment in time, thought and funds, in studying the problem of mediumship. Modern spiritualism had come into existence in the middle of the nineteenth century, and it was among the spiritualist mediums that many of the most interesting paranormal phenomena, phenomena involving telepathy, clairvoyance, and psychokinesis, appeared. There was, moreover, a deep-seated conviction among skeptics and intellectuals that the reality of existence beyond death was of enormous personal and philosophical importance to all serious persons, and was, moreover, a major issue with reference to the tenability or untenability of the widely held "materialism" of an agnostic era. The various kinds of evidence for survival beyond death, whether they derived from the study of apparitions and ghosts, from mediumship, or from the more complex lines of investigation to be discussed below, became for many the most important, the central problem of psychical research. Within the space available we shall try to give evidence from three types of paranormal events: (1) Spontaneous telepathic and clairvoyant events happening to ordinary persons, in which there is a suggestion of post-mortem action or commerce of the deceased with the living; (2) mediumistic phenomena; (3) the complex technical developments which carry the mediumistic studies to the challeng-

ing, perhaps insoluble, complexities known as "cross correspondences."

The following is a typical dream case announcing a death, under
circumstances suggesting survival: [3]

❧

. . . Some 35 years ago I took into my employment a tender,
delicate-looking boy, Robert Mackenzie, who, after some three or
four years' service, suddenly left. . . . A few years afterwards, my
eye was caught by a youth of some 18 years of age ravenously de-
vouring a piece of dry bread on the public street, and bearing all
the appearance of being in a chronic state of starvation. Fancying
I knew his features, I asked if his name were not Mackenzie. He
at once became much excited, addressed me by name, and informed
me that he had no employment; that his father and mother, who
formerly supported him, were now both inmates of the "poor-
house," to which he himself had no claim for admission, being
young and without any bodily disqualification for work, and that
he was literally homeless and starving. . . . Suffice it to say that he
resumed his work, and that, under the circumstances, I did everything in my power to facilitate his progress. . . . I was apparently
his sole thought and consideration, saving the more common concerns of daily life.

In 1862 I settled in London, and have never been in Glasgow
since. Robert Mackenzie, and my workmen generally, gradually lost
their individuality in my recollection. About 10 to 12 years ago my
employés had their annual soirée and ball. This was always held
. . . on a Friday evening. . . . On the Tuesday morning following,
immediately before 8 A.M., in my house on Campden Hill, I had
the following manifestation, I cannot call it a dream; but let me
use the common phraseology. I dreamt, but with no vagueness as
in common dreams, no blurring of outline or rapid passages from
one thing disconnectedly to another, that I was seated at a desk,

[3] Mrs. Henry Sidgwick, Notes on the evidence, collected by the Society,
for phantasms of the dead, *Proceedings of the Society for Psychical Research*,
1885, Vol. 3, 95–98.

engaged in a business conversation with an unknown gentleman, who stood on my right hand. Towards me, in front, advanced Robert Mackenzie, and, feeling annoyed, I addressed him with some asperity, asking him if he did not see that I was engaged. He retired a short distance with exceeding reluctance, turned again to approach me, as if most desirous for an immediate colloquy, when I spoke to him still more sharply as to his want of manners. On this, the person with whom I was conversing took his leave, and Mackenzie once more came forward. "What is all this, Robert?" I asked, somewhat angrily. "Did you not see I was engaged?" "Yes, sir," he replied; "but I must speak with you at once." "What about?" I said; "what is it that can be so important?" "I wish to tell you, sir," he answered, "that I am accused of doing a thing I did not do, and that I want *you* to know it, and to tell you so, and that you are to forgive me for what I am blamed for, because I am innocent." Then, "I did not do the thing they say I did." I said, "What?" getting same answer. I then naturally asked, "But how can I forgive you if you do not tell me what you are accused of?" I can never forget the emphatic manner of his answer, in the Scottish dialect, "Ye'll sune ken" (you'll soon know). This question and the answer were repeated at least twice—I am certain the answer was repeated thrice, in the most fervid tone. On that I awoke, and was in that state of surprise and bewilderment which such a remarkable dream, *quâ* mere dream, might induce, and was wondering what it all meant, when my wife burst into my bedroom, much excited, and holding an open letter in her hand, exclaimed, "Oh, James, here's a terrible end to the workmen's ball, Robert Mackenzie has committed suicide!" With now a full conviction of the meaning of the vision, I at once quietly and firmly said, "No, he has not committed suicide." "How can you possibly know that?" "Because he has just been here to tell me."

I have purposely not mentioned in its proper place, so as not to break the narrative, that on looking at Mackenzie I was struck by the peculiar appearance of his countenance. It was of an inde-scribable bluish-pale colour, and on his forehead appeared spots which seemed like blots of sweat. For this I could not account, but by the following post my manager informed me that he was wrong in writing of suicide. That, on Saturday night, Mackenzie, on going home, had lifted a small black bottle containing *aqua fortis* (which he used for staining the wood of birdcages, made for amusement), believing this to be whisky, and pouring out a wineglassful, had drunk it off at a gulp, dying on the Sunday in great agony. Here, then, was the solution of his being innocent of what he was accused of—suicide, seeing that he had inadvertently drunk *aqua fortis,* a deadly poison. Still pondering upon the peculiar colour of his countenance, it struck me to consult some authorities on the symptoms of poisoning by *aqua fortis,* and in Mr. J. H. Walsh's "Domestic Medicine and Surgery," p. 172, I found these words under symptoms of poisoning by sulphuric acid . . . "the skin covered with a cold sweat; countenance livid and expressive of dreadful suffering." . . . *"Aqua fortis* produces the same effect as sulphuric, the only difference being that the external stains, if any, are yellow instead of brown." This refers to indication of sulphuric acid, "generally outside of the mouth, in the shape of brown spots." Having no desire to accommodate my facts to this scientific description, I give the quotations freely, only, at the same time, stating that previously to reading the passage in Mr. Walsh's book, I had not the slightest knowledge of these symptoms, and I consider that they agree fairly and sufficiently with what I saw. . . .

My manager first heard of the death on the Monday—wrote me on that day as above—and on the Tuesday wrote again explaining the true facts. The dream was on the Tuesday morning, immediately before the 8 A.M. post delivery, hence the thrice emphatic "Ye'll sune ken." I attribute the whole to Mackenzie's yearning gratitude for being rescued from a deplorable state of starvation, and his earnest desire to stand well in my opinion. I have coloured nothing, and leave my readers to draw their own conclusions.

A good many dreams such as this, and a good many apparitions experienced while awake represent the deceased as *still existing:* and if they appear to contain a paranormal element—e.g., an element of knowledge received through no normal source, as in the Mackenzie case—they may be offered as evidence of the survival of the personality which is manifesting itself. If, however, the person has only recently died, it is not difficult to argue that the shock of death initiated the impression, and that the case is really simply a case of telepathy from the dying, not the dead.

Another class of survival evidence widely accepted is the communication of messages through spiritualistic mediums and amateur sensitives whose unconscious or automatic movements may convey messages (cf. page 4).

Despite skepticism, one has the sense of the eerie or uncanny as one first observes automatic writing, or even the operation of the Ouija board. The hand acts without conscious direction; but it acts intelligently and purposively. This becomes a little less mysterious as one notes that talking or walking in one's sleep is obviously done intelligently and at least with some degree of purpose, although if we may believe what is said by the subject when he awakes, he has no memory and was perhaps acting automatically in the same sense in which the writing is done automatically. We will not now enter into the very subtle question whether any writing can be done with *absolute* unawareness or whether the level of awareness is simply low, or whether there is a split-off awareness —a sort of awareness of which the fully integrated, conscious individual knows nothing. Indeed, we may take our choice among a considerable number of theories of consciousness and subconsciousness. All we are concerned with now is the fact that a considerable number of persons may show "automatisms" of this sort without suggesting in any way anything of the paranormal. Split-off or dissociated functions exhibiting the knowledge and skills available to the person may develop in moments of fatigue or suggestibility, a "brown study" or state of abstraction; or the more full-fledged hypnotic trance may bring into full awareness the motivation and the content of the communication which had appeared to be produced without awareness. Automatic writing is not in itself the subject for psychical research at all, nor are the ordinary "motor automatisms," as they are called.

Neither are the so-called "sensory automatisms," the automatic or split-off functions of the senses, such as hallucinations, as for example those seen in a glass ball, in which striking events may be observed, which are quite different from those suggested to other persons by the reflections on the surface of the glass. Indeed, after the reflections have faded out, the ball may "mist over," and from this, new hallucinatory images, often vital and active, may appear. These sensory automatisms do not, in themselves, involve the paranormal any more than the motor automatisms do. They are simply examples of involuntary or not-well-integrated aspects of mental function.

The first issue, however, for psychical research is whether the *content* of such communication is manifestly beyond that which could be achieved by the subject. If, for example, there is a communication which purports to come from the deceased, the primary question for psychical research is whether the content of such communication is manifestly beyond that which could be achieved by the subject. If, for example, he gives a communication which purports to come from the deceased, the primary question for psychical research is whether the communication contains any knowledge not known to the person. The following is a simple case which raises this question.[4]

A spiritualistic circle of six persons at Flushing, Holland, met on the evening of July 23rd, 1922. Of these persons, two had once known English but had not kept it up; the remaining four were unacquainted with English. By use of a simple wooden device held over the letters of the alphabet, messages were spelt out. On the evening in question, a "communicator" appeared, stated that he

[4] *Journal of the Society for Psychical Research*, 1923, Vol. 21, 170–175.

was an Englishman, and indicated that he would write a song for them, see 1-a below:

	Evening Song	Evening Song
1-a THE SUN HAS SET	1-b The sun has set,	1-c The sun has set,
AND NOW A new	And now a new	And now anew
WITH F A LL END EW	With fallen dew	With fallen dew
THE GRASS IS WET	The grass is wet,	The grass is wet.
FIrSt parT	And little burd	Each little bird
each little bird	is sing to rest	Has sunk to rest
Has sunk storest	Within his nest	Within its nest
witH ts netstn	No song is heard	No song is heard.
O Sng is hear		

Now, a fifteen year old boy lived opposite to the house where the seance took place; he longed to attend one of these mysterious meetings, but was not allowed to. On the evening of July 23rd, he watched the persons entering the house across the way, then, bored and vexed at not being invited, he got out an old school-book which contained the stanzas of an English poem he had once learned at school (see 1-c above). He drowsed over this poem for about a half hour, during which time the sitting across the street was continuing. On the following day one of the sitters learned what the boy had been doing, and asked him to type out from memory the poem he had been reading. The boy's version is found in 1-b above.

If there appears to be something in such a message which does not come from the mind of the automatist, a second question arises: from whom could it come, and by what means? In an extensive survey of such messages one occasionally finds one not easily attributed to a living source. In some instances the trance personalities represent themselves as being able to see and report on what is printed on certain pages of a given book, the location of which is described. The scientific problem is *usually* whether there is any evidence for *clairvoyance* for the book; in the following example, however, occurring during the course of a trance sitting with Mrs. Osborne Leonard, the issue is whether there is evidence for the survival of the alleged communicator.

č

A CASE WHERE THE MEMORY OF THE COMMUNICATOR SEEMS THE MOST LIKELY SOURCE OF INFORMATION[5]

I will next quote a case in which the memory of the communicator seems almost certainly to be the source of information—so much so that if accurately described it serves as evidence of the communicator's identity in the same kind of way as would the reading of a sealed letter after the writer's death. The test was received by Mrs. Hugh Talbot, and is one of the earliest book-tests of which we have a record. . . . It was given on March 19, 1917, but most unfortunately was not recorded in writing till the end of December of the same year. This, of course, greatly diminishes the value of the record, though happily we have the testimony of two witnesses, besides the sitter, who were aware of what Feda[6] had said before verification.

Mrs. Talbot's report, written out and sent to Lady Troubridge on December 29, 1917, is as follows:

Two sittings with Mrs. Leonard were arranged for me through Mrs. Beadon last March, one for Saturday 17th at 5 P.M. and the other at the same hour on Monday the 19th. Mrs. Leonard at this time knew neither my name nor address, nor had I ever been to her or any other medium, before, in my life.

On Monday the first part of the time was taken up by what one might call a medley of descriptions, all more or less recognisable, of different people, together with a number of messages, some of which were intelligible and some not. Then Feda (as I

[5] Mrs. Henry Sidgwick, An examination of book-tests obtained in sittings with Mrs. Leonard, *Proceedings of the Society for Psychical Research*, 1921, Vol. 31, 253–260.

[6] Feda is the "control" or purporting deceased personality dominating Mrs. Leonard's mediumistic trance. [G. M.]

am told the control is called) gave a very correct description of my husband's personal appearance, and from then on he alone seemed to speak (through her of course) and a most extraordinary conversation followed. Evidently he was trying by every means in his power to prove to me his identity and to show me it really was himself, and as time went on I was forced to believe this was indeed so.

All he said, or rather Feda for him, was clear and lucid. Incidents of the past, known only to him and to me were spoken of, belongings trivial in themselves but possessing for him a particular personal interest of which I was aware, were minutely and correctly described, and I was asked if I still had them. Also I was asked repeatedly if I believed it was himself speaking, and assured that death was really not death at all, that life continued not so very unlike this life and that he did not feel changed at all. Feda kept on saying: "Do you believe, he *does* want you to know it is really himself." I said I could not be sure but I thought it must be true. All this was very interesting to me, and very strange, more strange because it all seemed so natural. Suddenly Feda began a tiresome description of a book, she said it was leather and dark, and tried to show me the size. Mrs. Leonard showed a length of eight to ten inches long with her hands, and four or five wide. She (Feda) said "It is not exactly a *book,* it is not printed, Feda wouldn't call it a book, it has writing in." It was long before I could connect this description with anything at all, but at last I remembered a red leather note book of my husband's, which I think he called a log book, and I asked: "Is it a log book?" Feda seemed puzzled at this and not to know what a log book was, and repeated the word once or twice then said "Yes, yes, he says it might be a log book." I then said "Is it a red book?" On this point there was hesitation, they thought possibly it was, though he thought it was darker. The answer was undecided, and Feda began a wearisome description all over again, adding that I was to look on page twelve, for something written (I am not sure of this word) there, that it would be so interesting after this conversation. Then she said "He is not sure it is page twelve, it might be thirteen, it is so long, but he does want you to look and to try and find it. It would interest him to know if this extract is there." I was rather half hearted in responding to all this, there was so much of it, and it sounded purposeless and also I remembered the book so well, having often looked through it wondering if it was any good keeping it, although besides things to do with ships and my husband's work there were, I remembered, a few notes and verses in it. But the chief reason I was anxious to get off the subject was that I felt sure the book would not be forthcoming; either I had thrown it away, or it had gone with a lot of other things to a luggage room in the opposite block of flats where it would hardly be possible to get at it. However, I did not quite like to say this, and not attaching any importance to it, replied rather indefinitely that I would see if I could find it. But this did not satisfy Feda. She started all over again becoming more and more insistent and went on to say "He is not sure of the colour, he does not know. There are two books, you will know the one he means by a diagram of languages in the front." And here followed a string of words, in what order I forget "Indo-European, Aryan, Semitic languages," and others, repeating it several times, and she said "There are lines, but not straight, going like this"—drawing with her finger lines going out sideways from one centre. Then again the words, "A table of Arabian languages, Semitic languages." I have tried to put it as she said it, but of course I cannot be sure she put the names in that order. What I am quite sure of is the actual words she used at one time or another. She said all the names and sometimes "table," sometimes "diagram" and sometimes "drawing," and all *insistently*. It sounded absolute rubbish to me. I had never heard of a diagram of languages and all these Eastern names jumbled together sounded like nothing at all, and she kept on repeating them and saying this is how I was to know the book, and kept on and on "Will you look at page twelve or thirteen. If it is there, it would interest him so much after this conversation. He *does* want you to, he wants you to promise." By this time I had come to the conclusion that what I had heard of happening at these sittings had come to pass, viz. that the medium was tired and talking nonsense, so I hastened to pacify her by promising to look for the book, and was glad when the sitting almost at once came to an end.

I went home thinking very little of all this last part; still, after telling my sister and niece all that I considered the interesting things said in the beginning, I did mention that in the end the medium began talking a lot of rubbish about a book, and asking me to look on page twelve or thirteen to find something interesting. I was to know the book by a diagram of languages. After dinner, the same evening, my niece, who had taken more notice of all this than either my sister or myself, begged me to look for the book at once. I wanted to wait till the next day, saying I knew it was all nonsense. However, in the end I went to the book-shelf, and after some time, right at the back of the top shelf I found one or two old notebooks belonging to my husband, which I had never felt I cared to open. One, a shabby black leather, corresponded in size to the description given, and I absent-mindedly opened it, wondering in my mind whether the one I was looking for had been destroyed or only sent away. To my utter astonishment, my eyes fell on the words, "Table of Semitic or Syro-Arabian Languages," and pulling out the leaf, which was a long folded piece of paper pasted in, I saw on the other side "General table of the Aryan and Indo-European languages." It was the diagram of which Feda had spoken. I was so taken aback I forgot for some minutes to look for the extract. When I did I found it on page thirteen. I have copied it out exactly.

I cannot account now for my stupidity in not attaching more importance to what Feda was trying to say about the book, but I was so convinced, *if* any book was meant, it was the red book. This one I had never opened, and as I say there was little hope of getting the other, nor did I feel there could be anything in it my husband would want me to see. Also it was only my second sitting. I knew nothing of mediums and the descriptions seemed so endless and tedious. I can't see why now.

(Signed) LILY TALBOT.

1 Oakwood Court.

Page 13 of Notebook.

"I discovered by certain whispers which it was supposed I was unable to hear and from certain glances of curiosity or commiseration which it was supposed I was unable to see, that I was near death. . . .

"Presently my mind began to dwell not only on happiness which was to come, but upon happiness that I was actually enjoying. I saw long forgotten forms, playmates, schoolfellows, companions of my youth and of my old age, who one and all, smiled upon me. They did not smile with any compassion, that I no longer felt that I needed, but with that sort of kindness which is exchanged by people who are equally happy. I saw my mother, father, and sisters, all of whom I had survived. They did not speak, yet they communicated to me their unaltered and unalterable affection. At about the time when they appeared, I made an effort to realise my bodily situation . . . that is, I endeavoured to connect my soul with the body which lay on the bed in my house . . . the endeavour failed. I was dead. . . ."

Extract from Post Mortem. Author anon.
(Blackwood & Sons, 1881.)

I do not attempt to reproduce the diagram of languages, which is complicated, but Feda's description of it as having lines going out from a centre is correct; this branching out from points and from lines happens repeatedly.

Mrs. Talbot wrote, at Lady Troubridge's request, to her niece and her sister, asking them to write down what they remembered. Their account follows:

Miss Bowyer Smyth's Account

On March 19, 1917, my aunt, Mrs. Hugh Talbot, had a sit-

ting with Mrs. Leonard. When she came home, her sister, Mrs.
Fitzmaurice, and I, asked her about it. Among other things she
said she had been told to look for "a book, but not exactly a
book, a sort of note book." She would know the book by a "drawing about languages" in the beginning of it and on page 12 or 13
she would find something interesting.

My Aunt did not seem at all impressed or interested, in fact
she thought the whole thing sounded such nonsense that she was
sure it was no use looking for the book; the size of which had
also been indicated by the medium with her hands, namely about
eight or ten inches long.

It was not till after dinner that night that Mrs. Fitzmaurice
and I persuaded her to look for the book, she was so firmly
convinced it would be no use. She finally got out some old and
dusty note books of her late husband's, and in one found, first a
table of languages, and on page twelve or thirteen the sensations
of a man passing through death. I remember the whole incident
quite clearly, as it seemed to me so unusual and interesting,
especially as my Aunt had evidently never opened or read these
note books before, in fact it took her a considerable time to find
them and she at first thought she had not kept them.

(Signed) Doris Bowyer Smyth.

Charmouth, 18.12.17.

Mrs. Fitzmaurice's Account

On Monday, March 19, 1917, my sister, Mrs. Talbot, had her
second sitting with Mrs. Leonard. She had already had one very
interesting one, so that my niece, Miss Bowyer Smyth, and myself
were very anxious to hear about it. My sister repeated as far as
she could everything the medium had said and mentioned particularly that she had been asked to look for a certain book. She
asked the medium what kind of book, and she was told it was a
book with a diagram or table of languages in the front. My sister
said, is it what they call a "log" book and the medium immediately said "yes, yes, a log book," and that she was to find page

twelve or thirteen. My sister in telling us spoke as if this were nonsense and I personally did not pay much attention about the book. I was so much more interested in certain remarks purporting to come from my brother-in-law, for to me who knew him so well they seemed so exactly like what I could imagine his saying; they seemed to bear his personality.

Later on, at the end of dinner, my sister went to a book case in the dining room to look for the book (I do not remember asking her to do so, though my niece says we both asked her to), but she suddenly gave an exclamation of surprise and handed me across the table a leather note book open at page twelve and thirteen and there we found an extract which was plainly what she had been told to look for. It described the sensations of a man who had died, or nearly died. I have forgotten it exactly, but I know it described a man whose spirit was passing away, and what he felt when he saw the faces of his people round his bed. And on turning to the front pages of the book we found the diagram of languages which had been mentioned in his effort to describe through the medium *which* book the extract was in, for it appears there were two books somewhat similar.

To us my sister's interview seemed intensely interesting and I have written it down as far as I can exactly how I remember it.

(Signed) MABEL FITZMAURICE.

December 20, 1917.

It is evident that even the discovery of the diagram of languages revived no recollection in Mrs. Talbot of ever having seen it before, and this makes it difficult to suppose that the knowledge shown by the communicator was derived telepathically from her. At the same time it will be generally agreed I think that the coincidence is quite beyond what can reasonably be attributed to chance. Further, the quotation on page 13 of the notebook seems quite appropriate; and we may even regard it as probable that had contemporary notes been taken of what was said at the sitting, the truth of the statement attributed to the communicator that the quotation "would be so interesting after this conversation" would have been still more apparent. The incident must, I think, rank among the best single pieces of definite evidence we have for memory of their earth life in communicators, and therefore of personal identity. But it is scarcely, strictly speaking, a book-test.

MRS. PIPER AND THE "CROSS CORRESPONDENCES"

Shortly after the founding of the S.P.R. in London, William James, very deeply identified with the new investigations, got wind of an extraordinary sensitive with whom he and his wife had sittings. This was Mrs. L. E. Piper, of Boston, a quiet seeker after the meaning of the new spiritualism, who had herself fallen in a trance in the presence of a medium. Her trance appeared to be genuine, and her sensitivity extraordinary. James early reported that the material conveyed in the communications could not by any reasonable quirk be interpreted as normally acquired. It was rich in intimate personal matters which were not known except in the family circle. He and others of the period began to believe that special research efforts should be expended to study such mediumship. Some believed, within a few years, that some of the messages plainly came from the deceased; others believed that information not reaching the medium's mind through normal channels might reach it telepathically from living persons. We cannot here discuss the intricacies of the evidence as it existed even in those days. We shall, however, try to show, as the Piper mediumship developed, some of the classes of problems which led to fuller documentation in the heyday of the S.P.R. investigations of Mrs. Piper.

She worked for a long series of sittings in England and for a long series of sittings in the Boston area; was a modestly paid employee of the S.P.R. for many years; was shadowed by a detective for a three-week period; was constantly under direct or indirect observation; was never involved in any suspicious circumstances. Nor, so far as I know, has any responsible person ever asserted that she was involved in scraping together information by questionable means. In her sittings she was apparently in a very deep trance (from the point of view of the medical and psychological observers who worked with her), and the question of "responsibility" is a different one here. Many of the personalities who spoke through her in the early years were plainly the products of suggestion, while in her middle period, it can be argued, the interaction of suggestion effects and genuine paranormal effects are prominent. Our problem here is to try to make as real as we can the fact that during her deep trance there is communication through the automatic writing of the busy hand, while the heavy and sometimes laboring body of a deeply entranced figure betrays no sign of waking awareness except this hand and the capacity to hear what is slowly and carefully spoken.[7]

Prominent in the evolution of Mrs. Piper's phenomena was Dr. Richard Hodgson, an Australian scholar who became Research Officer for the A.S.P.R., and for many years had control of the Piper sittings. Originally an arch skeptic, Hodgson's first report on Mrs. Piper stressed essentially the products of suggestibility and the inadequacy of serious evidence for communications from the deceased.[8] The experience, however, of appearing to receive messages from a young man, G. P., who had died tragically during the midst of the investigations, satisfied Hodgson that G. P. was actually communicating.[9] Not long thereafter the control of the Piper phenomena appeared to pass into the hands of a group of entities who claimed to have lived long ago, known as the Imperator Band, who acted as administrators, so to speak, of the communication

[7] I had three years of sittings with Mrs. Piper in 1922 to 1925, near the end of her career. For the most part, my sittings were uneventful and lacking in the types of phenomena which characterized the zenith of her career. There were, however, some phenomena of interest, as appears for example, in the experiences of Jane H. Sagendorph: *A Vision and its Sequel,* Boston Society for Psychic Research, 1926.

[8] Richard Hodgson, A record of observations of certain phenomena of trance, *Proceedings of the Society for Psychical Research,* 1892, Vol. 8, 1–167.

[9] ———, A further record of observations of certain phenomena of trance, *Proceedings of the Society for Psychical Research,* 1897–98, Vol. 13, 284–582.

process for some years. During the first decade of this century, after the death of both Myers and Sidgwick, the entities communicating through Mrs. Piper stressed the urgency of messages emanating from Myers; and after Hodgson's death in 1905, the Hodgson personality likewise took an important part. During these early years of the century occurred an extraordinary development combining *soi-disant* messages from Myers with a new feature: the "cross correspondences."

A cross correspondence is a series of fragmentary phrases or sentences each essentially without significance, but which, when put together, give a clear message. One of the sensitives taking part in the work of the S.P.R. gives, through automatic writing, a veiled but inescapably clear reference to the appearance of Attila before the gates of Rome and the successful plea of the Pope that the city not be sacked. At approximately the same date another automatic writer, not in normal communication with the first, writes "Ave Roma Immortalis" and immediately adds the phrase: "How could I make it any plainer without giving her the clue?"[10] What appears regularly in all these cross correspondences is not so much a sheer repetition of the same words through different sensitives, as the establishment of a series of fragments or links which, when put together in the right way, form an integrated picture puzzle. The principle can be illustrated from one of the classic cross correspondences involving Mrs. Piper: the "Hope, Star and Browning" case. The other two women who figure prominently in the cross correspondence are Mrs. A. W. Verrall, a classical scholar who taught at Newnham College, Cambridge University, and her daughter, Helen de G. Verrall. The Verralls appear with a number of other automatists in many of the cross correspondences in the opening years of this century.

[10] Alice Johnson, On the automatic writing of Mrs. Holland, *Proceedings of the Society for Psychical Research*, 1908–09, Vol. 21, 297–303.

"Hope, Star and Browning."[11]

Immediately following the extract from the sitting [with Mrs. Piper] of Feb. 11, 1907 . . . came these words:—

> (Myers communicating) Did she [i.e. Mrs. Verrall] receive the word.
> Evangelical.

J. G. P.   "Evangelical"?

> yes.

J. G. P.   I don't know, but I will enquire.

> I referred also to Browning again. [I had chosen on Dec. 18, 1906 some words from Browning's *Flight of the Duchess* for transmission to Mrs Verrall by Myers[P],[12] and he had claimed, though wrongly, to have succeeded in getting them written. It is to this that I think "again" refers. *J. G. P.*]

J. G. P.   Do you remember what your exact reference to Browning was?

> I referred to Hope and Browning.
> yes. (assent to reading as above.)
> I also said Star.
> (Miss Newton enters to announce the arrival of the sitter, Mr Macalister.)

· · ·

J. G. P.   Yes; I'm sorry, but we can, I hope, have a good talk the time after next.

> Mean while look out for Hope Star and Browning

· · ·

I [J. G. P.] will now quote the scripts of Mrs Verrall which I take to correspond with the words "Hope, Star and Browning":—

---

[11] J. G. Piddington, A series of concordant automatisms, *Proceedings of the Society for Psychical Research*, 1908, Vol. 22, 59–77.

[12] The subscript, as in "Myers[P]," means the entity purporting to be Myers communicating through Mrs. Piper. [G.M.]

Script of Jan. 23, 1907.

<u>Justice holds the scales.</u>
That gives the words but an anagram would be better
Tell him that—rats star tars and so on. Try this.
It has been tried before RTATS rearrange these
five letters   or again t e a r s
                    s t a r e

s e a m
s a m e
and so on
Skeat takes Kate's Keats stake steak.
But the letters you should give tonight are not so many
—only three

                    a s t

Script of Jan. 28, 1907 . . .

Aster [star]
τέρας [wonder or sign]
The world's wonder
And all a wonder and a wild desire—
The very wings of her
A WINGED DESIRE
ὑπόπτερος ἔρως [winged love]
Then there is Blake
and mocked my loss of liberty.
But it is all the same thing—the winged desire
ἔρως ποθεινός [passion] the hope that leaves
the earth for the sky—Abt Vogler for earth
too hard that found itself or lost itself—in the sky.
That is what I want
On the earth the broken sounds
                              threads
In the sky the perfect arc
The C major of this life

But your recollection is at fault

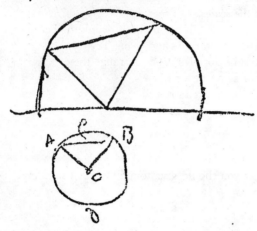

ADB is the part that unseen completes the arc.

Mrs Verrall had handed this script to me on Jan. 29, and pencilled on the envelope was this note:—

"Jan. 29,/07. Is enclosed attempt at *Bird?* 'winged,' ὑπόπτερος, and 'Abt Vogler' (Vogel) suggest it. The later part is all quotations from R. B.'s *Abt Vogler* and earlier from the *Ring and the Book*. 'Oh, Lyric Love' etc."

Mrs Verrall might have added that "bird" was also suggested by the line which in the original precedes "And all a wonder and a wild desire", namely,

"O lyric Love, half angel and half bird". . . .

Now as to the correspondence with the words "Hope, Star and Browning":—

Hope is found in the words "the hope that leaves the earth for the sky".

These words are a misquotation of

"The passion that left the ground to lose itself in the sky".

"Hope" has been substituted for "passion"; and it seems to me that by means of this very misquotation or substitution emphasis is thrown on the word "hope." . . . Mrs. Verrall knew of the misquotation. She wrote to me on Feb. 15, 1907:—"I knew perfectly when I read the script that it should have been 'passion' which left the ground for the sky—and I was annoyed at the blunder! The ἔρως ποθεινός, which came straight out of a passage that I had been translating in the course of my work, represents 'passion.' And I wondered why the silly thing said 'Hope.'"

Browning pervades the whole script, and is besides definitely mentioned in Mrs Verrall's pencilled note.[13]

Star is given prominently at the head of the script of Jan. 28 in the form Aster, the Greek for star. . . .

• • •

When, by reason of the coincidences involved, my mind began to concentrate itself on these two pieces of script and the words "Hope, Star and Browning" given in the Piper trance, a vague impression came over me that the string of words, "rats arts star," had somehow and somewhere come under my eyes before. At first I thought this must be mere fancy, and, when, after a little, I seemed to remember having seen them written on a piece of paper in Dr Hodgson's handwriting when I went through his private papers in the early summer of 1906, at Boston, I was inclined to accuse myself of suffering from a delusion of memory. Still the memory—real or fancied—persisted, and to satisfy myself I wrote to Dr Hodgson's executors in Boston, Mr George Dorr and Mr Henry James, Jr., and asked them to search among the odds and ends which, with other matter such as letters, I had handed over to them, for a scrap of paper with the words "rats arts star" upon it. On August 23, 1907 Mr James sent me the sheet of paper containing a rough draft of anagrams in the handwriting of Dr. Hodgson. . . .

[13] Some of these comments which Mrs. Verrall appends to her scripts bear, I fancy, much the same relation to the subject-matter of her scripts, as do the utterances of Mrs. Piper during the later part of the waking-stage to her trance-script. [J. G. P.]

. . .

But the coincidence does not end here.

We naturally were all considerably elated by the "Hope Star and Browning" correspondence (though the full significance of the incident was not apparent till months later), and by way of encouragement Mrs Verrall, on Feb. 15, gave her daughter a general description of the incident, being, however, careful to substitute imaginary words for the original ones. For "Star" "Planet Mars" was substituted, for "Hope" "Virtue," and for "Browning" "Keats." The script of Jan. 23 was not mentioned, and a general description only of the script of Jan. 28 was given. One correct detail only was Miss Verrall told, and that was that a *five* letter anagram had constituted a part of the success on Jan. 28.

Before, however, Miss Verrall had been told anything at all, she had on Feb. 3, written the following script:—

> Vulliamy not to be confused with the other.
> Williams more precious than rubies what was
> the name of the younger child Cecil Atl Mundellier
> (scribbles)

> quam ob rem in Siciliis proficiscitur [wherefore in Sicily he
> sets out.]

> a green jerkin and hose and doublet where the
> song birds pipe their tune in the early morning
> therapeutikos ek exotikon [a healer from aliens]

 a monogram

the crescent moon

remember that and the star

like a thunder riven oak the grim remains
stand on the level desolation of the plains
a record of all ages of the span
which nature gives to the weak labour of a man.

 bird.

After she had been told about the coincidence between her mother's script and that of Mrs Piper, Miss Verrall wrote the following on Feb. 17, at which time she was away from home and at a distance from Mrs Verrall:—

androsace (?) Carthusian candelabrum

 many together

 that was the sign she will understand

when she sees it
No arts avail
diapason $\delta\iota\alpha$ $\pi\alpha\sigma\omega\nu$ $\rho\upsilon\theta\mu\sigma\varsigma$ [rhythm through all]
the heavenly harmony $\omega\varsigma$ $\epsilon\phi\eta$ $\sigma\pi\lambda\alpha\tau\omega\nu$ [as Plato says]
the mystic three (?)

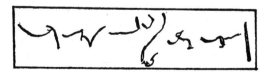

and a star above it all
<u>rats</u> everywhere in Hamelin town
now do you understand   Henry (?)

❦

The initiative for this cross correspondence appears to have come partly from the investigators; partly from the entities, whatever they are, that take part in the communications. The latter are willing to attempt to get messages through at other points, and although they do not consistently understand all that is said about what has been done elsewhere, they keep up the effort as if they were deaf persons at the telephone. In the case of the entranced Mrs. Piper, the confusion is often considerable. In the case of the waking and very alert Helen Verrall, the slips appear to be such as would occur in the course of ordinary fantasy. Not all that has been communicated has actually been recorded, but a good deal of it has been. It is evident that most of the Hope, Star, and Browning plan was effectively consummated, and in a fashion very much in the spirit of the Browning-lover and aspiring star-seeker, F. W. H. Myers.

Unless one believes that the precautions reported in these studies were really never taken, and assumes that messages were being "spilled" from one automatist to another by fraud or carelessness, the line of least resistance would be to assume that there is a set of channels of telepathic communication between the various automatists. It would not be very far-fetched to assume that each of these automatists, as she writes, assumes a sort of attitude or mental set: "This is the way F. W. H. Myers would communicate; this is his classical style; this is the way in which cross correspondences might emanate from him." A considerable amount of this material having been produced, there could be some coincidences anyway, and the number could be very greatly increased by a telepathic interchange. Then, of course, after the material has been worked up and published, all of the various minds participating have been enriched by further associations, and the cross correspondences will have to become more subtle or complex if they are to be interesting. Actually a good many ran their course as if this were the correct interpretation.

To conclude at this point, however, would not give a full report of all the facts. For one thing, note that the *initiative* has to come from somewhere, and in many instances the initiative appears to lie with the entity, F. W. H. Myers, who keeps reappearing as if moving from one hiding point to another. There seems to be no central focus of the Myers entity among the various automatists, as if the Myers of Miss Verrall were dominant over the others. There is, so to speak, a Myers impersonator or actor, well developed and fully cognizant of his task, in *each* of these communicating centers. Moreover, though the process of "incubation" of a secondary personality is something we know very little about, it must be granted time to initiate and carry out vigorously and strategically the various lines of communication required, and this would seem to call for a very active "subconscious mind." Maybe there is such an active subconscious mind at work, but we do not know whose it could be.

One guess would be that it could be the subconscious mind of Mrs. Verrall, as we do have during her lifetime many brilliant Myers communications, and not very much after her death. This hypothesis has at times been pressed among those unwilling to consider the hypothesis of survival. Actually, if we follow a law of parsimony, it is simpler to say that the instigating agency is something beyond the minds of the various living automatists, and this is actually psychologically a better fit, in the sense that to one who knows the Myers personality and the personalities of the automatists, it is simpler than a theory of complex origins. This, of course, settles nothing, but tries to keep all avenues of speculation open until the final evidence comes in. We may summarize the cross correspondence situation by saying that there are many dozens of successful attempts to create the sense of a hidden unity through many messages, and that they are compatible either with a vigorous and unrelenting hypothesis of telepathy among many living automatists or with the hypothesis of a single discarnate entity devoted to the task of demonstrating its continued existence.

But the issue is worth pursuing a little further. In connection with the "extended telepathy" hypothesis there must be (as already noted) within some subconscious stratum of each automatist's mind a play actor which says, "I am Myers. I will produce Myers-like scripts." What is the real *alternative* to this view? Ordinarily it has been stated in terms of a doctrine of direct intervention by a discarnate mind influencing the processes of association going on in an incarnate mind. The deceased Myers causes Helen Verrall's or Mrs. Piper's mind to move in a certain course and to write certain sentences. Is this view tenable? If in fact the reader is willing to consider the hypothesis of survival of death, and the possibility of making contact with the deceased, can he take the further step of saying that the mind of the living is subordinated, to some degree, to the intentions and thought patterns of the deceased?

This issue turns out, in fact, to be very complicated. In the first place, the mind of the automatist can never be completely pushed aside, erased, made vacant. Any communication will show the automatist's mind at work, however much evidence there may be of a discarnate contribution. Secondly, certain fundamental biases, or ways of working, which characterize the automatist, his way of looking at matters, his way of expressing himself, will appear over and above the sheer content of his thought. In the third place, these subconscious strata are often suggestible and pushed into incorrect or self-contradictory statements. The spiritualist who believes that trance utterances are literal expressions of the intent of the deceased is caught in many embarrassing instances in which the message simply could not emanate from the deceased at all. A celebrated instance is that in which G. Stanley Hall at a sitting with Mrs. Piper, speaking to the purporting control, Richard Hodgson, asks to speak with his niece, Bessie Beals.[14] The purporting Hodgson brings Miss Beals, who proceeds to communicate. Actually, no Bessie Beals existed. The Hodgson personality, when informed of

[14] Amy E. Tanner, *Studies in Spiritism*, New York, D. Appleton and Co., 1910, 254.

this fact, tries nevertheless to squirm out of the predicament into which he has been pushed. Often it appears that the consciousness which communicates through such automatisms is plastic, mobile, easily controlled by inner and outer factors, lacks that resolute firmness and integrity which we associate with human personality in its mature form.

Facing this fact, Mrs. Henry Sidgwick[15] formulated, nearly sixty years ago, the classical and still the most useful doctrine of the nature of automatic communications. Working with Piper material, which she exhaustively analyzed (and the analysis would apply to many other cases of mediumship), she argued that the communicating intelligences with which we directly deal are in all instances split-off, subconscious portions of the automatist, acting under the impact of the situation and eager to act out the characterizations which they have taken upon themselves. When, however, favorable conditions exist for communication and these subconscious portions of the automatist's mind are favorably geared to the task, they can obtain telepathic fragments of the information they need to act out their part. This is not essentially different from the telepathic acting out of instructions from a distance, reported by Pierre Janet[16] and encountered not infrequently in hypnotic studies of telepathy. The Sidgwick view, then, is that telepathic material may enter the stream of communications and express the relation of the communicator to sitter or friend who wishes to hear from this communicator.

"Now," asked Mrs. Sidgwick, "is the telepathic process necessarily limited to any particular person or group of persons?"

Apparently not. If, therefore, there be survival of death, telepathic messages may be received, so far as we know, as well from

[15] Mrs. Henry Sidgwick, Discussion of the trance phenomena of Mrs. Piper, *Proceedings of the Society for Psychical Research,* 1900–1901, Vol. 15, 16–38.

[16] Pierre Janet, Note sur quelque phénomènes de somnambulisme, *Revue Philosophique,* 1886, Vol. 21, 190–198; and Deuxieme note sur le sommeil provoqué à distance et la suggestion mentale pendant l'état somnambulique, *Revue Philosophique,* 1886, Vol. 21, 212–223.

the deceased who are interested and oriented to the process as from distant living persons. The Myers personality can influence the communications through Mrs. Verrall, Miss Verrall, Mrs. Piper, and others, by a telepathic control process. He can, to some degree, become aware of what is happening at the various sittings at which communications are recorded; and he can, subject to the types of confusion already noted, make plans and beam messages to the subconscious strata of the various automatists' minds, hoping that he will "get through." This is not equivalent to stating that the "real Myers" appears *in full form* through any automatist. It is, rather, a telepathic impact which is impressed. This hypothesis of telepathy from the deceased makes more sense than any other hypotheses that have been offered. This, of course, will do nothing to lessen the strain upon the mind of the reader who cannot conceive of the possibility of survival on any terms. It must be admitted that such a reader will either have to make massive use of the hypothesis of fraud or will have to invent very complex mechanisms of telepathic interchange regarding which we know but little. He can, however, if he is resolute, do exactly this, and can therefore reject survival evidence if he is so determined.

But we have written as if the entire stream of unconscious activity of the automatist were involved. Do we not in fact have a mixture, at any given time, involving both normal and paranormal components in the automatic script or utterance? Yes, and if so, we must recognize that, in a certain sense, part of what appears in such a message is the actual thought pattern of the source of the telepathic impulse. James H. Hyslop,[17] pushing this point forward, asked if there were not *degrees* of self-realization on the part of the discarnate intelligence; asked if there were not instances in which quite a large part of the personality of the deceased could force itself through? Do we not have mixtures which vary all the way from almost pure dominance of the automatist to almost pure dominance of the discarnate communicator? If we do, have we not

[17] A record and discussion of mediumistic experiments, *Proceedings of the American Society for Psychical Research,* 1910, Vol. 4, 1–812.

in essence reduced the telepathic contribution at times to a sheer detail? Have we not recognized that a massive intervention, almost an "incarnation" has occurred in which the mind of the deceased becomes almost wholly effective in controlling the living system, the body of the automatist? If this be so, the Sidgwick hypothesis would pass by gradations over into the Hyslop hypothesis.

My own personal preference here is for the Sidgwick hypothesis, simply because we need at no time to assume the full abrogation of self-control on the part of the automatist; we need never assume that the automatist's mind has been made empty and replaced by the mind of the discarnate, as would be involved in a classical case of demonic possession. Nevertheless, it must be admitted that the conception of very great passivity in the mind of the automatist, yielding to the telepathic control by the deceased, is not really very different from the conception of direct invasion, and we do not know enough about the psychology of these states to say much more. The survival hypothesis can fare very well on the basis of the Sidgwick approach if once one can persuade oneself that an immaterial mind can exist independently of the living system which is its substrate in all of our traffic with psychological matters in this here-and-now world.

It is the biological and the philosophical difficulty with survival that holds us back, not really the unacceptability of the evidence as such. If it were solely a matter of evidence and not at all a question of *a priori* objections, I believe that almost all of my readers would go along with something like the Sidgwick interpretation of the cross correspondences, the "Diagram of Languages" book test (pp. 192 ff.), and the other survival evidence recounted here.

The literary puzzles, the complex designs involving literary fragments put together to give meaning, are not, however, the only types of cross correspondence available. Relatively infrequent, but very important, are the instances in which a complex and full-bodied message rather than a fragment is involved, and in which a question put to various automatists is answered in different ways at different times by the same *soi-disant* communicator, so that the result adds up to cumulative evidence of personal identity through different automatists, rather than simply affording literary jigsaw puzzle materials. Outstanding among the instances of the type of cross correspondence involving highly complex but independent messages from the same apparent communicator appearing through different channels is the Lethe case. This case is of such great importance that, despite its length and complexities, a rather large part of it will be reproduced here.

F. W. H. Myers had died in 1901; Richard Hodgson in 1905. Most of the investigators of the Piper phenomena (J. G. Piddington and Alice Johnson, particularly) were in England. An American, George B. Dorr, was conducting sittings with Mrs. Piper in Arlington, Massachusetts, and attempting to get from the purporting communicator, F. W. H. Myers, a characteristic expression of his knowledge of the classics (Mrs. Piper had no classical education and Mr. Dorr not much). The following is the response:

ॐ

THE LETHE CASE[18]

Extract from record of sitting held on March 23, 1908.
(Present: G. B. Dorr.)

G. B. D.   Now shall I ask you a question? What does the word "Lethe" suggest to you?
(Myers$_P$[19] communicating.) Leaflet?

G. B. D.   No, "Lethe". (G. B. D. spells word.)
Lethe. Do you refer to one of my poems, Lethe? . . .

. . .

G. B. D.   These last words are not clear to me.
he saves them by taking them across River—Athens—

---

[18] J. G. Piddington, Three incidents from the sittings: Lethe; the Sibyl; the Horace Ode Question, *Proceedings of the Society for Psychical Research,* 1910, Vol. 24, 86–104.
[19] See footnote No. 12, p. 202.

It is all clear. Do you remember Cave?

G. B. D. I think you are confused about this. I ought to have waited until another day to bring it up, when the Light [Mrs. Piper, G. M.] was fresh. It was a water, not a wind, and it was in Hades, where the Styx was and the Elysian fields. Do you recall it now?
Lethe. Shore—of course I do. Lethe Hades beautiful river—Lethe. Underground.—
What is the matter that I do not hear better? Is it lack of Light? I think it is.

• • •

Waking-stage[20]

Fish Mermaid Saturn . . .
Hero . . . —Olympus
(Then followed a word which was written down as "pavia." In response to Mr. Dorr's requests the word was whispered several times, but never distinctly enough to be caught with certainty.)
Sybil—Olympus—water—Lethe—delighted—sad— lovely—mate.—
Put them all together. (This was followed by inarticulate whispering.)
Entwined love—beautiful shores.—Ask him if he cannot hear me.
Muses.—I wrote "church" long ago. . . .
      Olympus.—There's Mercury. . . . —Love—He has drawn a cross with ivy over it. Pharaoh's daughter came out of the water . . . —Warm—sunlit—love.
Lime leaf—heart—sword—arrow
          I shot an arrow through the air
          And it fell I know not where.

---

[20] The phrase "waking-stage" refers to a period of a few minutes during which Mrs. Piper returned to normal consciousness. She frequently uttered a few words or sentences during this period. [G. M.]

(Mrs. Piper then puts her hands up before her face, palms outward as though warding something off, but smilingly like a child in play.)

Oh! point it the other way!

G. B. D.   Whom do you see?

Lady.—I want to say that the walls came out, and in the air was a lady who had no clothes on; and in her hand she had a hoop and two pointed things, and she pulled a string, and she pointed it straight at me, and I thought it would hit me in the eye. And Mr. Myers put his hand up and stopped her. She had a hoop, and there was only half of the hoop there. . . .

Extract from record of sitting held on March 24, 1908.

(Present: G. B. Dorr.)

● ● ●

[The control today is apparently Hodgson throughout, Myers being indicated by him as present and occasionally speaking. *Note by G. B. D.*

I think it is clear that some of the passages that follow are to be attributed to Hodgson$_P$, and some to Myers$_P$; but I do not think it necessary to attempt to apportion their respective parts, as anything which Hodgson$_P$ says about the Lethe question he evidently says on behalf of Myers$_P$. *Note by J. G. P.*]

I wrote in reply to your last inquiry Cave—Lethe.

G. B. D.   I asked him (*i.e.* Myers) whether the word Lethe recalled anything to him.

He replied Cave—Banks—Shore.

G. B. D.   But these last two (*i.e.* "Banks Shore") were not written until after I had told him it was a water.

Yes, but he drew the form—a picture of Iris with an arrow.

G. B. D.   But he spoke of winds.

Yes, clouds—arrow—Iris—Cave—Mor M O R Latin

for sleep Morpheus—Cave. Sticks in my mind can't you
help me?

G. B. D.   Good. I understand what you are after now. . . . But
can't you make it clearer what there was peculiar about
the waters of Lethe?

Yes, I suppose you think I am affected in the same way
but I am not. . . .

G. B. D.   Capital. That's as clear as can be.

Did you understand Cave?

G. B. D.   Yes, the Cave of Sleep.

(Hand bows assent energetically.)

Hoping you would understand clouds I R I S

(A bow is here drawn for rainbow, and also wavy lines.
G. B. D. asks what the lines mean.)

clouds—C L O U D S

. . .

Yes, I cannot possibly tell you all my thoughts at once.

G. B. D.   Tell me *anything* that any of the questions I ask you
may bring up. *Lethe* for instance may bring back other
memories to you.

(Hand here makes drawings upon the paper.)

G. B. D.   What does that mean?

Flower—Banks

. . .

Did the Light quote Picture I made for her spirit as it
returned [*i.e.* in the waking-stage]?

G. B. D.   The picture of Iris?

Yes.

. . .

Waking-stage

(The first whispered word caught is the same as that
not understood in the previous waking-stage, whose
sound was then written down as "pavia"; but it is still
impossible to catch it clearly.) . . .

Mr. Myers is writing on the wall.

G. B. D.   What is he writing?

(Mrs. Piper is got with difficulty to repeat "C", and then afterwards, as though something came in between, "Y X".)

• • •

Extract from record of sitting held on March 30, 1908.

(Present: G. B. Dorr.)

G. B. D.   Shall I read you my record of the [utterances made in the] waking-stage at our last meeting?

(Myers$_P$ communicating.) Yes, do kindly.

(G. B. D. then goes through the utterances in the waking-stage of the trance of March 24, 1908, *seriatim,* omitting, however, to ask for an explanation of the word recorded as "pavia".) . . .

G. B. D.   The next thing I heard . . . was that Mr. Myers was writing on the wall.

Good.

G. B. D.   All that I could get Mrs. Piper to repeat was C-y-x.

Chariot.

G. B. D.   Is that the meaning of the word which he was writing?

Yes. Pronounce the word for me.

G. B. D.   I do not know the word. Won't you spell it out for me?

Cynx—C Y N X.

G. B. D.   Is that a Greek word?

Yes. . . .

• • •

G. B. D.   "Lovely—mate—entwined love".

We walk together, our loves entwined, along the shores. In beauty beyond comparison with Lethe. Sorry it is all so fragmentary but suppose it cannot all get through.

. . . .

G. B. D.   Then came the picture of Iris which you showed the

Light and which she described to me as real.

Yes, that was to answer your question.

G. B. D.   But I see no connexion between Iris and Sleep, or Lethe rather.

No, only Iris shot an arrow into the clouds and caused a rainbow. . . . It brought it to my mind simply.

• • •

Extract from record of sitting held on April 7, 1908.

(Present: G. B. Dorr.)

G. B. D.   Let us take up [the record of] yesterday's waking-stage and go over it together. . . . "He keeps saying something about C Y X."

(Myers$_P$ communicating.)

S C Y X   C S Y X.

G. B. D.   You cannot get the word now, can you?

(Hand makes gesture of dissent.) . . .

Waking-stage.

. . . .

Mr. Myers says: "No poppies ever grew on Elysian shores."

• • •

The only point which Mr. Dorr saw in the answers to his question was the allusion to the Cave of Sleep, which he thought was probably due to an association of ideas between the oblivion produced by the waters of Lethe and the oblivion of sleep. In November, 1908, Mrs. Verrall went carefully through the records of Mr. Dorr's sittings, and—though she found a good many instances where answers given in the trance to questions on literary and classical subjects, which to Mr. Dorr had seemed vague or meaningless, were really indicative or suggestive of real knowledge—she failed to trace any coherence in the answers given to the question about Lethe. Another classical scholar, Gerald Balfour, when he

read through the records, likewise saw no sense in these answers.
Nor did I, when I first considered them. But I was struck by the
way in which Myers_P and Hodgson_P at the sitting of March 24,
1908, spontaneously repeated, amplified and emphasised the answer given to the Lethe question on the previous day; and showed
themselves apprehensive of its not having been understood, and
confident of its relevancy. When confidence of this kind is exhibited
by the trance-personalities it is usually well-founded. Accordingly
I thought it worth while to search for passages in classical authors
which might throw light on the matter; and by good luck came on
a passage in the eleventh book, hitherto unknown to me, of the
Metamorphoses of Ovid, which explains and justifies the main part
of the answers given in the trance. In this book Ovid tells the story
of the transformation of Ceyx, king of Trachin, into a kingfisher,
and of his wife, Alcyone, daughter of Aeolus, into a halcyon. I ap-
pend what is partly a summary and partly a literal translation of
the passage in question.

Summary of Ovid, Metamorphoses XI. 410–748.

Ceyx, in order to consult the oracle about the fate of his brother
Daedalion who had been changed into a hawk, starts on a voyage
to Claros; but is shipwrecked on the way and drowned.

Meanwhile, Alcyone, who sorely against her will has been left
behind at home, in ignorance of her husband's death importunes
the gods and especially Juno for his safety. But to make supplica-
tion on behalf of one who is dead is an unholy act, and so unac-
ceptable to Juno; who, in order that her temple may no longer be
polluted by the prayers of Alcyone, bids Iris, the messenger of the
gods, "seek speedily the drowsy court of Somnus [*i.e.* Sleep], and
order him to send to Alcyone a vision, in the form of the dead
Ceyx, to reveal the sad truth." Thereupon "Iris clothes herself in
raiment of a thousand hues, and, imprinting her bended bow upon
the sky, seeks, as bid, King Sleep's abode that lies hidden beneath
a cloud. Near by the Cimmerians' land is a cave with deep recess,
a hollow mount, the home and sanctuary of slothful Sleep, . . . It

is the home of silent rest. Yet [the silence is not absolute, for] from the foot of the rock issues the stream of the water of Lethe, and as the wave glides purling through the stream among the babbling pebbles, it invites sleep. Before the cavern's entrance abundant poppies bloom and herbs innumerable, from the juice whereof Night brews sleep. . . . No watchman on the threshold stands; but in the centre is a couch . . . whereon lies the god himself [*i.e.* Somnus] with limbs in languor loosed." . . . Iris enters the cave, irradiating it with the colors of her apparel, delivers her message to Somnus, and quickly departing returns to the heavens along the rainbow-path by which she came. From among his thousand sons, Somnus chooses Morpheus, whose special gift it is to mimic the form, visage, gait and speech of man, to execute the task that Iris has enjoined. Morpheus flies to Trachin, and appears in the form of Ceyx to Alcyone, who thus learns her husband's fate. Overcome by despair Alcyone goes down to sea to drown herself, and as she stands upon the shore the body of a drowned man is washed up close to her. She recognises it as her husband's corpse, and flings herself into the water. In the act of falling she is transformed into a halcyon. The gods take pity on her sorrow, and after a time transform Ceyx into a kingfisher; and thus Alcyone rejoins her beloved mate. "For seven tranquil days in winter-time Alcyone sits brooding on her nest as it floats on the face of the waters. Then lulled is the wave of the sea; and Aeolus guards and confines the winds, and secures a calm surface for his daughter's brood."

Let me now compare the allusions in the trance with Ovid's story:

Trance	Ovid. *Met.* XI
March 23	
1. Cave	1. Cave of Sleep
2. Vision of female figure with half a hoop	2. Iris with her bow (the rainbow)

3. "Sad lovely mate. Entwined love."

3. cf. ll. 733–8, especially the words *miserabilis—moesto—rostro—dilectosartus amplexa,* and the whole story (ll. 410–748) generally for the passionate love of Ceyx and Alcyone.

March 24

4. "Cave—banks—shore —Flower——banks—

Clouds

4. *Ante fores antri foecunda papavera florent Innumerae-que herbae* (11. 605–6). *Tecta sub nube latentia* (l. 591). *Nebulae . . . exhalantur* (ll. 595–6).

5. "Iris—Morpheus— Latin for sleep" [*i.e.* Somnus].

5. Iris—Morpheus—Somnus.

6. C yx and apparently a letter lost between c and y.
March 30. Cynx
April 6. Cyx.
April 7. Scyx, csyx:

6. Ceyx.

7. *March* 23. } Word re-
March 24. } corded as
March 30. } "pavia."
April 7. "Mr. Myers says no poppies ever grew on Elysian shores": a remark which suggests (1) that they grew on some other shores; (2) that this was not the first mention of poppies in the trance: which it was not, if "pavia" = *papavera.*

7. *Papavera* (l. 605) *i.e.* the poppies which grew before the entrance of the Cave of Sleep, and consequently by the banks of the Cimmerian river of Lethe.

The references in the trance to "cave", "flower banks", "clouds" and "poppies" show that the recollections of the trance-personality were not confined to the general outline of the story of Ceyx and Alcyone, but extended to details of the story as told in Ovid's *Metamorphoses,* and especially to details there closely connected with the river of Lethe. . . .

. . . when after the preliminary muddles a relevant recollection did emerge, it was heralded by the words "It is all clear", and that these words were emphasised by being underlined.

Neither Mrs. Piper nor Mr. Dorr had read any Ovid. . . . Accordingly, if Mrs. Piper's own memory furnished the reminiscences of the Ceyx and Alcyone story displayed in the trance, or if she obtained them telepathically from Mr. Dorr, our next step must be to enquire what book or books other than Ovid could have supplied Mrs. Piper or Mr. Dorr with the details of the story given in the trance. . . .

. . .

I know of two books only, other than Ovid, from which Mrs. Piper or Mr. Dorr could have derived the details of the Ceyx and Alcyone story as given in the trance. These two books are Bulfinch's *The Age of Fable* and Gayley's *The Classic Myths in English Literature:* the latter, as stated on the title-page, being "based chiefly on Bulfinch's *Age of Fable*", and being, in fact, an enlarged and modernised edition of it.

Neither Mrs. Piper nor Mr. Dorr had, until I mentioned it to them, ever heard of Gayley's book. Mrs. Piper affirms in the most positive manner that she had never read, seen or heard of Bulfinch's book. . . . Mr. Dorr, however, had read Bulfinch as a boy . . . and consequently, *if the allusions in the trance had been confined to the Ceyx and Alcyone story only,* he might, in spite of the fact that he retains no recollection of it and failed to recognise the allusions to it in the trance, be regarded as the source from which Mrs. Piper telepathically derived her knowledge.

But the allusions in the trance were not confined to the story of Ceyx and Alcyone. Allusions to other Ovidian stories followed them, and were combined with them and with each other in such a way as to leave no reasonable doubt that the person responsible for this combination was reproducing his recollections of a combination of stories peculiar to Ovid. . . .

❧

So far we have given material from the first answer to the Lethe question. The same question, however, was asked about two years later in England in such a way that another automatist could in turn act as an avenue for the classicist, F. W. H. Myers, to tell what he recalled about Lethe. The second Lethe question and answer belong to the investigation of the English sensitive, Mrs. Willett, by Sir Oliver Lodge:

❧

THE LETHE CASE (continued) [21]

Members of the Society who have followed the subject of Cross-correspondence are aware that in recent years several ladies, some of them previously strangers to us, have proved able to produce script containing evidential matter which purports to come from deceased members of the S.P.R., among others from the late Mr. Myers; and one of these ladies, now known to us as Mrs. Willett, seems to be endowed with exceptional power and productiveness. . . .

• • •

Supplementary Preliminary Statement by O. J. L.

For my own part I am assured not only of Mrs. Willett's good faith, and complete absence of anything that can be called even elementary classical knowledge, but also of the scrupulous care and fidelity with which she records her impressions, and reports every trace of normal knowledge which seems to her to have any possible

---

[21] Sir Oliver Lodge, Evidence of classical scholarship and of cross-correspondence in some new automatic writings, *Proceedings of the Society for Psychical Research*, 1911, Vol. 25, 113–175.

bearing upon the script. We are able in fact to regard her as a colleague in the research. . . .

. . .

Edmund Gurney is supposed to be the chief communicator or manager of Mrs. Willett's automatism, and many messages come from him; but occasionally we are told that "Myers" is in touch with "the machine," and some episodes connected with . . . Myers$_W$ shall be narrated.

The chief portion of what I have first to report takes its origin in a question which Mr. Dorr, of Boston, U.S.A., asked of a Myers control, through Mrs. Piper, in America in March, 1908. The answers then and there received have been studied by Mr. Piddington, were found to be of singular interest, and were reported on by him to a private meeting of the Society held on Oct. 28, 1909—his paper being read to the meeting by Miss Helen Verrall. At this date Mrs. Willett was living in a remote part of the country and there is no reason to suppose that she ever saw the *Journal* of the Society. Moreover, no details at all are given of this paper in the *Journal*. It is only referred to (in October and November, 1909) under the title, "Some Classical Allusions in Mrs. Piper's Trance," and was not published in the *Proceedings* (Part LX.) until April, 1910.

I myself had heard of the paper beforehand and had read parts of it; so in September it occurred to me that it would be instructive to ask the Myers-like influence operating through Mrs. Willett the very same question as had been asked of the Myers control working through Mrs. Piper. At this period I had not had first-hand experience of Mrs. Willett's phenomena, though I had made her acquaintance in London on the 17th of May, 1909; but inasmuch as the character of the "Myers" communications coming through her had favourably impressed me, I wrote with some care to her on 28 Sept., 1909, enclosing a question in a sealed envelope for her to open at any convenient time when it seemed likely that script would be forthcoming.

Letter from O. J. L. to Mrs. Willett, dated 28th Sept. 1909.

I want to ask F. W. H. M. a question *à propos* of nothing, and propose to enclose it for you to use when you have an opportunity. It is a very short one, but more important than it will sound.

It may be best not to open it till you feel ready to communicate it.

The answer may take some time before it is complete, but a record of everything said, gibberish or otherwise,—perhaps especially on the first occasion—may be important.

The envelope enclosed in this letter of mine to Mrs. Willett was stuck up and endorsed by me as intended for F. W. H. M. through Mrs. Willett, under date 29 Sept., 1909.

It happened that she was not doing any automatic writing at this time, and therefore did not open the envelope till some months later. It was subsequently returned to me at my request for inspection, and on the tongue is now written in Mrs. Willett's writing:

"Opened by me
Feb. 4, 1910
at ——."

The sheet of paper enclosed in the envelope runs as follows:

Mariemont, Edgbaston, 29 Sept. 1909.

My dear Myers, I want to ask you a question—not an idle one. WHAT DOES THE WORD LETHE SUGGEST TO YOU?

It may be that you will choose to answer piece-meal and at leisure. There is no hurry about it.

OLIVER LODGE

My object of course was to see whether what we may call the "Willett-Myers" could exhibit a train of recollection similar to that of the "Piper-Myers," when stimulated by one and the same question. And the circumstances were such that even if identically the *same* train of memories were tapped—which on any hypothesis was improbable—the evidence would be good for something supernormal, though in that case it might have to be assumed that the supernormality was limited to telepathy from the living.

But the answers that I got through Mrs. Willett were supplementary to, and by no means identical with, those obtained through Mrs. Piper. They contain a common element, and in my judgment are characteristic of the same personality, but they are not identical.

In speaking for the moment of "the same personality," I must guard against the supposition that I regard the Piper-Myers, the Willett-Myers, the Verrall-Myers, the Holland-Myers, as all exactly the same. On the assumption that they all include something of a real "Myers," the mixed or compound personalities should all contain a common element, and this common element may be dominant or recessive, according to circumstances; but on any hypothesis we must expect the messages as we receive them to be more or less sophisticated by the instrument through which the communications are made. . . . and we may expect that the range of "Myers" reminiscences which can be tapped by such means must be limited, or at least curbed to some extent in power of expression, by the range of memory and association—or as some might say by the brain deposit—of the person through whom the answers are obtained.

. . .

A statement made by Myers [through Mrs. Willett] is of interest in this connexion. He recognises that the use of different automatists to convey a single idea necessitates attention to various forms or modes of expressing that idea; for in a Willett script of Feb. 10, 1910 . . . occur the words:

That I have to use different scribes means that I must show different aspects of thought, underlying which unity is to be found.[22]

Willett Script

I shall now give the answers which were written through Mrs.

[22] It will be observed that the Willett script, like that of Mrs. Holland, uses the word "scribe" in the sense of automatist. [O. J. L.]

Willett's hand, when she, in solitude, on Feb. 4, 1910, had opened my question and read it (so to speak) to the intelligence which at the time was controlling her hand and producing automatic writing.

I must first explain that in the automatic writings of Mrs. Willett, the name of the ostensible communicator not only comes at the beginning, but is repeated at intervals throughout the script. The object of this repetition of the name is not quite clear, but it seems to be a plan adopted of fixing the communicator's own attention to the matter in hand; while it occasionally serves as a sort of punctuation-mark or break, like a full stop or the beginning of a new paragraph. It also has the effect of keeping constantly before us the identity of the ostensible communicator; but in reading it is best to ignore most of these interruptions.

* * *

Script of Feb. 4.

Here is the Script in as near facsimile as ordinary printing can make it, the two portions in parentheses near the beginning being the words of Mrs. Willett herself:

(Scribble)
> Myers yes I am here
> I am now ready to deal
> with the question from Lodge
> Before you open the envelope
> reread his letter to you
> the one that accompanied
> the letter to me

(I did so—

> "I want to ask F. W. H. M. a question *à propos* of nothing,
> and propose to enclose it for you to use when you have an
> opportunity. It is a very short one, but more important
> than it will sound. It may be best not to open it till
> you feel ready to communicate it. The answer may take

some time before it is complete, but a record of everything
said, gibberish or otherwise,—perhaps especially on the
first occasion—may be important."
The script continued)
    Yes now open the Question—the envelope containing the
    question
(I did so and read it through twice

                    • • •

The script began at once)

    Myers the Will again to live
    the Will again to live the
    River of forgetfulness
    not reincarnation
    Once only does the soul
    descend the way that leads
    to incarnation   the blending
    of the Essence with the
    instrument Myers tu Marcellus
    Eris you know that line
    you [Mrs. Willett]
    I mean
    Write it nevertheless and add
    Henry Sidgwicks
    In Valle Reducta
    Add too the Doves and the
    Golden Bough amid the
    Shadows add too
    Go not to Lethe
    Myers
    Myers there was the door to
    which I found no key
    and Haggi Babba too
    This is disconnected but not
    meaningless the shining souls

shining by the river brim   The pain forgotten but there
is another meaning another
more intimate link and connection
that now I cannot give
it does not escape me I see
the bearing Rose fluttering rose leaves blown
like ghosts from an enchanter
fleeing Myers and Love
Love the essential essence
not spilt like water on
the ground far off forgotten
pain   not   not (A break and pause here)

Darien the Peak
in Darien the Peak
Peak P E A K (Another pause)

m Myers I have not done yet
to Lodge this may have meaning
to Lodge this may have meaning
Let him remember the occasion
Myers I am not vague
I am not vague
I want an answer to this   to this
Script from Lodge
Myers tell
him I want an answer
Does he recognise my recognition
Does he recognise my recognition
Myers   pause   (did so)   Let Lodge speak (?)
speak let him speak
Myers enough for to-day Myers
let Lodge speak
          F.

(*End of Feb. 4 Script.*)

. . .

. . . on the very next day (February 5th), and therefore before I had been made aware of the existence of the script of Feb. 4, Mrs. Willett was conscious of a special effort being made, and she obtained a remarkable script, concerning the coming of which she makes the statement annexed:

Statement by Mrs. Willett concerning her reception of the script of February 5th, a facsimile and a transcription of which follow.

5 Feb., 1910.

Note about 6.10 P.M. I came downstairs from resting and suddenly felt I was getting very dazed and light-headed with a hot sort of feeling on the back of my neck—I was looking at the *Times* newspaper—I did not think of script until I felt my hands being as it were drawn together—I could not seem to keep them apart and the feeling got worse—and with a sort of *rush* I felt compelled to get writing materials and sit down, though [people] were in the room and I have never tried for Sc. except alone (with the exception of the time with Mrs. V.). The enclosed Sc. came—the most untidy Sc. I ever had—a long pause after the word "spell it."

After the sheet (1) I thought the Sc. was finished and began in a few minutes to copy it out when I felt my hands "going" again and took another sheet (2) when some more Sc. came.

I am giving the *original* Script and this note to ———— now, as I do not feel a copy can be made of the writing, some of which is unlike any I ever had.

I still feel very dazed and uncomfortable. The Sc. has no meaning whatever to me. I take the word in large letters to be

Dorr,

and this I know is the name of some man in America concerning whom Mrs. Verrall sent a message [to the Willett communicators] in the summer to say that his sittings (with Mrs. Piper, I think) had brought good evidence—I know she has written a paper about these sittings—but I know nothing whatever about them, nor about the person named "Dorr," except that he exists, and is American.

• • •

Copy of Sc. of 5 February, 1910, ended 6.25 P.M.

You felt the call   it   I it is I who write Myers. I need urgently to say this tell Lodge this word Myers   Myers   get the word   I will spell it   (scribbles)   Myers   yes the word (?) is DORR

[end of sheet 1]

We (?)   H   (scribbles, perhaps M)
Myers the word is
(Scribbles)   D   DORR
Myers enough
     F

[end of sheet 2]

• • •

Miss Johnson informs me that Part LX. of *Proceedings,* though dated March, 1910, was not issued from the printer till April 9, also that she posted a special copy to Mrs. Willett on April 19. Before that date Mrs. Willett was entirely in ignorance of the answers which Mr. Dorr had obtained through Mrs. Piper, and indeed of the fact that any such question had been put.

Further references to this matter, emphasising the importance of it as seen from "the other side," appear in later scripts.

On February 10th, 1910, for instance, the script begins as follows:

Myers   yes   I am ready   I know what Lodge   WANTS he wants to prove that I have access to knowledge shown elsewhere
Myers.

• • •

The first intimation that the normal and supraliminal Mrs. Willett had of the real meaning of the name Dorr in this connexion was through Part XL. of the *Proceedings* S. P. R., containing Mr. Piddington's paper. This was received by her for the first time on 20th April, 1910.

• • •

[Thus] In any communications subsequent to this date, April 20, 1910, it must be remembered that the newly-published Part LX. has been seen by Mrs. Willett.

• • •

. . . on June 5th, 1910, I received the following script by post from Mrs. Willett:

> PLUTO and BEES
> Re LETHE
> I said there was a pun *somewhere*
> I meant in my own Sc not in Plu (scribble) not in either plato or others   I MYERS made a pun I got in a WORD I wanted by wrapping it up in a QUOTATION
> Later I got the WORD itself   after an effort which disturbed my Machine and which Gurney deprecated as being an exp exemplification of the End justifies the Means Gurney tell me Lodge can you find it now Myers I got the WORD in by choosing a quotation in which it occurs and which was known to the Normal Intelligence of my Machine   Write the word SELECTION
> WHO SELECTS MY FRIEND PIDDINGTON?
> I address this question to Piddington   Who SELECTS.

• • •

The statement about the pun had come in a script of March 7th, 1910, before Mrs. W. had received Part LX. of *Proceedings,* in this way:

> Write again the Nightingale
> I want that seen to[23]

[23] The Nightingale was mentioned on Feb. 10, 1910, in the second Lethe

Pluto not not Plato this time but PLUTO
Bees Bees the hum of Bees
Myers there was a pun but I do not want to say where.

We had taken this to refer to some classical pun, and I had a long and fruitless hunt for it. The script of June 5th, 1910, which I have already quoted, was in answer to a written statement about my failure to find a pun in connexion with either Bees or Pluto or Lethe. The explanation given on June 5th clearly showed me what pun was intended, especially when taken in connexion with the following communication which had come on May 6, 1910:

Edmund Gurney   Tell Lodge I don't want this to develop into trance. You have got that, we are doing something new.
[It then went on to say that the method now usually employed was telepathic, not telergic, and added—].
If you want to see the labour of getting anything telergic done here [you] can see the word Dorr.
That word had to be given in that way, after efforts had been made to convey it telepathically without success.
It was a great strain on both sides.
We don't want to move any atoms in the brain directly.

Very well then, the meaning clearly is that the pun was in connexion with the word "Dorr" . . .

I naturally looked back, therefore, to see what familiar quotation was intended, in the script that had come immediately after the envelope had been opened (Feb. 4), and it quite plainly was the following:

Go not to Lethe   Myers
Myers there was the door to which I found no key and Haggi Babba too

---

script . . . and was at once identified as Keats' "Nightingale" . . . The desire expressed by Myers$_W$ to have it again written and "seen to" suggests that at this time the whole point had not been apprehended; and in fact the complete associations with the word were not worked out till considerably after March 7, 1910. . . . [O. J. L.]

This is disconnected but not meaningless.

. . .

Lethe and "The Will to Live."

I now take the more literary references in this same piece of Willett script recorded above . . . as produced on 4th Feb., 1910, and quote them in order.

The first answer, given directly the question had been read, was:

> The Will again to live   the Will again to live
> the River of forgetfulness.

Now, to anyone familiar with the Sixth Book of the *Aeneid* (as I regret to say I then was not, though perhaps for evidential reasons my ignorance was in this case useful), "the Will again to live" is an admirable sentence to be suggested by the idea of Lethe. For it is when Aeneas, while visiting the Underworld in company with Anchises, sees the river of Lethe, that he also sees mustering on its banks the souls who have been purified from the stains of their former existence, and who are destined to live on earth once more. They assemble on the banks, like bees humming round lilies, waiting until their turn comes to drink the water of forgetfulness so that they may wish for a new terrestrial existence.

This is a famous passage of Virgil, and has been translated by Myers himself in his Essay on Virgil (*Classical Essays,* p. 174):

> "And last to Lethe's stream on the ordered day,
>   These all God summoneth in great array;
>   Who from that draught reborn, no more shall know
>   Memory of past or dread of destined woe,
>   But all shall there the ancient pain forgive,
>   Forget their life, and will again to live."

Thus the actual words, "will again to live," occur in connexion with Lethe in F. W. H. Myers's poem; and these words, it must be noted, had not long ago caught the eye of Mrs. Willett herself, for in her annotations on the script, when it was sent to me, there is at these words the following note:

> I recognise this as a quotation from one of Mr. Myers's Poems, —I think, but am not certain—from his Essay on Virgil. . . .

She did not appear to have noticed any connexion between these words and Lethe—and she had not yet seen Part LX. of *Proc.*, Vol. XXIV., where in a footnote a connexion is indicated.

Nevertheless, if this were the only incident, we should have to assume that this part of the answer emanated from her subconscious and lapsed memory.

I find, indeed, that the stanza just quoted occurs not only in the Essay on Virgil, but was incorporated by Mr. Myers, in modified form, in his original and published poem called "The Passing of Youth." (See the *Renewal of Youth and other Poems*, p. 136.)

> "God the innumerous souls in great array
>   To Lethe summons by a wondrous way,
>   Till these therein their ancient pain forgive;
>   Forget their life, and will again to live."

It may be noted here that the very first answer given by the Piper-Myers to Mr. Dorr's question, as soon as he had got the word, was

Lethe. Do you refer to one of my poems? (See *Proc.* XXIV., p. 87.)

A recollection of the above quoted passage may well be supposed to underlie and to justify this reference; which hitherto has been thought by us to be inappropriate, since Mr. Piddington had failed to discover a reference to Lethe in F. W. H. Myers's *original* poems.

Coming back now to Mrs. Willett again, I say that if "the will again to live" had been the only answer to the question about Lethe, although we should have recognised its extreme appropriateness . . . we should have had to refer it to the subconsciousness of Mrs. Willett, because she had certainly read the translation in Mr.

Myers's Essay on Virgil. But the script goes on, after "the River of forgetfulness,"—which being an idea in general popular knowledge is useless for our purpose—first of all, singularly enough, to contradict what would appear to be the significance of the phrase, "will again to live," and to say:

> Not reincarnation
> Once only does the soul descend the way that leads to
>   incarnation.

. . .

Then the script goes on:

> The blending of the Essence with the instrument
> tu Marcellus Eris. . . .
> In Valle Reducta
> Add too the Doves and the Golden Bough amid the shadows.
> Add too Go not to Lethe.

And then, after the Omar Khayyam Door episode, which appears in rather smaller writing, as if interpolated in the main message, it continues:

> The shining souls shining by the river brim
> the pain forgotten.

. . .

The script goes on:

> Tu Marcellus Eris.

and breaks off to tell Mrs. Willett that she knows that line; which was true. The reason she knows it is because it had already been quoted in Miss Verrall's script of dates between April 29 and May 20, 1909, which had been given her to annotate . . . a fact explained to me later by Mrs. Verrall.

It is not therefore the mere occurrence of these words, but the occurrence of them in a Lethe connexion, that is important; for there had been nothing previously to show any such connexion. But there is a connexion; for, in Virgil's Sixth Book, Aeneas was told that one and the most notable of the souls standing by the river bank ready to be incarnated, would, when his time came, be Marcellus. This reference to Marcellus is reproduced in Church's "Stories," but the word "Lethe" does not occur in them. The complete sentence *"Tu Marcellus eris, Manibus date lilia plenis"* is quoted in *Proc.* Pt. 57, p. 300, in connexion with the "Thanatos—mors—death" cross-correspondence; and this Part of the *Proceedings* Mrs. Willett had read; but again there is no mention of Lethe there. The *episode* of the young Marcellus is referred to obscurely in the conclusion of Myers's "Essay on Virgil," and is associated with the strewing of lilies:

> "Give, give me lilies; thick the flowers be laid
> To greet that mighty, melancholy shade";

but the *name* Marcellus is not there given. He is only spoken of as "that last and most divinely glorified of the inhabitants of the under world" (AE. vi. 883), about whom it was prophesied that he should die prematurely. I am of opinion that there was no normal association of Marcellus with Lethe in Mrs. Willett's mind.

Then her script goes on:

> Write it nevertheless and add
> Henry Sidgwick's
> In Valle Reducta.

Now *In Valle Reducta* (in a sheltered vale) is the opening phrase of Virgil's description of the river of Lethe (AE. vi. 703). It and its context are thus translated by Bryce (*Bohn's Series*):

> "Meanwhile Aeneas, in a winding vale, observes a lonely grove, and brakes that rustle in the woods, and the Lethean stream which skirts those peaceful homes. All around were flitting countless crowds and troops of ghosts; even as when, on a peaceful summer's day, bees in the meadows settle on the various flowers,

and swarm around the snow-white lilies; the whole plain buzzes with their humming noise." . . .

I quote the whole passage now, though the reference in the script to the bees and the lilies comes later. Note that the sheltered or lonely vale through which Lethe runs is expressed in Virgil by the phrase *In valle reducta;* and these words in the script are called "Henry Sidgwick's" because Henry Sidgwick had been represented as communicating them, through what is called the "Mac" script, in July, 1908. This, it is true, had been seen by Mrs. Willett, but it contained no reference to Lethe, though the phrase *in valle reducta* is followed by the words "Aeneid 6," and preceded by "Aeneas." There is no mention of Marcellus in the Mac script, and therefore at no time any reason for her connecting *In valle reducta* with Marcellus or Lethe. There may have been . . . an obscure reason in her mind for connecting the Golden Bough with Marcellus, but none for connecting "the Golden Bough" with *In valle reducta.* . . .

The fact, however, that both these Latin phrases, *tu Marcellus eris* and *in valle reducta,* had passed through her mind, seems to have made it possible for Myers . . . to make her quote these two passages in the original Latin—a thing usually difficult or impossible.

It is the combination and juxtaposition that is notable, not the occurrence of the phrases themselves.

• • •

Not yet, however, are we through the truly remarkable piece of script which came on Feb. 4, 1910. Immediately after the line about "the shining souls shining by the river brim" we get,—

The pain forgotten but there is another meaning another more intimate link and connexion that now I cannot give It does not escape me I see the bearing

Rose fluttering rose leaves blown like ghosts from an enchanter fleeing and Love Love the essential essence not spilt like water on the ground far off forgotten pain.

"Forgotten pain" may readily refer to Lethe; and as for "Love the essential essence not spilt like water on the ground"—the eternity of love, no matter what happens to the Physical Universe, is the burden of *The Renewal of Youth* as well as of many another poem by F. W. H. Myers.

For instance in *Classical Essays,* p. 99:

> "Now from about thee, in thy new home above,
> Has perished all but life, and all but love."

. . .

Appendix B.
O. J. L.'s normal knowledge.

On February 6th, 1910, the day I received the important script of Feb. 4 hitherto commented on, I was very busy, but I sent three hasty replies to it at different periods of the day. These replies had better be reproduced, as showing

(1) how little information could at that time have been extracted from my mind,

(2) how much, or little, information was imparted to Mrs. Willett when she read them.

They were in three sealed envelopes, and she opened and read them to Myers$_W$ on Feb. 10, as is reported later.

(No. 1) Well Myers, but I want more from you about Lethe and its suggestions than that. It must awaken literary and classical reminiscences in your mind. What you have said so far seems naturally sophisticated a little with what your Scribe has been reading. . . . But, while you have been thinking, perhaps more has occurred to you. I had better say no more at present.

(No. 2) The phrase "peak in Darien" occurs in your book—I remembered it dimly and have looked it up. Miss Cobbe collected some cases of clairvoyance of the dying, wherein, shortly before death, they showed themselves aware of someone in the spirit who had only recently died, and of whose death they had no normal means of knowing. She seems to have published this little collection of cases under the title "The Peak of Darien." (So says *Proc.* S.P.R., Vol. V., p. 459. Paper by Gurney completed by Myers.)

(No. 3) "A Peak in Darien" is reminiscent of Keats. Perhaps that is what you wanted me to perceive. But do not be afraid of my literary ignorance, which is great; because I have means of ferreting out any literary allusions if they are known to man. So don't think of me or of what I shall understand, but let your own thoughts luxuriate, and trust to their being understood—though perhaps not immediately.

O. J. L.

• • •

Part II
Concerning the Script of 10 February, 1910.

Evidence of supernormal access to knowledge.

We now pass on to consider more particularly the matter written by Mrs. Willett's hand on Feb. 10, 1910. And in the first instance it may be convenient to quote the whole of it, as it stands, just as I did with that of Feb. 4. . . .

Complete Copy of Willett Script of Feb. 10, 1910.

Myers yes I am ready   I know
what Lodge wants   he wants me

to prove that I have access to
knowledge shown elsewhere
Myers give me his 3 answers
all all together

(The answers, printed on p. 146 [of *Proc.* S.P.R.], were here opened and read.)

Myers there is an Ode I want
an Ode Horatian
Lydia   I referred to the
Ode elsewhere

Write   write the word
Seneca
Again Filial piety that was
the motive that led him
the son to the Father
Virgil
But Ulyss   there is a
paralel   Ulysses
this is confused in   Myers
confused in the script but not
in my mind.   The confusion
is not in my thought   but
in the expression of it as it
reaches you   Lodge
The nightingale   but
but   I no no no
Myers begin again
the nightin   Nightingale but Shelley
too Myers as well
Once more ye Laurels
Myers this seems incoherent
Myers but don't be discouraged ·
Myers
Myers Dorrs scheme
Excellent Myers that
I have to use different Scribes
means that I must show different
aspects of thoughts underlying
which unity is to be found
Strew on her Roses   Roses
Ganymede.
Myers Mrs. Verrall might
make something of that
Myers homeless in the heart of
Paradise   Myers

Where was the Sybil
flavicomata.
Myers I have not finished
Myers Myers   wait
Myers the draught of forgetfulness
What is Anaxagoras for   not
Anchises   that is not what
I want
Which only I remember   which
only you forget   there is a line
of Swinburne's I want
that Pagan singer of fair
things and all dead things
Go thither and all forgotten
days   Myers something
like that   Swinburne
By the Waters of Babylon
we sat down and wept when
we remembered thee oh
Zion
Myers Myers get thee to a
Nunnery
The Shepherds pipe the Muses
dance and   Better to Rule among
no to slave among the living
that King it mid the
Dead
Sleep the dream that flits by
night   Sleep and his twin
Brothers   not Brothers
single   Brother
His name was writ
in water
Myers Homer and Horace the
thought allied but I cannot

get it clear
Watts   Watts
you are getting Myers
you are getting <u>dim</u>   Enough
                    F

(*End of Script of 10 Feb. 1910, ended at 12:40* P.M.)

. . .

Lethe and Knowledge of other Scripts

But we have been led on to the end of this script of Feb. 10, 1910, without having nearly exhausted its earlier part.

Let us, therefore, return to a plainly Lethean reference, written at an earlier stage, immediately after the reference to Virgil and Ulysses:

The Nightingale but but (scribbles) no no (scribbles)
Myers begin again
the Nigh in   Nightingale but Shelley too Myers as well
Once more ye Laurels   Myers this seems
incoherent but don't be discouraged

Further on, as we have already seen, the script makes a very plain reference to Keats, by the phrase,

His name was writ in water

—itself a simple and easy Lethean reference to any man of letters, or, for that matter, to Mrs. Willett.

So there is no doubt that it is Keats' poem, *Ode to a Nightingale,* that is here referred to by the word "Nightingale." It is evident, also, that the reference constitutes a good answer to the question, "What does Lethe suggest to you," for its first verse begins thus:

"My heart aches, and a drowsy numbness pains
    My sense, as though of hemlock I had drunk,
Or emptied some dull opiate to the drains
    One minute past, and Lethe-wards had sunk."

So that reference is quite clear. . . .

• • •

Then the script of March 7, 1910, goes on:

> Write again the Nightingale
> I want that seen to
> Pluto not not Plato this time but PLUTO
> Bees Bees the hum of Bees.

Now, "Nightingale," as we have seen, is a recognised reference to Lethe, and so is the "hum of Bees". . . . Upon it Mrs. Verrall noted in May, 1910:

> There is no doubt in my mind that the reference here is to *Aen. vi.,* the bees round the lilies at Lethe's stream. The word *hum* represents the Latin *"strepit* omnis *murmure* campus." This I think very remarkable,—the reference I mean to "hum of bees" as a reminiscence evoked by Lethe. J. G. P. will tell you of the special interest that the passage has in connexion with "lilies and poppies" in his Lethe paper. And if I have not sent you a reprint of a recent article of mine in the *Classical Review* I will do so.

This paper of Mrs. Verrall's in the *Classical Review* for March, 1910, has reference to the association of Bees and Lilies in Virgil, with the special significance which he probably attached to the symbolism. But I confess that the actual communications of scholars on these subjects are so like the scattered references in the scripts,— both of those which have now appeared in Vol. XXIV. and of those which I obtained through Mrs. Willett at a date before that part of the *Proceedings* had been published,—that it requires some effort to discriminate between them; which tends to confirm my impression that we are tapping a mind full of literary feeling and classical scholarship. And the advantage of the fact that these communications have come to *me* is obvious, since my mind is only potentially, but not actually, either the one or the other.

Evidence for Scholarship

• • •

Prayer of Ajax

When speaking of the difficulty which people have in following up anything which negatives the trend of their own life work, and of the absence in most cases of any strenuous longing for illumination whatever might be the result, Myers . . . communicating with me orally in May 1910 . . . said:

> Light more light though it should blind me.
> A prayer, that is, a prayer long ago.

To which I replied:

> "Yes I know, the prayer of dying Goethe."

On which I got the response:

> Yes but there is a classical analogy.
> Prayer of Ajax.

This I then dimly remembered, and with assistance found it, in the *Iliad*, XVII., 647, ἐν δὲ φάεϊ καὶ ὄλεσσον. [24]

This may be regarded as common knowledge, and its occurrence is therefore not remarkable. The line is quoted and accurately translated in the biographical *Memoir of Henry Sidgwick*, which Mrs. Willett had read; but she does not know the Greek letters. The same English phrase "though it blind me," without the Greek, had occurred in the script of Miss Helen Verrall, who had made a note associating it with both Goethe and Ajax; and this, too, had been seen by Mrs. Willett. Mrs. Willett herself associates it with Goethe, so she tells me in reply to an enquiry, but with nothing else.

[24] The prayer is made by Telamonian Ajax in the midst of the strange darkness which the gods had sent to protect the body of Patroclus and to assist the Trojans. The appeal is for light, even though it be fatal, and may be paraphrased thus—If thou wilt destroy us, yet destroy us in the light; or, let us have light whatever be the consequence; or, let us perish in the face of day. Goethe of course used the word "Light," as it was used in the above script, for mental illumination. [O. J. L.]

Now comes the notable incident of which the above is a necessary though detached and independent prelude.

About a week later I had another opportunity of receiving communications personally; and after a great number of other subjects the question came orally:

Now Lodge do you want to say anything to me?

I then said, "May I ask a question?" and on permission being given I asked, à *propos* of nothing, what a certain sentence meant, namely,

$$\text{ἐν δὲ φάεϊ καὶ ὄλεσσον.}$$

The oral conversation through Mrs. Willett which followed I had better give in full; it will be perceived that Mrs. Willett speaks of the communicator in the third person, as "he," though at the beginning and the end a few words are reported in the first person:

O. J. L.   Do the words [just cited,—spoken thus, without translation or explanation] mean anything to you?

Mrs. W.   Greek.   How shall I make this clear.
Where comrades wander.
Then he says a word with a g and s's.
Glossolally, that's the word.
He says that that's a separate faculty.

O. J. L.   Very well, perhaps I had better not bother him through this machine, but ask it through a trance medium.
Wait a minute, give him a chance.

O. J. L.   Shall I repeat the sentence?
No he has got it pretty clear.
[Mrs. Willett murmured it over nearly correctly, except that the last word was pronounced by her more like the English word "lesson" or "lessen"; which she immediately corrected, saying, "He says it is oless-on."]
He says it makes him think of comrades, but it is difficult to explain why; and of change, complete change.

It makes him think of his own death, something of his own life.

That sort of question has a better chance when asked through an entranced subject.

Will you try it with Mrs. Piper?

What you have got down he knows will appear to you fearful rubbish, but it's not altogether rubbish.

Think of trying to dictate to a First Standard child, that is the condition.

Then he says, Ajax.

Then he says, Cassandra; and surely any fool can see the connexion between Cassandra and a god with wings, no that's not it, Mercury.   And then he says

Though it should blind me.   Though it should blind me (repeated).

And he says he fell, struck by a fork,

And then he says, he will. . . .

Mother and Lover of Men the sea,[25]

The Pagan singer of sweet things.

Now Lodge she has groped far enough,

Stop writing.

Upon this I have to note that the first idea—that about comrades—evidently emanates from Mrs. Willett herself, since "comrades" occurs in a Greek line well known and often repeated in connexion with Myers, about which I had spoken to her some months previously.

But the detection of the identity of these last Greek words with what had been said previously, and their close connexion with the phrase "Though it should blind me," cannot be due to chance, and is surely beyond Mrs. Willett's normal knowledge. There was nothing to indicate any connexion with what had been a mere episode on a previous occasion among a mass of other material. I was

[25] Swinburne, *Triumph of Time:*
"I will go back to the great sweet mother,
Mother and lover of men, the sea." [O. J. L.]

present, but I gave no sort of indication, when the word Ajax was said, that it was specially acceptable.

The Ajax who insulted Cassandra and who fell struck by a fork —whether of lightning or Neptune's trident does not matter—and was drowned in the sea, is not the greater Ajax who made the prayer, but is Ajax Oïleus.

The immediate reference to Swinburne when the sea has been thought of is very natural.

The phrase "Then he says 'he will' " may *possibly* be intended to refer to the bragging of this latter Ajax, which resulted in his sudden doom.

I consider the mention of Ajax in connexion with the Greek sentence, and the virtual though not literal translation of it, to be quite good; but the apparent confusion between the greater and lesser Ajax must be counted as an exceptional unscholarly defect.

• • •

Discussion of the Possibility of a Normal Explanation of the Facts.

Most of the script of major importance received by me, and dealt with above, seems to have been started into activity by my question about Lethe. At first the answers were confined to reminiscences of Lethe itself, but the idea was speedily caught that I wanted to detect in $Myers_w$ knowledge of matters that had been referred to by other Myers controls,

> I know what Lodge wants, he wants me to prove that I have access to knowledge shown elsewhere.

This was, indeed, exactly the object of my question,—and Myers . . . entered into the game *con amore,* flooding me with literary and classical allusions.

But, of all the scripts thus received, I think none excelled in interest the one obtained on the first occasion—immediately after the envelope containing my question had been opened by Mrs. Willett—namely, on February 4, 1910. The extraordinary appropriateness of the answers then given, to the idea of "Lethe" as treated in classical and modern literature, seems to me a truly remarkable fact.

. . .

It may be said—for such things are often said—that it is the most scientific course to press a normal explanation at all hazards, and in face of every obstacle, before admitting anything else. With this contention, plausible as it sounds, and true though it is in many cases, I do not agree. The scientific attitude is to find if possible the *true* solution, not the most plausible or superficial one, of any problem. And it is by no means scientific to ignore a number of the facts and conditions, when devising even a provisional explanation. Some view which occurs to a casual reader ought not to be allowed to supersede and overpower the deliberate judgment of a careful student of the facts. I assert that no careful student of the phenomena—that is no one who painstakingly scrutinises the whole of the evidence—can be permanently satisfied, in this case, with a normal explanation; and I have not scrupled to indicate throughout my own view.

For instance, at the outset, the kind of references and classical allusions which would be given by a fraudulent writer would surely be of an inferior and less scholarly description than those which have actually been obtained. Moreover, although the hypothesis of fraud may manage to survive in connexion with the occurrences on one particular date, when Mrs. Willett was alone, it will not explain what happened on other days, when I was present myself and put questions and received answers without giving any sort of opportunity for "hunting things up."

People will no doubt say,—oh that was telepathy! Yes, but that is not a normal explanation; and it is entirely different from the hypothesis of fraud. The same explanation will not fit the two sets of circumstances; telepathy will not explain the one, fraud will not explain the other.

The only alternative which will explain both, is the supposition that Mrs. Willett is a classical scholar in disguise.

But then that will not explain the obtaining of the word "Dorr," nor for the knowledge shown of the writings of other automatists. Some other hypothesis has to be invented for all that: and no doubt one will be forthcoming. But it is almost proverbial in science that whenever a fresh hypothesis has to be invented to account for every fresh case, it is an indication that the explorer is off the track of truth. He feels secure and happy in his advance only when one and the same hypothesis will account for everything—both old and new—which he encounters.

The one hypothesis which seems to me most nearly to satisfy that condition, in this case, is that we are in indirect touch with some part of the surviving personality of a scholar—and that scholar F. W. H. Myers.

That has gradually come to be, I confess, my own working hypothesis, which I am ready to abandon freely on good grounds— but on good grounds only,—not in deference to sentimental prejudice. I admit that it is a momentous conclusion—when it comes to be a "conclusion,"—I doubt if we any of us realise, to the full, how momentous. But in science we are not unused to discoveries of considerable magnitude; and if, after due scrutiny facts become compulsory, men of science must be ready to enlarge their scheme of the universe so as to admit them.

This second answer to the Lethe question is remarkable mainly for its degree of independence from the first. The classicist who is able to answer a difficult question by referring to a different poet, a different art form, a different series of episodes, a different chain of associations, just as in the first answer to the Lethe question, shows some confusion. Indeed, his confusion in mixing Ajax Oileus with Telamonian Ajax is awful. Basically, however, if we recall the Sidgwick conception of telepathic communication from the deceased, we shall find in the second answer to the Lethe question a more complete array of strengths and weaknesses, a richer pattern of triumph and confusion, than we have in the earlier answer. If the experiment by Dorr and the experiment by Lodge were properly planned, and if the automatists, Piper and Willett, were unaware of each other's contributions, we have here a signally striking effort on the part of the discarnate F. W. H. Myers to indicate through different channels his abiding interest in the beauty of the classics, and his rich competence to handle their content in response to a challenge.

We have, up to this point, the problem whether there is any way in which a personality could manage to give impressive evidence of its existence (a) through a simple channel, (b) through multiple channels. If there should seem to be any success the skeptic could usually say that the information given is derived from the mind of someone still living, or is perhaps achieved by clairvoyance from documentary evidence. The cross correspondence might have emanated from the minds of living classicists, perhaps Mrs. Verrall, and the "Diagram of Languages" (pp. 192 ff.) might have been seen clairvoyantly (though even here the fact of *aim* or purpose supports the hypothesis of a deceased communicator).

Several attempts have been made to get around these difficulties and to provide more convincing survival evidence. An outstanding instance is the scheme represented in the "Ear of Dionysius" in which two deceased personalities are reported to have met "on the other side" and devised a plan for survival evidence free from the objections raised. This is one of the few generally recognized classics of survival evidence, and is worth very close study indeed:

The Ear of Dionysius: Further Scripts
Affording Evidence of Personal Survival[26]

On the 26th of August, 1910, the automatist who is already well

---

[26] G. W. Balfour, *Proceedings of the Society for Psychical Research,* 1918, Vol. 29, 197–243.

known to members of the Society under the name of Mrs. Willett sat for a script with Mrs. Verrall.

The script produced on this occasion, partly written and partly dictated—I use the word script for convenience' sake to include the spoken as well as the written word—contained the phrase "Dionysius' Ear the lobe." . . .

No further reference was made in any Willett script to the Ear of Dionysius until more than three years later. The subject was first revived in a script written in the presence of Sir Oliver Lodge on the 10th of January, 1914. The sitting was a very long one, and in the course of it occurred the following passage.

A
(Extract from Script of Jan. 10, 1914.)

Do you remember you did not know and I complained of your classical ignorance   IGNORANCE

It concerned a place where slaves were kept—and Audition belongs, also Acoustics

Think of the Whispering Gally

To toil, a slave, the Tyrant—and it was called Orecchio— that's near

One Ear, a one eared place, not a one horsed dawn [here the automatist laughed slightly], a one eared place—You did not know (or remember) about it when it came up in conversation, and I said Well what is the use of a classical education—

Where were the fields of Enna

[Drawing of an ear.]

an ear ly pipe could be heard

To sail for Syracuse

Who beat the loud-sounding wave, who *smote* the moving furrows

The heel of the Boot

Dy   Dy   and then you think of Diana   Dimorphism

To fly to find Euripides

not the Pauline Philemon

This sort of thing is more difficult to do than it looked.

. . . The communication must be taken as purporting to come from Dr. A. W. Verrall, the incident recalled in the extract having actually happened very much as described. I will relate it in the words of Mrs. Verrall's own note, written on Jan. 19, 1914, after this portion of the script had been shown to her.

My typed note on the Willett Script of Aug. 26, 1910, is as follows: " 'Dionysius' Ear the lobe' is unintelligible to me. A. W. V. says it is the name of a place at Syracuse where D. could overhear conversations." This makes clear what was instantly recalled to me on hearing the Willett Script of Jan. 10, that I did not know, or had forgotten, what the Ear of Dionysius was, and that I asked A. W. V. to explain it. . . . he expressed considerable surprise at my ignorance. . . .

• • •

The "place where slaves were kept" refers of course to the stone quarries where the Athenian captives were imprisoned. The words that follow describe the Ear of Dionysius, with its peculiar acoustic properties. Dionysius himself is not named either in this or in the succeeding scripts to which I shall presently call attention. . . .

• • •

The next reference in the script is almost certainly to the ill-fated Athenian expedition against Syracuse. The words "who beat the loud sounding wave, who smote the moving furrows" are probably reminiscent of Tennyson's *Ulysses*.

• • •

Before I enter upon these further developments it will not be out of place to make a brief statement concerning the conditions in which the Willett Scripts are produced. Many of these are written when the automatist is alone, awake, and fully aware of her surroundings. The remainder, produced in the presence of a "sitter,"[27]

[27] A few of Mrs. Willett's scripts have been produced in the presence of some member of her family, and two in the presence of a friend who does not belong to the investigating group. Apart from these rare occasions, she has never sat for automatic writing save with Mrs. Verrall, Sir Oliver Lodge, or myself; and never at any time in the presence of more than one person. [G. W. B.]

fall mainly into two classes. Either the automatist is in a normal or nearly normal state of consciousness, much as when she writes scripts by herself, or else she is in a condition of trance. There have been a few intermediate cases, when it is hard to say whether the sensitive is in trance or not. But these are a very small number: in general there is no difficulty whatever in distinguishing. Scripts obtained in a normal state of consciousness, whether in presence of a sitter or alone, are always annotated by Mrs. Willett shortly after they have been produced. The originals are carefully preserved in the custody of the investigating group; but she keeps copies to which she can at any time refer. Of scripts produced in trance, on the other hand, she remembers nothing, even immediately after waking; and the contents are carefully kept from her knowledge. The script of Aug. 26, 1910, in which the first reference to the Ear of Dionysius occurred, was a trance-script. That of Jan. 10, 1914, from which Extract A has been taken, was written in normal conditions of consciousness. All the remaining scripts I shall have occasion to quote in this Paper were trance-scripts. Until May of this year (1916), Mrs. Willett had never been shown any of them or any portion of any of them: there is no doubt in my own mind that in a normal state of consciousness she was totally ignorant of their contents. In that month I allowed her to see, not the entire scripts, but just those passages which I am about to cite, and which have been printed for distribution among the audience. The date of the last of these scripts was August 19, 1915. It is clear, therefore, that Mrs. Willett's having been shown the extracts nine months later could in no way weaken any "evidential" value which the episode they relate to may be thought to possess.

I now proceed to read and comment on Extract B from the Willett sitting of Feb. 28, 1914, at which I was myself present.

B.

(Extracts from Sitting of Feb. 28, 1914.)
(Present: G. W. B.)

Some confusion may appear in the matter transmitted but there is now being started an experiment not a new experiment

but a new subject and not exactly that but a new line which joins
with a subject already got through
 a little anatomy if you please
 Add one to one
 One Ear [*sic*] one eye

 the one eyed Kingdom
 No, in the K of the Blind the 1 eyed man is King
 It is about a 1 eyed MAN[28] 1 eyed
 The entrance to the Cave Arethusa
 Arethusa is only to *indicate* it does not belong to the 1 eyed
 A Fountain on the Hill Side

What about Baulastion [*sic*]

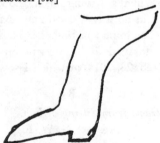

[28] "man" crossed out in the original. [G. W. B.]

[Laughs] Supposed to be a Wellington Boot
12 little nigger boys thinking not of Styx
Some were eaten up and then there were Six *Six*.

[At this point Mrs. Willett ceased to write and began dictating to the Sitter.]

Some one said—Oh I'll try, I'll try. Oh! Some one's showing me a picture and talking at the same time.

Some one said to me, Homer—and some one said—I'm so confused, I'm all with things flitting past me; I don't seem to catch them. Oh dear!

> Nor sights nor sounds diurnal.
> Here where all winds are quiet.[29]

Oh!

Edmund says, Powder first and jam afterwards. You see it seems a long time since I was here with them—and I want to talk to them and enjoy myself. And I've all the time to keep on working, and seeing and listening to such boring old—

Oh, ugh! [Expression of great disgust.]

Somebody said, Give her time, Give her time. . . . Oh, if I could only say it quickly and get done with it. It's about a cave, and a group of men. Somebody then—a trident, rather like a toasting fork *I* think.

Poseidon, Poseidon.

Who was it said, It may be that the gulfs will wash us down —find the great Achilles that we knew?[30] He's got a flaming torch in his hand. And then some one said to me, Can't you think of Noah and the grapes?

Optics—Oh! *that,* you know [putting a finger to her eye].

Oh, if I could only say what I hear! Oh, I *will* try, I *will* try.

Somebody said to me, Don't forget about Henry Sidgwick, that he pleased not himself. Do you know he used to work when he hated working. I mean sometimes he had to grind along with-

[29] Swinburne: *The Garden of Proserpine.* [G. W. B.]
[30] Tennyson: *Ulysses.* [G. W. B.]

out enjoying what he was doing. That's what I'm trying to do now.

Do you know that man with the glittering eyes I once saw? He hit me with one word now. [Here Mrs. Willett traced a word with one finger along the margin of the paper. I failed to make it out, and handed the pencil to her, whereupon she wrote]

Aristotle.

[Dictation resumed] And Poetry, the language of the Gods. Somebody killed a President once and called out—something in Latin, and I only heard one word of it, Tironus, Tiranus, Tiranius —something about sic.[31]

What is a tyrant?

Lots of wars—A *Siege* [spoken loud and with emphasis]. I hear the sound of chipping [here Mrs. W. struck the fingers of one hand repeatedly against the palm of the other]. It's on stone. Now, wait a minute. Oh, if I could only get that word.

Fin and something gleba Find [pronounced as in the Latin *finditur*]—oh! it's got to do with the serf. It's about that man who said it was better—oh! a shade among the shades. Better to be a slave among the living, he said.[32]

Oh, the toil—Woe to the vanquished.

That one eye has got something to do with the one ear. [Sighs] That's what they wanted me to say. There's such a mass of things, you see, rushing through my mind that I can't catch anything.

[A pause and then sobbing] He was turned into a fountain that sort of Stephen man, he was turned into a fountain. WHY? that's the point: WHY? . . .

Oh, dear me! Now I seem to walking about a school, and I meet a dark boy, and—it's the name of a Field Marshall I'm trying to get, a German name. And then something says, All this is only memories revived: it's got nothing to do with the purely

[31] *Sic semper tyrannis*—uttered by Booth when he murdered President Lincoln. The phrase had already appeared in Mrs. Piper's trance of Apr. 17, 1907. See *Proceedings*, Vol. XXIV., p. 30. [G. W. B.]

[32] Spoken by the shade of Achilles to Ulysses in Hades. [G. W. B.]

literary—There are two people in that literary thing, chiefly concerned in it. They're very close friends—they've thought it all out together.

Somebody said something about Father Cam walking arm in arm—with the Canongate?! What *does* that mean?

Oh! [sniffing] what a delicious scent!

No rosebud yet by dew empearled.

I'll try and say it. Hold me tight now while I try and say it. [Pause.]

It may take some considerable time to get the necessary references through. But let us peg away; and keep your provisional impressions to yourself. May [Mrs. Verrall] is to hear nothing of all this at present; *because this is something good and worth doing,* and my Aristotelian friend—

[At this point the subject is abruptly broken off and not referred to again until the very end, when E. G. (Gurney) intervenes to close the sitting.]

Enough for this time. There is sense in that which has been got through though some disentanglement is needed. A Literary Association of ideas pointing to the influence of two discarnate minds.

You will doubtless have noticed the recurrence in this extract of most if not all of the topics already found in Extract A. I will briefly enumerate but need not dwell on them further. References are once more made to

The Ear of Dionysius;

The stone quarries in which the vanquished Athenians worked;

Enna (by means of a quotation from *The Garden of Proserpine*);

Syracuse ("Wars—a Siege," and "Arethusa");

The heel of Italy (Wellington Boot);

The Adventures of Balaustion.

There is also, however, much in the Extract that is new.

We are now told that an "experiment" is being attempted; and that this experiment consists in "a literary association of ideas," some of which have already appeared, while others are now being introduced for the first time. Much importance is attached to the experiment: it is "something good and worth doing." There are additional references yet to come, which may take a "considerable time" to "get through." Meanwhile Mrs. Verrall ("May") is not to be told about it: any provisional impressions the other investigators may form are to be kept to themselves.

The literary riddle—for such it proves ultimately to be—which is thus in the course of being propounded is the work, we are told, of two intimate friends no longer in the flesh. It is intended to be characteristic of them, and to serve as evidence of their personal survival.

The identity of the two friends, indicated without disguise in the later extracts, is made sufficiently clear even in the present one to anybody acquainted with previous Willett Scripts. They are Professor S. H. Butcher and Dr. A. W. Verrall.[33]

The "man with the glittering eyes I once saw," from whom proceeds the word *Aristotle,* is Professor Butcher. The incident referred to is a vision of Professor Butcher seen by Mrs. Willett on the night of Jan. 21, 1911, a few weeks after his death. . . .

. . .

Two other symbolic references to Prof. Butcher are contained in Extract B. "Father Cam walking arm in arm with the Canongate" signifies the association, in the persons of Verrall and Butcher, of the Universities of Cambridge and Edinburgh. . . .

. . .

To resume: We have now learnt that the subjects associated together in Extract A and reproduced in Extract B are intended to find their place in some kind of literary scheme carefully thought out and devised by two friends who in their lifetime were eminent classical scholars. They are, as it were, pieces which have to be

[33] Professor Butcher died in December, 1910, and Dr. Verrall in June, 1912. [G. W. B.]

fitted into a single whole more or less after the manner of a jig-saw puzzle. . . .

. . .

. . . We are told to join the one ear to the one eye; but I doubt if any one . . . can say how the Ear of Dionysius and the stone quarries of Syracuse are connected with the stories of Polyphemus and Ulysses and of Acis and Galatea except by the geographical accident of their all belonging to Sicily. Such a mere geographical unity would hardly justify the communicators in describing their scheme as "something good and worth doing" which it had taken the united industry of two distinguished scholars to think out.

Let us see what assistance we can get from the next script.

C.
(Extract from Script of March 2, 1914.)
(Present: G. W. B.)

The Aristotelian to the Hegelian friend greeting. Also the Rationalist to the Hegelian friend greeting.[34] These twain be about a particular task and now proceed with it.

a Zither that belongs the sound   also stones, the toil of prisoners

and captives beneath the Tyrant's rod

The Stag   *not* Stag, do go on

Stagyr   write   rite

[Here Mrs. W. ceased writing and proceeded to dictate.]

Somebody said to me Mousike.

---

[34] "The Aristotelian friend" is S. H. Butcher. "The Rationalist friend" is A. W. Verrall, possibly with allusion to his book *Euripides the Rationalist.* "The Hegelian friend" is myself. It would have been natural for Butcher and Verrall so to describe me in old Cambridge days. [G. W. B.]

Do you know, it's an odd thing, I can see Edmund as if he were working something; and the thing he is working is me. It isn't really me, you know; it's only a sort of asleep me that I can look at. He's very intent—and those two men I don't know. One's very big and tall, with a black beard. The other man I don't see so well. But he holds up a book to me.

Oh! Somebody wrote a book about something, and this man, who's holding up the book, wrote a book about *him*. And the reference he wants isn't just now to what *he* wrote, but to what this person he wrote about wrote.

What does Ars Poetica mean?

Edmund said to me Juvenal also wrote satires—and then he laughed and said, Good shot.

The pen is mightier than the sword. Oh, it's so confusing—stones belong, and so does a pen. Oh!

Somebody said, Try her with the David story. She might get it that way. The man he sent to battle hoping he'd get killed, because he wanted him out of the way.

A green-eyed monster.

Now, all of a sudden I had it. Jealousy, that first infirmity of petty minds.

What does Sicilian Artemis . . . mean? [Pause]

Such an odd old human story of long ago

He that hath an ear to hear, let him hear.

What is an ear made for?

Oh, this old *bothersome rubbish* is so *tiresome*.

[As she said this Mrs. W. banged her arms down on the table as if in disgust. Presently she seized my pencil and drew the same figure as in the previous sitting, of an ear and the oval of a face. From this point onwards she wrote instead of dictating.]

Find the centre   [Here she added the eye.]

Not to you to Golden numbers golden numbers,[35] but add 1 to 1 two singles, dissimilar things, but both found normally in pairs in human anatomy—Good.

Gurney says she has done enough now but there is more, much more, later Until the effort is completed the portions as they come are not to be seen by any other AUTOMATIST.

E. G.

. . . an answer has been given to the emphatic question asked in the previous script concerning the cause which led to Acis having been changed into a fountain. The cause was Jealousy—a lover's jealousy, like that which sent Uriah to perish in the forefront of battle. Jealousy, then, is one of the pieces which have to be fitted into the finished picture of our jig-saw puzzle.

Next, mention is made for the first time of a *Zither*—the sound of which instrument, we are told, "belongs"—also of *Mousike,* the Greek word for the Art of Music. Further, the references to Aristotle seem to carry with them a significance beyond what they possessed in the previous script. There they appeared to serve merely as a symbol of S. H. Butcher. Here they are apparently introduced on their own account as well. "The Stagirite" is a correct description of Aristotle, who was born at Stageira, a sea-port in Macedonia. It would seem, however, an odd title to use in this place unless with the deliberate purpose of inviting attention. Again, a few sentences later it is explicitly stated that a reference is wanted not to what Butcher wrote about Aristotle, but to something which Aristotle himself wrote; and we are left to infer from the words *Ars Poetica* which follow that this something is to be found in Aristotle's Treatise on Poetry. . . .

Here is a list of the leading topics so far given:

The Ear of Dionysius.

The stone-quarries of Syracuse in which prisoners were confined.

---

[35] From Dekker's *Patient Grissel:* "To add to golden numbers golden numbers." There seems to be no special point in the quotation here. [G. W. B.]

The story of Polyphemus and Ulysses.
The story of Acis and Galatea.
Jealousy
Music and the sound of a musical instrument.
Something to be found in Aristotle's *Poetics*.
Satire.

• • •

. . . Mr. Piddington and I, who were studying the scripts, were accordingly content to wait without troubling our heads overmuch about an answer to the conundrum, until more light should be vouchsafed, either by further scripts from Mrs. Willett, or by means of cross correspondences elsewhere.

• • •

D.
(Extract from Script of Aug. 2, 1915.)
(Present: Mrs. Verrall)

Someone speaks a tall broad figure with a dark beard & eyes that emit light with him stands the man who said I am Henry Butcher's ghost, do you remember?
Ecate
(Mrs. V.   Yes.)
not the one who holds a Rose in his hand. His hand is resting on the shoulder of the younger man & it is he who calls.
The Aural instruction was I think understood *Aural* appertaining to the Ear.
(Mrs. V.   Yes.)
and now he asks HAS the *Satire* satire been identified
(Mrs. V.   I don't know.)
Surely you have had my messages concerning it [it] belongs to the Ear & comes in
(Mrs. V.   I have not had any messages.)
It has a thread. Did they not tell you of references to a *Cave*
(Mrs. V.   No, not in connection with the Ear of Dionysius.)

The mild eyed melancholy Lotus Eaters came.

That belongs to the passage[36] immediately before the one I am now trying to speak of.   men in a cave   herds

(At this point Mrs. V. repeated, half aloud, the last two words.)

listen don't talk, herds   & a great   load   of   firewood &
the EYE
olive wood staff

 Ai [37]

the man clung to the fleece of a Ram & so passed out   surely that is plain

(Mrs. V.   Yes.)

well conjoin that with Cythera & the Ear-man

The Roseman said Aristotle then Poetics   The incident was chosen as being evidential of identity & it arose out of the Ear train of thought.

There is a Satire

write Cyclopean Masonry, why do you say masonry   I said Cyclopean

Philox   He laboured in the stone quarries and drew upon the earlier writer for material for his Satire   Jealousy

The story is quite clear to me & I think it should be identified a musical instrument comes in something like a mandoline

thrumming   thrumming   that is the sense of the word. . . .

He wrote in those stone quarries belonging to the Tyrant

Is any of this clear?

[36] *I.e.* to the passage in the *Odyssey* preceding that which tells the story of Polyphemus. [G. W. B.]

[37] "Ai," perhaps an expression of pain, representing the Greek *alaî*. [G. W. B.]

(Mrs. V.   Yes, a great deal, and when I know some things I have not been told, probably all.)

[Drawing of an Ear.]

You have to put Homer with another . . . & the Ear theme is in it too. The pen dipped in vitriol that is what resulted & S H[38] knows the passage in Aristotle which also comes in There's a fine tangle for your unravelling & he of the impatience . . . will

Let her wait   try again   Edmund

Sicily

He says when you have identified the classical allusions he would like to *be told*.

(Mrs. V.   Yes.)

In this Extract, again, there is little with which we are not already familiar. But that little contains the key to the puzzle.

"Cythera"; "Cyclopean, Philox, He laboured in the stone quarries and drew upon the earlier writer for material for his Satire, Jealousy"—in these words I will not say that he who runs may read the riddle, but he will certainly have a fair inkling of it if he first takes the trouble to read up the account given of a certain Philoxenus of Cythera in *Smith's Dictionary of Greek and Roman Biography and Mythology,* or in the *Encyclopedia Britannica.*

Those of us who are not specialists in classical literature need not blush to confess ignorance of the very name of Philoxenus. He was nevertheless a poet of considerable repute in antiquity, though only a few lines from his works have actually come down to us.

Philoxenus was a writer of dithyrambs, a species of irregular lyric poetry which combined music with verse, the musical instrument most generally employed being the Kithara or Zither, a kind of lyre. He was a native of Cythera, and at the height of his reputation spent some time in Sicily at the Court of Dionysius the Tyrant of Syracuse. He ultimately quarrelled with his patron and was sent to prison in one of the stone-quarries.

[38] Professor Butcher was familiarly known among his old friends by the first initials of his name. [G. W. B.]

So far the accounts that have come down to us agree; but they differ as to the cause of the quarrel. Most writers, according to the *Dictionary of Greek and Roman Biography and Mythology*, ascribe the oppressive action of Dionysius "to the wounded vanity of the tyrant, whose poems Philoxenus not only refused to praise, but, on being asked to revise one of them, said the best way of correcting it would be to draw a black line through the whole paper." This version of the quarrel is also followed by the writer in the *Encyclopedia Britannica*, and by Grote in his *History of Greece*. . . . There was, however, another account, mentioned in the *Dictionary of Biography and Mythology* only to be rejected, which ascribed the disgrace of the poet "to too close an intimacy with the tyrant's mistress Galateia."

I now come to the heart of the mystery which has hitherto baffled us. The most famous of the dithyrambic poems of Philoxenus was a piece entitled *Cyclops* or *Galatea*. Of this poem only two or three lines have been preserved; and any attempt to reconstruct its plot must depend on other sources of information. The *Encyclopedia Britannica* says of it: "His masterpiece was the Cyclops, a pastoral burlesque on the love of the Cyclops for the fair Galatea, written to avenge himself upon Dionysius, who was wholly or partially blind of one eye." This falls in well with the references in the scripts to *Satire;* but does not provide much of a foundation for the references to the stories of Ulysses and Polyphemus and of Acis and Galatea, and to the topic of jealousy. The *Dictionary of Biography and Mythology* helps even less. Moreover, it states that the poem was composed in the poet's native island; whereas the script affirms that it was written in the stone-quarries.

I have searched through various other English authorities and books of reference as well as a few foreign ones, in order to discover, if possible, whether there was any single modern source from which the story told or implied in the scripts could be supposed to be derived. Apart from works in German or Latin—languages which Mrs. Willett does not understand—there are only two books, so far as I have been able to discover, which can fairly be said to fulfil this condition. One of these is Lempriere's *Classical Dictionary*. Lempriere's account is as follows: "A dithyrambic poet of Cythera, who enjoyed the favour of Dionysius tyrant of Syracuse for some time, till he offended him by seducing one of his female singers. During his confinement Philoxenus composed an allegorical poem, called Cyclops, in which he had delineated the character of the tyrant under the name of Polyphemus, and represented his mistress under the name of Galatea, and himself under that of Ulysses." The other is a work on the *Greek Melic Poets* by Dr. Herbert Weir Smyth, Professor of Greek at Bryn Mawr College, Pennsylvania, obviously intended for scholars, and not in the least likely to attract attention from the general public. The copy I have seen was a presentation copy sent by the publishers to the late Dr. Verrall, who thought well of the book and used it (so Mrs. Verrall told me) as a textbook in connection with some of his lectures.

"Like Simonides," writes Professor Smyth, "Philoxenus was a man of the world, a friend of princes, and many stories are told of his nimble wit at the Syracusan Court. His friendship with Dionysios the Elder was finally broken either by his frank criticism of the tragedies of the tyrant or in consequence of his passion for Galateia, a beautiful flute-player, who was the mistress of Dionysios. Released from prison by the prince to pass judgment on his verse, the poet exclaimed: . . . [take me back to the quarries]. In his confinement he revenged himself by composing his famous dithyramb entitled either *Kyklops* or *Galateia,* in which the poet represented himself as Odysseus, who, to take vengeance on Polyphemus (Dionysios), estranged the affections of the nymph Galateia, of whom the Kyklops was enamoured."

Here evidently is the literary unity of which we were in search and which was to collect the scattered parts of the puzzle devised by the two friends on the other side into a single whole. It is to be found in the version just given of the plot of the *Cyclops* of Philoxenus. Dionysius and his "Ear," the stone-quarries of Syracuse, Ulysses and Polyphemus, Acis and Galatea, Jealousy, and Satire— all these topics fall naturally and easily into place in relation to this account of the poem.[39] Music and the thrumming of a musical instrument can be fitted in without much difficulty, as belonging to the characteristics of dithyrambic poetry. . . .

Extract D closes with a request from Gurney that he should be told as soon as the classical allusions had been identified. This request was complied with about a fortnight later, as will be seen from Extract E, the last with which I shall have to trouble you.

E.

(Extract from Script of Aug. 19, 1915.)

(Present: G. W. B.)

(G. W. B. First of all, Gurney, I want to tell you that all the classical allusions recently given to Mrs. Verrall are now completely understood.)

Good—at last!

(G. W. B. We think the whole combination extremely ingenious and successful.)

& A W ish—

(G. W. B. What is the word after "A. W."?)

A W-ish

(G. W. B. Yes.)

Also S H-ish

(G. W. B. Yes.)

• • •

. . . the extract I have just read is chiefly interesting for its insistence upon the claim that the whole scheme is characteristic of the two friends [A. W. Verrall and S. H. Butcher] who have devised it, and therefore points to the survival of their distinctive personalities.

❦

[39] The ancient authority followed by both Lempriere and Prof. Smyth is Athenaeus, a late Greek writer, whose work may well have been known to Butcher or Verrall, but could not possibly be known to Mrs. Willett. [G. W. B.]

It remains only to note that for those not accepting the case as survival evidence, there remain three hypotheses discussed in the psychical research literature: (1) The hypothesis of telepathy from Mrs. Verrall. This hypothesis, to say the least, would have to be stretched. (2) The hypothesis of snooping and fraud by Mrs. Willett, capped by brilliant scholarly success in fitting together the pieces. There is no evidence for anything of this sort. (3) The hypothesis that the trance personality of Mrs. Willett draws not upon the surviving personalities of Verrall and Butcher, but upon a cosmic reservoir of knowledge. This seems to be a "fudge" hypothesis put forth to avoid simpler hypotheses.

We come now to the end of our long section on survival evidence. While anyone seriously interested in psychical research in the era of William James would have taken for granted the importance of the issues which emerge in the material just presented, it is probable that almost no modern reader will respond in this way. A few of the old-timers are still to be found, and a few of the younger readers have become interested in the survival issue, but the problems tend to seem less and less real to the generation trained in experimental and quantitative parapsychology, as exemplified by J. B. Rhine's Duke University Laboratory and the many related movements in psychical research today.

It will be noted, of course, that the era of the great mediums— roughly from 1880 to 1925—has passed, at least as far as Britain and the United States are concerned. Only one of the great old-time mediums is still living—Mrs. Osborne Leonard—and Mrs. Leonard has not, for many years, done the type of work for which she was long justly famous. One question is why the species of the great mediums has moved on, and why we have failed by search and training to replace them. Perhaps we have here a circular relationship: doubt inhibiting the development of mediumship and the failure of mediumship adding to doubt. Some will even take issue with the present editor for including so much of the classical survival material. The editor does not, however, feel guilty about this any more than he would in emphasizing any other material which waxes and wanes with various cultural circumstances, especially in view of the likelihood that in many cases cycles may recommence themselves; and especially in view of the fact that what is really important, like the work of Galileo or Darwin, remains important. The music of Palestrina, or of Schubert, is important though no Palestrinas and Schuberts are to be found today. Ultimately it is perspective, not finalities, with regard to facts, that our book is aiming to create, and the era of great mediumship is a part of the necessary perspective.

What then, does the editor seriously offer the reader in this survival material? Does he expect the reader to take seriously, in the midst of modern skepticism and hostility to "outrageous hypotheses," first that a soul could exist independently of its material body, and secondly that this soul could communicate with the living? The editor suggests that these data were collected within the framework of these beliefs and that these beliefs have a prima-facie reason to be studied in their cultural context and offered as serious hypotheses with reference to such evidence as can be marshaled. He believes that a strong case has been offered for communication from the deceased, and that in this modern empirical era no theological or philosophical argument will any longer be taken seriously without empirical evidence.[40]

If, on the other hand, he is asked whether he thinks the evidence is "convincing," he will reply in terms of two rather broad philosophical issues. First, as the biological evidence comes in, decade by decade, year by year, he cannot find any easy way to conceive of a soul, a spiritual entity independent of the living system known to biology, psychiatry, and psychology. Difficulties which were already serious three centuries ago as the physiology of the brain began to be understood, have become more and more serious, and the inti-

[40] After completion of the preparation of this book, Hornell Hart's *The Enigma of Survival: the Case For and Against an After Life,* Springfield, Illinois: Charles C Thomas, 1959, has appeared. No one concerned with modern evidence or with modern opinion on the subject can afford to be unfamiliar with Hart's work.

mate unity of psychological and physiological processes known to us through anatomy, physiology, psychopathology, even biochemistry and histology, makes the conception of an independent soul recede more and more into the land of the utterly incredible and unimaginable. The editor, as a modern psychologist, finds himself forced, as most psychologists find themselves forced, into this Never-Never land in which theoretical objections are so enormous that no empirical material could stand up against them. Hand in hand with this comes the fact that there is, so far as he knows, no survival evidence which is completely unambiguous, complete in itself, and free of all competing or alternative explanations. The theory offered by Mrs. Sidgwick, already quoted (according to which secondary personalities are dissociated fragments of sensitives or mediums acting under the influence of suggestion, vividly impersonating the personalities of the deceased) can be maintained *if* one gives it a very great capacity to use telepathic information from the living, or telepathic and clairvoyant information combined. Even the "diagram of languages" (pp. 192 ff.) and the "Ear of Dionysius" *can* be looked at in this way. It is true that it takes forcing, but this can be done and will always be preferred when the alternative is an utterly incredible hypothesis.

But is that the only honest way of looking at the survival hypothesis? No, in all candor, there are three types of evidence which still remain essentially as they have remained through all psychical research, and which, so far as I know, cannot be swept aside or essentially weakened. First, there is the patent fact in the case of many apparitions, in the case of some dreams, and in the case of a great many mediumistic performances, in which the *initiative*, the directing force, the plan, the purpose of the communication, seems pretty plainly to come from no living individual, however fragmentary, dissociated, or subconscious the vehicle appears to be. At the time of death, or some time after death, there seems to be a will to communicate. It appears to be autonomous, self-contained, completely and humanly purposive. It is at its best in the Myers type of material given above, pp. 214 ff., and it assumes formidable and unescapable directness in the "Ear of Dionysius," in which not one, but two highly organized purposive and directed activities expressing two individualities are combined. The intent is *didactic, clear, sure of itself, shows initiative.* It is true that these individualities do not act exactly like the individualities of incarnate persons; they forget, for example, what they have started, and need to be brought to the point at which they had gone off the track. But when they resume, they continue at the same extraordinary level, a level completely characteristic of themselves and characteristic of no living person. It is the autonomy, the purposiveness, the cogency, above all the individuality, of the source of the messages, that cannot be by-passed. Struggle though I may as a psychologist, for forty-five years, to try to find a "naturalistic" and "normal" way of handling this material, I cannot do this even when using all the information we have about human chicanery and all we have about the far-flung telepathic and clairvoyant abilities of some gifted sensitives. The case looks like communication with the deceased.

Where, then, do I stand? To this the reply is: what happens when an irresistible force strikes an immovable object? To me, the evidence cannot be by-passed, nor on the other hand can conviction be achieved. It is trivial and childish to ask whether I believe fifty-five—forty-five or forty-five—fifty-five. Trained as a psychologist, and now in my sixties, I do not actually anticipate finding myself in existence after physical death. If this is the answer that the reader wants, he can have it. But if this means that in a serious philosophical argument I would plead the antisurvival case, the conclusion is erroneous. I linger because I cannot cross the stream. We need far more evidence; we need new perspective; perhaps we need more courageous minds.

VIII.

An Interpretation

IT IS hoped that this book has suggested the kinds of materials with which psychical research deals. Though little attention has been given here to the strands that connect these types of phenomena with one another, it must be evident that they all have an affinity. They all belong to a class of events not ready for inclusion in systematic science, mainly because the events do not easily fall into the time-space-motion-energy system with which physical science has acquainted us. Science is selective: to use what "fits in," so that the data, including those given in this book, reflect the method of investigation used.

Not only are the present data difficult to accept, but when the problems of authentication are met, there are problems of conscious and unconscious self-deception on the part of those who experience or witness the phenomena and on the part of the investigators that study them, and perhaps still more on the part of those who read what they have not themselves encountered. Then comes a formidable scientific block, if we accept some of them as "facts": the difficulty of obtaining information as to the precise conditions—physiological, psychological, sociocultural—in which these events occur. Finally, hand in hand with this last point, comes the difficulty of duplicating the conditions so that a repeatable experiment can be devised, or conditions specified in which fresh spontaneous phenomena are likely to occur. What we have in the meantime are large masses of more or less authenticated materials, of which a few fragments have here been presented, and a rather considerable body of psychological and philosophical speculations as to the conditions, the dynamics, the explanatory principles which will bind these diverse classes of phenomena together.

There is indeed a very considerable theoretical literature, and, as is always true in science, there is a continuum from the hypotheses evoked to throw light upon one *specific* event to the broadening areas of philosophical interpretation in which "models" or systematic philosophical systems are sketched out to explain wider and wider reaches of phenomena. This is clearly no place for the more comprehensive theoretical systems. It is, however, a place in which there may be some obligation on the author's part to sketch a few of the simpler hypotheses from which models are beginning to be devised and in the light of which theoretical systems are today being mapped out.

First, a very general principle which has already been noted above is that psi phenomena are often expressions of unconscious or deep-level dynamic principles reflecting the relation of the person to his physical environment or more commonly to his personal-social environment. When two or more persons are involved, the assumption is that there is deep-level interaction between them. Secondly, hand in hand with this principle goes the assumption that the phenomena are expressions of need, impulse, drive, or purpose; that in harmony with the modern trend to see stress-reduction or goal-seeking as expressions of all life, psi phenomena may well be regarded as directed expressions of conscious or unconscious needs. From this point of view, the act of clairvoyance makes a contact to round out the cognitive grasp of a situation, while a telepathic process may convey and receive information, thus linking two minds together, or might represent empathy, a *feeling with,* a groping toward other individuals psychologically close to the receiver.

Hand in hand with these two principles—the assumption of unconscious dynamics and the assumption of need fulfillment or purpose—comes the assumption of some kind of fundamental dualism, some basic difference, between normal and paranormal processes. One way of stating the situation is that paranormal processes do not represent a part of the time-space-event system which the physical sciences describe. As we have suggested above, there is a certain timeless, spaceless, or we might say transtemporal and transpatial character at the very heart of the paranormal. This is indeed one of the major reasons why the phenomena do not belong to and are rejected by official science. It is at the same time a distinguishing criterion which marks off situations with which a psychology allied to physics can deal and those calling for a somewhat different kind of psychology.

From the foregoing it follows that there is a state of mutual exclusion, or even opposition, between the conditions under which ordinary contact with the environment is made and those in which the rules are suspended and the paranormal supervenes. This may appear at first sight to be in contradiction to the principle of potentiation described below (page 277). We must choose our words carefully. Let us say that the evidence tends to suggest that the normal and the paranormal are as a rule found under somewhat different conditions; the paranormal does not appear if the normal is doing its work well. There seem nevertheless to be special cases in which the normal may call upon the paranormal for aid and the two kinds of functions may be blended.

Now if all this is so, it would appear to follow that ideal conditions for the study of the paranormal would involve a certain blunting or limitation of the possibility of normal function.[1] We have studies of semisleeping and sleeping conditions, which together with half-wakeful conditions, drowsiness and hypnosis, as well as various drug states and deliria and toxic states, all seem to offer more than their share of paranormal output. It would appear then to be literally true that the paranormal emerges "when the coast is clear" and the "impediments"[2] to its appearance are removed. One of the paradoxes confronting the experimental parapsychologist is evident: he must use all the psychology he knows

[1] Jan Ehrenwald, *Telepathy and Medical Psychology*, New York, W. W. Norton and Co., 1948.
[2] Gardner Murphy, "Removal of impediments to the paranormal," *Journal of the American Society for Psychical Research*, 1944, Vol. 38, 2–23.

with reference to getting motivation and a favorable attitude toward the task and the experimenter. He must structure his task so that it can be paranormally perceived and the results evaluated; he must be alert for incline effects, decline effects, grouping of hits, and other expressions of normal perceptual activity. And at the same time he must keep in mind constantly that he is dealing with a process which probably would not be there at all if conditions were favorable for normal perception, exemplifying the normal range of psychological laws relevant to its occurrence. Parapsychologists must, as it were, create all the conditions under which cognition in general (or perception in particular) would be expected to occur, but then blunt, inhibit, or block the special conditions which favor normal perception! He must use opaque envelopes, screens, or long-distance conditions, so that when once he has aroused the urge to perceive he can prevent all perception of a normal sort from occurring. It is in fact this very paradox which has made the clear formulation of a model for repeatable experiments so difficult to achieve.

What has been implied here about paranormal cognition (including experimental telepathy, clairvoyance, and precognition) applies almost in full force likewise to PK, and indeed in all likelihood to every type of paranormal process. We are dealing, if not with a basic dualism in human nature between a normal and a paranormal process, at least with a practical functional dualism in the sense that we must strenuously exclude every possibility of normal physical action upon external objects or events if we are to include our observed phenomena as PK. At the same time we must make the most of all the psychology we know to get the mood, attitude, and "stance" of the subject favorable for the production of movement. It is as if we said to him, "Take all the conditions that will make the production of movement impossible and then produce the movement."

There remains, however, an escape: the possibility that there may be conditions under which some kinds of normal perception and action may actually potentiate or predispose toward paranormal perception or action. The faint sights and sounds may offer a matrix upon which paranormal information is grafted, as we have often suspected.

In most ESP experiments we wish to make absolutely certain that sensory cues are eliminated; and while in ordinary precognition experiments they are by definition eliminated, it may be that for certain purposes we are throwing babies out with their baths. It may be more appropriate to study the exact conditions under which normal and paranormal *interact,* and while statistically controlling the maximum which the normal by itself alone can produce, we may be able to see what will happen when normal and paranormal occur in juxtaposition or in *coalescence* or *reinforcement,* one of another. We may, for example, use sensory material which can be perceived under ordinary conditions, but which will be perceived in different ways depending upon a paranormal factor operating at the moment. Thus, the Jastrow "duck-rabbit"[3] figure was used by Kahn and Ehrenwald in an experiment in which the ordinary oscillations between duck and rabbit (see Fig. 13) were to be controlled by the experimenter's looking at a duck or at a rabbit at a particular moment. The theory was that the oscillations which occur normally for normal persons would be to some degree attuned to the experimenter's perception of the duck on some occasions and of the rabbit on other occasions.

An ancient question is whether the psi functions are part of the primitive endowment of living things which have on the whole tended to deteriorate, or assume vestigial form, as higher and more efficient sensory and motor powers have developed, *or* whether the paranormal functions are a property of all life, so that more and richer phenomena appear as we ascend the evolutionary tree. There is not much evidence on this point, but it is of some significance that the attempts to prove the presence of psi phenomena in invertebrates have been failures. There are a few very suggestive

[3] *Journal of the American Society for Psychical Research,* 1957, Vol. 51, 74–75.

Fig. 13   Jastrow "Duck-Rabbit" Figure

experiments with dogs, cats, and horses, sometimes working in association with members of their own species, sometimes with their human masters. Even if all problems of scientific control of these experiments be completely waived, the fact appears that the animal results are typically below the level of paranormal function which is found both spontaneously and experimentally in humankind.[4]

Deterioration through injury, disease, and old age seems to have a slightly adverse effect upon extrasensory capacities at least. It is

[4] I dare not venture an opinion as to the realities underlying the homing of pigeons and other birds. Cf. J. G. Pratt, The homing problem in pigeons, *Journal of Parapsychology,* 1953, Vol. 17, 34–60.

of interest that the two groups of subjects identified in terms of age who have in general been most successful are children of elementary and junior-high-school age and young adults. This would look as if the paranormal were at its height when other biological functions are at their height. This is, however, a tiny shred of evidence upon which to base any conclusion at all.

If we turn now to the question as to the most favorable *states* in which to manifest such phenomena, we shall have to re-emphasize what is said above, page 276, about the importance of need, structure of task, removal of impediments to paranormal function. But something must be added about a fundamental capacity to function outside of the ordinary time-space categories; an ability to accept, if you like, the reality of telepathy, clairvoyance, precognition, psychokinesis, and to go ahead and function in these ways regardless of plausibility or antecedent expectation. To believe that one can and will function in this way, to be free from barriers, and to take the plunge, these are the primary suggestions that can be given. They do not work infallibly, but they seem in the long run to be clues worth pursuing and worthy of better experimental documentation than they have as yet received.

If we turn now to the attributes of *individuals,* the fundamental personality dispositions which seem to favor the exercise of psi capacities, we can certainly note an apparent hereditary factor in the sense that there are many good instances of apparent telepathic interchange between relatives, including those cases in which an accident to one could in no way normally be foreseen by the other, and likewise a considerable number of cases in which a broad psi predisposition seems to run in families, of which an outstanding illustration is the case of Mrs. and Miss Verrall, noted above on pp. 201 ff. There are also some cases in which twins seem paranormally responsive to one another. It may be that the biological relationship involves having similar needs or similar modes of cognitive organization, or similar barriers, or similar ways of removing barriers, or finally similar ways of transcending the time-space relationships. All of these possibilities remain unexplored.

Turning now to more immediately obvious attributes which may predispose toward psi success, there are the physical attributes, such as special physiological conditions, as long noted in the literature in connection with paranormal exchanges during fever states and delirium, and the very curious data of Schmeidler[5] indicating high success during the passive states following concussion, as compared with a control population in the hospital which was not similarly passive, and likewise the data of Gerber and Schmeidler[6] in which the extraordinary passivity and sense of fulfillment of the mother recovering from parturition was likewise found to be a favorable state. It may be that it is here in fact that the absence of impediments, the absence of a nervous preoccupied effort to make sensory contact with the environment is most effectively removed. Finally, there is the assumption that a state of profound dissociation or splitting of the mind—capacity to carry out one activity with the hand and think about something utterly different, or capacity to pass into a "brown study" or "absent" state while still carrying on normal interchange with the environment—may be a favorable state, so that people with such tendencies may be used as clairvoyants, tea readers, mediums, priests. Even in a society which ridicules the whole business, such individuals may cultivate for their own interest and that of their friends those moments of abstraction in which paranormal impressions seem to come.

We have then a few suggestions about favorable states and favorable personalities, but no one has undertaken experimentally to develop the favorable personality and the favorable state; no one, unless one takes into account the bold persons with the courage of

---

[5] Gertrude R. Schmeidler, Rorschachs and ESP scores of patients suffering from cerebral concussion, *Journal of Parapsychology*, 1952, Vol. 16, 80–89; also in Schmeidler and McConnell, *op. cit.*, 75–84.

[6] Rebecca Gerber and Gertrude R. Schmeidler, An investigation of relaxation and of acceptance of the experimental situation as related to ESP scores in maternity patients, *Journal of Parapsychology*, 1957, Vol. 21, 47–57.

their convictions who have undertaken to "train" mediums for regular work as spiritualist instruments for communication between the deceased and the living. Such training, whatever it involves, certainly involves a focusing of need, a strengthening of favorable attitude, and a capacity to remove barriers. Perhaps experimental psychologists, unwilling to commit themselves to spiritualist modes of thought, may still find something here which could be converted into an experimental program for the cultivation of states favorable to the psi process. Of very real promise here are methods for developing relaxation and freeing the mind from distractions; methods for increasing single-minded intent in the task of functioning paranormally, and in the specific persons and targets involved in the task; and methods in studying the process of *learning* to function paranormally.

Before the curtain falls, however, I wish to deal now explicitly with the question: what can be *believed* in a field in which the data appear to conflict with the basic assumptions of science?

Many thoughtful readers will certainly reach the view that we cannot accuse large numbers of scholars and scientists of fabricating data, bribing confederates, or grossly distorting evidence. In connection with the modern skepticism about the positive findings of psychical research, we often find ourselves confronted with the statement: either the data are genuine, or you are accusing a group of scholars of collusion and fraud.

Yet in point of fact, this black-white mode of thinking does not work very well whether in orthodox science or in parapsychology. There is an extraordinary number of instances in ordinary science in which unconscious bias causes people to "see" events that were not really capable of being seen but only inferred; subtle errors arise from assumptions made or oversights regarding unexpected or unpalatable evidence; and almost as common are those forms of self-deception in which one gives the positive evidence the benefit of the doubt. Indeed in my years in ordinary normal research in fields like social psychology, attitude measurement, clinical psy-

No! in my research attempts esp psych have been methodologyually weak —at that time ...

chology, psychology of personality, I have seen literally dozens of shaky conclusions follow from shaky assumptions and have myself often been deceived. Even an independent repetition of a good experiment is no guarantee of the soundness of the original conclusions. Some of the faulty assumptions of the original study may have been built into the replication. I have known a considerable number of cases of refusal to publish evidence unfavorable to a position which had once been taken by a person dominant in the field. Psychologists working as I have done through many years with the subtle influence of wishes upon perception would be in a very foolhardy position in asserting that as a rule, a psychological experiment can easily be repeated and the truth quickly confirmed. This is very far indeed from reality. Truth is come by only after an enormous amount of labor, anxiety, and discipline.

In the field of parapsychology all of this is likewise the case. In addition, a pretty large proportion of the investigators are persons inadequately trained in experimental psychology; a considerable number of loose experiments have gotten into print; a number of statistical errors have been made; and what is far more important, a certain feeling has developed that one must not admit errors or even what looks like fraud because it would cause derision and sweeping rejection on the part of the scientific public.

Now here the moral issue is complex and baffling. Suppose that a certain psychologist, ABC, is known to have made errors in certain experiments, but that these are not the ones that he has published. The *published* work is all right so far as we can tell. Do we have an ethical obligation, if we know the details about the unpublished work, to drag this into the light, and "wash dirty linen in public"? Ordinarily this is considered to be ethically inappropriate. But suppose the point be pressed: If you are an honest man, and you know that ABC did certain incompetent things and that he *may* well have also done these in his published work, the argument can get very slippery and complex, with a good deal of underhand name-calling. Those who know normal psychology and also parapsychology will think of cases of this sort. They will also think of cases, of which there are several, in which the heated or frightened investigator has defended what could never properly be defended, by way of withholding certain malodorous data.

But then he must immediately admit that to define the case legally and morally involves the use of specific names, dates, and other facts which involve a personal ventilation of an ethical and legal charge in public, of a sort which our culture does not ordinarily condone unless huge social or national danger is involved. This issue about what to do with incompetent and unethical procedures both in general psychology and in parapsychology has worried me considerably for some twenty-five years, and I do not pretend to see the light clearly. I do wish, however, to make clear to my reader that I cannot, with good conscience, accept the simple statement that "men of integrity and good will do not deceive themselves, do not get caught in ethical traps, do not withhold data, do not give false impressions." On the contrary, my impression is that normal human beings get involved to some degree in just such complications; that as William James is said to have said, "No man tells the truth under fire"; and that life is a matter of complexities and probabilities, in which you proceed at the risk of your life. In this volume I am not choosing material which I consider likely to be spurious, but I am in no position to "guarantee" cases. I attempt to give the reader a sense of the difficulties, and of the relative conclusiveness or inconclusiveness of the scientific effort in psychical research, and he will reach his own conclusions.

WHAT DOES PSYCHICAL RESEARCH INCLUDE AND EXCLUDE?

Samples have now been given of a few major types of materials gathered by psychical research. These have been arranged under the headings: Spontaneous Cases, illustrated by some of the classical and some of the recently gathered cases; Experimental Telepathy, illustrated by the experiments at the University of Groningen immediately after the First World War; Experimental Clairvoyance, illustrated by the work of Pearce and Pratt at Duke University and of Gertrude R. Schmeidler at Harvard and at City College; Precognition, as represented by the experiments of S. G. Soal and his collaborators; Psychokinesis, as studied by Laura A. Dale at the American Society for Psychical Research and by Pratt and Forwald at Duke; finally, a considerable amount of material, largely the classical British material, on the issue of survival of death.

While striving to avoid doctrinaire judgments that this or that investigation is good, or sound, or conclusive, or that this or that other study is superficial, unsound, or incredible, I have attempted in each case to make a few comments as to the issues on which it would be useful to have more information; and a few suggestions as to possible alternative interpretations of the reported findings. The reader has surely suspected, or indeed become convinced, that the compiler and interpreter of these materials is himself frequently uncertain as to the soundest position to take, and trembles at the prospect that his readers might accept on authority what cannot for a long time be confidently accepted or rejected at all. We are dealing with the first steps that lead *up to* the gateway of science; not with a single step within the hall *beyond* those gateways. We have no science of parapsychology; no theoretical system tightly and beautifully organized in the manner of the architect; no solid beams of repeatedly confirmed findings, reproducible by a careful experimenter who can exactly follow the specifications, sure of the general trend of the results that he will get.

Parapsychology is important as a challenge. If it prematurely achieves the position of a closed, massive, monolithic body of data, all thoughtful men will be the losers. There is often a *presumptive* case and the reader will discover this as he moves through the data. This presumptive case will stand out for thoughtful readers, at least this has always been the case in psychical research. It has not been the thoughtful readers, but those who will not read at all but who "know in advance" what can and what cannot happen, that make the most serious problem. A jury of those who will thoughtfully read is the only kind of jury that we have any intention of invoking in the present task.

But have we sampled all the major fields of psychical research? Far from it. In exemplifying certain types of investigations, we have, in general, followed the tradition of the Society for Psychical Research in London, which has likewise been the tradition of the American Society for Psychical Research in New York, and we have at times relied heavily upon university laboratory work. The following are examples of types of phenomena on which we have *not* succeeded in finding the kinds of data which we could offer the readers of a book like this with the assurance that it would be worth their time to study them:

1. The reports of the human "aura," the luminous capsule or shroud frequently reported to surround the body, usually with colored light. The aura is frequently stated to be constant for a given individual, so that the same observer or a number of independent observers will all report the same aura for a given individual. There are dozens of published claims, often very dogmatic ones, about the aura, but I have not seen a serious experimental report on it.

2. Suspended animation. From many parts of the earth, notably from India, there are reports of persons who, in a special state of trance or ecstasy, have become in a sense like hibernating animals, with greatly diminished respiration and heart beat, indeed often like figures more dead than alive, yet capable, after a long period, of resuscitation and resumption of normal human activities. Apparently many have seen tombs into which persons had gone and from which they were later seen to emerge under conditions which convinced them that suspended animation was a fact. I have never encountered a first-hand report of any individual who saw a person pass into a state of suspended animation, or recover from one; indeed I have seen nothing which would compare in interest with the very common cases of persons placed in therapeutic cubicles in which the body was chilled, and continued to function at subnormal temperatures.

3. Stigmatization. Here the line is much harder to draw. Graff and Wallerstein have reported an interesting case in which a tattoo

mark on a sailor's arm became periodically engorged with blood under conditions of psychological stress.[7] Dr. Montague Ullman has carefully reported a fever blister on the lip which was induced and removed by suggestion.[8] Phenomena of these types are a commonplace in the "psychosomatic medicine" of today. The usual view is that circulatory and biochemical changes controlled by the central nervous system, though of course not fully understood, are at least understood a great deal better than are such phenomena as clairvoyance or psychokinesis, and that we should push on from where we are in our knowledge of normal psychology and physiology rather than involving the paranormal in these instances.

4. Out-of-the-body experiences; experiences of trance, ecstasy, depersonalization, loss of individuality. All of these phenomena appear to be real, and they all seem to be consonant with a modern conception of the unity of the living system in which mental phenomena, such as changed conceptions of the self, sense of identification with the universe, tendency to undergo bilocation (in which one looks down on one's body and feels that the observer and the observed body are two different and equally real things), are experiences not very far from the known terrain of general psychology, which we are beginning to understand more and more without recourse to the paranormal.

On the other hand, it is the hard core of telepathy, clairvoyance, precognition and psychokinesis that we do *not* know how to cover at all, even by stretching our concepts from normal psychology. It is for these reasons that they are regarded as the core data of psychical research or parapsychology. The other phenomena in the groups listed above, then, are rejected because no good evidence is known that could be presented to the reader, *or* because no reason can be offered for believing that they belong in a separate category of the psychical, rather than belonging to general psychology. We

[7] Norman T. Graff and Robert S. Wallerstein, Unusual wheal reaction in a tattoo: psychosomatic aspects in one patient, *Psychosomatic Medicine,* 1954, Vol. 16, 505–515.

[8] Montague Ullman, Herpes simplex and second degree burn induced under hypnosis, *American Journal of Psychiatry,* 1947, Vol. 103, 828–830.

are likely to be wrong at any one of these points. If these other classes of data prove to offer us something interesting, capable of investigation, and capable of pushing us into concepts which do not belong at all to the psychology of today, then we will have to accept them as part of psychical research.

5. But what about astrology, theosophy, numerology, and the many systems of occultism, secret wisdom, old and new, which are often offered as fundamental and systematic, while psychical research is fragmentary and superficial?

My answer is that psychical research is not, and cannot be, a systematic world philosophy. It is a field of investigation. Indeed, Jesuits and atheists have both made signal contributions to psychical research as they have to various exact sciences. Psychical research cannot pretend to be a systematic view of the world, however much its protagonists may incline toward certain interpretations rather than others, regarding the meaning of the data observed.

More specifically, if a system of very broad connotations, like astrology, were to point to specific *verifiable* relationships between events in the skies—let us say the absolute or relative positions of the planets—and specific human events, astrology could quickly turn into a science, and this might or might not have some point of contact with observations coming from psychical research. So far as I know, astrology does not gather verifiable observations of this sort. Theosophy is a religious system derived in large part from the ancient religious systems of India, given a modern form by Madame H. P. Blavatsky, and now quite widely heralded as a channel of intellectual, spiritual communication between the East and West. The only reason for mentioning it here is that the theosophist is very frequently among those who concern themselves with psychical phenomena. Often he believes that these phenomena are self-evident, and often he believes that the spiritual implications will become plain along theosophical lines to any earnest student. I have, myself, not discovered where to find the factual material gathered by theosophists.

Numerology is an intriguing system connected with ancient mystery cults of the Mediterranean world in which certain numbers are conceived to have certain spiritual significances and certain portentous implications for human life. Thus the earth is the fourth heavenly body, counting out from the sun, with Mercury as number two, and Venus as three. It is very simple from this point of view to see why the predominant color of the vegetation of the earth's surface is green, because the fourth color in the spectrum (in the order, red, orange, yellow, green) is green. There is a resonance of numbers which gives all things a harmony, in tune with which one could predict from any man's number (whether given by astrology or otherwise) the fundamental things about his character and fate. Here again, I am unfamiliar with factual material to support numerology, although some of the same philosophical ideas, emanating from the Pythagorean school, have been subjected to disciplined scientific form, and have become central to the structure of modern science. The difference between science and numerology is that numerology makes the assumptions, while the method of science formulates them in such a way that they can be tested.

In these and in all other movements in which one feels something of the near scientific, the would-be scientific, the not-quite scientific, claiming to deal with aspects of human nature less mundane than those with which science is concerned, the question is always whether they offer anything like verifiable facts. It would be ridiculous for me to set myself up as arbiter here, or elsewhere. I can only say that so far as I know, the consistent differentiation between psychical research and these many other fields is that despite many maddening difficulties and much ridicule, the areas noted by the psychical researcher are marked here and there with what appear to be facts, which are at least capable of gradually improved analysis and authentication; while the other fields noted are best known by their repeated *assertions,* in the absence of those orderly research techniques which might work toward ultimate authentication, corroboration, and repetition of the claims.

Since psychical research aims not to become a cult, but a branch of science, many of the problems with which it deals overlap the problems of psychology, physiology, anthropology, medicine. It is often difficult to tell whether a problem is a relevant one for the psychical researcher, or whether these other groups are adequate to the task.

Let us take, for example, the celebrated social institution of the "firewalk." In various parts of the world, e.g., southern India, a man grateful for the restoration of health to himself or some member of his family may announce that he will walk through the fire. A trench is dug. A very hot fire blazes for some hours within it. As the fire subsides the man leaps in, walks upon the embers very rapidly, and emerges at the other end. In many cases the performance is astonishing, but whether it goes beyond the normal physiological response of the foot, and indeed whether any special psychological state of exaltation, dissociation, anaesthesia, etc., needs be presumed, is not clear. Only when we are sure that normal psychology and physiology have failed to cover the situation can the psychical researcher say that he certainly belongs in the picture, and that he has an important area of investigation which the other scholars are not fully qualified to handle within the accepted scope of their disciplines.

Finally, a good many readers will wonder why so much "fuss" is made about the special challenges or wonders that are associated with that which goes beyond the existing disciplines. Is not the whole world full of wonders? Is not every physiological or psychological event largely inexplicable? Are there not miracles moment by moment? These are questions of definition. It is true that we understand very little, but we are beginning to systematize; indeed, the systematizations of the last 300 years since the time of Galileo have given us a rather good world view, and a rather good conception of the unity of the living system in which physiology and psychology are intimately fused. It is where something occurs that is *not* a part of this intimate fusion—it is where something occurs that appears to *transcend* the ordinary known relations of the organism to time, space, matter, and energy—that we have a breakthrough into something which at present we must call unknown, tying it to the known as best we can, but ready always to emphasize the unknown and see whether *new principles*—utterly and genuinely new principles—may be necessary in order to give a rounded interpretation. In this *World Perspectives* series, psychical research may turn out to harmonize and integrate with other new perspectives. It is more likely that it will be a "thorn in the flesh," necessitating some basic rethinking in basic new research, and playing a large role in the functional shift to a new way of looking at life and mind.

World Perspectives

WHAT THIS SERIES MEANS

WORLD PERSPECTIVES is the expression of a new vision of reality. It is a program to mark the spiritual and intellectual revolution through which humanity is passing. It aims to provide an authoritative perspective on the fundamental questions of our modern age, taking into account the changing cultural, scientific, religious, social, political, economic, and artistic influences upon man's total experience. It hopes to define through its universal principle and its individual volumes man's greater orientation in the world and the unprecedented development in men's feeling for nature and for each other.

Through the creative effort of the most responsible world leaders in thought, who have a paternity in the new consciousness and in the enlarged conceptual framework of reference of our epoch, this Series attempts to evoke not a rebirth of good will but vigorous ideas capable of overcoming misconceptions and confusing traditions and of restoring man's faith in his spiritual and moral worth and in his place in the cosmic scheme.

World Perspectives has been conceived out of a concern for the overwhelming accretion of facts which natural science has produced but upon which this science has failed, by virtue of the present limitations of its method, to bestow any adequate meaning. It is the thesis of the Editor that man has lost himself as the living center in a world created by himself. He has been fragmented into different categories which are the subject matter of various scientific approaches to reality with the result that he has become a heterogeneous mass of isolated pieces of reality, of spheres of objects. And the subjectivity left to him has been either driven into the cognitively irrelevant, remote corner of the emotions or his self has been formalized into the logical subject of scientific analysis, leaving him impotent to grasp the inner synthesis and organic unity of life.

There are, however, manifestations of a slow, if reluctant, awakening, and man as the experiencing, responsible and deciding self, endowed by nature with freedom and will, yet beset with confusion and isolated from the dynamic stream of living reality, begins to recognize the ominous implications of the loss of his center and to see that the different realms of scientific approaches to life, to man in relation to himself and his world, have become clouded. It is submitted that he is increasingly aware that his predicament consists in his inhuman situation of being treated and of treating himself as an object among objects, and as a consequence his image of the unity, order and beauty of the universe has collapsed. It is this new consciousness which *World Perspectives* endeavors to define, and thus to present a critically examined doctrine of man which may become a healing and preserving force capable of counteracting the procedural obsessions that afflict the modern mind in our apocalyptic era.

The conceptual framework of man's thinking in the West and in the East has become inadequate for understanding our world. The models and symbols that have served in the past no longer suffice; the old metaphors have lost their relevance and mankind has been emptied of its spiritual orientation and moral certitude. Our chief anxiety issues not from new experiences but from the fact that space and time, that implicit framework of all experience, have changed. Both actual life and theoretical thinking have outrun our powers of imagination. And yet our imagination is deeply influenced by those scientific notions which our reason is unable to fathom. The theoretical constructions on which the marvels of our world age are erected transcend the very language we speak, for finally they can be expressed only in mathematical symbols.

As space and time have changed their appearance and shattered our most elementary foothold in the physical world, and as language itself has undergone a mutation, we have been thrown into a state of anarchy and suspicion, conscious that science which has fathered these changes is itself threatened unless it too can be attuned to the wider and deeper range of human thought and human experience.

For it appears that unless great spiritual resources are present men tend to lie prostrate, to droop as mere victims of conditions and circumstances.

World Perspectives is born out of this consciousness of man's spiritual poverty and conceptual failure. For now the question of the human meaning of man's knowledge can no longer be repressed. The qualitative uniqueness of every life process and especially the uniqueness of that process which is called human is the subject of scrutiny of this Series. It attempts to point to a dialectic of polarity in which unity and diversity are accepted as simultaneous and necessary aspects of the same essence. It is a revolt against that philosophy which neglected the existing man and turned exclusively to the structure of the world. It is an effort to show that not causality alone but relationship as well constitute the living reality capable of creating a meaningful doctrine of man. It warns of the tragic implications of the atomization of our knowledge of man and nature which though a matter of expediency is at the same time a cause for distortion. And finally, this Series is a co-operative endeavor to contribute to the construction of the new, yet ancient, morality of the new world age in the new world community by analyzing and re-defining not only the traditional and obvious ethical aspects of life but the nature of life itself including the nature of man's relationship to the universe, to himself and all mankind. Only through such reflections may those basic concepts emerge which will permit the human spirit to ride disaster and wring victory out of the extremity of defeat, vindicating human freedom and the power of human personality. For finally seminal concepts must replace rampant ideologies.

World Perspectives presents powerful thinkers, unafraid and unimpeded, fiercely and unremittingly dedicated to the universal, unitive yet paradoxical meaning of life which may emerge out of the disciplined vision of reality. The authors of this Series endeavor to be the architects of the edifice constituting this new reality through poignant concepts, basic, powerful, novel, in order that the human mind may encompass and control what the human spirit may envisage and what human hands may touch. Implicit in this Series is the commitment to new ideas which come only through the quiet dissolving of prejudices, through the influence of new conditions that give birth to new prepossessions, through a certain necessary oblivion in the handling of tradition from one generation to another and through a process of elision by which mankind can surrender to novel and enlarged points of view without at first even knowing it.

The authors of *World Perspectives* hope to articulate the deep changes in men's minds that cannot be reached by the analytical method alone, for it is a mysterious virtue in the nature of man that he is capable of working for purposes greater than those of which he may be conscious and greater than any act of volition he may make, however mighty; as though there were an invisible creative force at work in the universe, subtle and inexplicable, in the midst of confusion.

In this way, it is submitted, *World Perspectives* attempts to show that man is that unique organism in terms of matter and energy, space and time, which is urged to conscious purpose through reason, his distinguishing principle. In this way the parochial society of the past may be ultimately transformed into the universal society of the future. In this way man may be unlocked from systems of thought which imprison and destroy. And this may be achieved only if the human heart and the human mind remember that principle of life, that law of the universe, that dynamic process and structure affording man a rocklike foundation while nourishing the maximum elasticity of his intellect. And this principle, this law, remains now as ever before: Hold to the truth, to the unity of man and the unity of knowledge, to the unmediated wholeness of feeling and thought, the unity of the knower and the known, of the outer and inner, of subject and object, particle and wave, form and matter, self and notself. As to the fragmented remainder, let us be totally uncommitted while at the same time we explore, enrich and advance the unfolding of the life process which relentlessly presses forward to actualize new forms.

New York, 1961   RUTH NANDA ANSHEN

WORLD PERSPECTIVES

Volumes already published

Index

73   12 11 10 9 8 7 6 5 4 3 2